The Family Context of Adolescent Drug Use

The Family Context of Adolescent Drug Use

Robert H. Coombs, PhD
Editor

Routledge
Taylor & Francis Group
New York London

First published 1988 by Haworth Press, Inc.

Published 2019 by Routledge
52 Vanderbilt Avenue, New York, NY 10017
2 Park Square, Milton Park, Abingdon, Oxon, OX14 4RN

Routledge is an imprint of the Taylor & Francis Group, an informa business

Notice:
Product or corporate names may be trademarks or registered trademarks, and are used only for identification and explanation without intent to infringe.

***The Family Context of Adolescent Drug Use* has also been published as *Journal of Chemical Dependency Treatment,* Volume 1, Number 2 1988.**

LIBRARY OF CONGRESS
Library of Congress Cataloging-in-Publication Data

The Family context of adolescent drug use / Robert H. Coombs, guest editor.
p. cm.
"Has also been published as Journal of chemical dependency treatment, volume 1, number 2."
Includes bibliography references.
ISBN 0-86656-799-2. ISBN 0-86656-828-X (pbk.)
1. Teenagers – United States – Drug use. 2. Drug abuse – United States. 3. Narcotic addicts – United States – Family relationships. I. Combs, Robert H.
HV5824.Y68F35 1988
362.2'93'088055 – dc 19 88-10965
CIP

ISBN 13: 978-0-86656-828-9 (pbk)

Dedication

For Loni, Craig and Trevor

ABOUT THE EDITOR

Robert H. Coombs, PhD, is Professor of Biobehavioral Sciences (Medical Sociology) at UCLA School of Medicine, and Director of the Office of Education at UCLA Neuropsychiatric Institute and Hospital. Dr. Coombs is the Associate Editor of several journals and the author of eight books and over 100 articles on the processes of human development, especially that of adolescents and young adults. He was involved in the 1980 White House Conference on Families and the 1986 California Commission for the Prevention of Drug and Alcohol Abuse.

The Family Context of Adolescent Drug Use

CONTENTS

II. FAMILY STYLES, STAGES AND VARIETIES

The Family Context of Adolescent Drug Use

Introduction

The drug problem in America, now several decades old is mestastasizing all segments of society. It is a self-defeating spiral downward, a process that is gathering momentum.

Decades of strategic advertising have glamorized chemical substances—tobacco, alcoholic beverages, prescription medications—by linking them to popularity, sex appeal, fun and well-being. The idea that personal pleasure and attractiveness can be enhanced by substances has become uncritically accepted and incorporated into the lifestyles of countless Americans. Millions of chemically dependent victims can attest that physical and emotional impairment are an excessive price to pay for these illusory rewards.

Despite the fact that two Presidents of the United States have declared war on drug abuse and marshalled enormous national resources, large numbers of young people continue to use substances. Because traditional efforts have been based on the questionable assumption that drug use is primarily a form of escape or an indication of personal deficiency, ameliorative efforts, usually aimed at later stages of drug involvement have rarely been effective. Little progress will be made as long as policymakers and helping professionals continue to focus on rehabilitation rather than prevention, and to ignore the familial and other social roots of adolescent initiation and escalation.

Traditional efforts to ameliorate drug-related problems have focused on individuals rather than families and social environments. As one probation officer observed, "We take a problem youth out of the dirty puddle, clean him up, and then toss him back into the puddle." Only recently have professionals recognized the potential of the family to prevent and ameliorate drug-related problems.

Because the family is the crucible of mental health and the locus of social control, its potential for preventing and resolving youth problems is enormous. "Our government spends a great deal of effort and money repairing damages resulting from weak and ineffective families," a President of the United States remarked shortly after announcing the first White House Conference on the Family. "The stronger families are," he said, "the less role there is to be played by the government."

What is needed is not more depersonalized efforts to combat substance abusers at advanced stages of involvement, but greater effort in helping families direct and redirect adolescent offspring at the initiation and escalation stages of drug involvement into productive lifestyles. Rather than stigmatizing, punitive approaches that label youths as delinquent or sick, what is needed are efforts that educate and strengthen families.

Adolescents undergoing rapid and sometimes confusing developmental changes are especially vulnerable to substance abuse and related problems. Only by dealing with the primary network of significant others who surround and influence children and youth, can effective, long-range solutions be implemented. By focusing on families, more promising directions can be developed, ones that are positive rather than negative, instructional rather than punitive, and preventive instead of remedial.

This book is composed of three parts. Part I provides a comprehensive literature review and offers background information about societal forces that affect families and make it difficult to raise drug free youngsters. Part II deals with family differences—family styles, stages and varieties. Part III, the final section, focuses on interventions—at home, at school and with peers.

In the first article, "The Institutionalization of Drug Use in America: Hazardous Adolescence, Challenging Parenthood," by Robert H. Coombs, Morris J. Paulson and Risa Pally, an overview is provided about the extent and cost of adolescent drug use and the institutionalized forces that entice youngsters to use drugs. Also discussed is the need for a federal family policy.

The second article, "Family Theory and Research on Adolescent Drug Use: A Review," by Thomas J. Glynn and Marianne Haenlein, provides a systematic review of family theory and research pertaining to adolescent drug use. Theoretical and methodological issues are highlighted. Adopting a systems-lifespan perspective, the authors identify the patterns of family interaction and coping that contribute to adolescent drug initiation, reinforcement and maintenance. The dynamic structures of parent-child relationships and parents as teachers/models are explored. Four areas of future research are identified that the authors believe will significantly advance current understanding of the relationship between adolescent drug use and families.

"Contrasting Family Patterns of Adolescent Drug Users and Nonusers," by Robert H. Coombs and Morris J. Paulson, contrasts the family styles of two adolescent groups—teenagers who drink and use other substances and those who refrain. Focusing on the initiation and escalation stages of drug involvement, this article discusses family structure, parenting life-styles, parent-youth interaction and parent versus peer loyalties.

The developmental stages of drug involvement, and the changing family circumstances at each stage, are explored in "Developmental Stages in Drug Use: Changing Family Involvements." Authored by Robert H. Coombs and Kathryn Coombs, this article explicates the developmental patterns and family involvements at each stage: initiation, escalation, maintenance, discontinuation, and renewal. Data derived from several study populations are reported—children, adolescents, and young adults—with colorful quotations from those at each stage.

"Ethnic Family Differences in Adolescent Substance Use," by Edward Kaufman and Linda Borders, discusses the influence of ethnicity in affecting adolescent substance use. Reviewed are the drinking and drug related characteristics and treatment needs in the Irish, Italian, Jewish, White Anglo-Saxon Protestant, Black, Hispanic, Asian and Native American families. The authors make clear that to be successful, intervention efforts must take into account the cultural patterns that legitimize and encourage the use of substances. Basic family structures in each ethnic group must be recognized and techniques utilized that respect and incorporate these inherent ethnic characteristics.

"Personality, Family and Ecological Influences on Adolescent Drug Use: A Developmental Analysis," by Judith S. Brook, Martin Whiteman, Carolyn Nomura, Ann Scovell Gordon and Patricia Cohen, reviews several developmental approaches to adolescent drug use. As the title indicates, this article examines the interplay between personality, socialization, and ecological factors related to adolescent drug use. Based upon data from a longitudinal study, the interrelation of childhood and adolescence factors and the adolescent's frequency of marijuana use are analyzed. More than 400 children and their mothers were studied at two times during an eight-year period. The authors conclude that childhood personality, family and ecological factors influence adolescent personality and parent-adolescent relationships, which in turn impact the adolescent's use of marijuana.

"Families with Attention Deficit Disordered Children and Others at Risk," by Dennis P. Cantwell focuses on youngsters with learning disabilities. Because they are often in trouble at school, and subsequently at home, they may be at greater risk for drug involvement. Failing at school does little to encourage parental praise or to enhance positive self-esteem. Ongoing ego-deflating interactions may predispose these youngsters to withdraw, to spend more time on the streets where substances are more available. The author reviews the literature on this topic and describes the learning handicaps that hamper these youngsters.

"Empirical Guidelines for a Family Intervention for Adolescent Drug Use," by Thomas J. Dishion, John B. Reid and Gerald R. Patterson, discusses empirical guidelines for designing and evaluating interventions aimed at adolescents who are at risk or already drug involved. The factors that effectively intervene to either prevent or curtail adolescent drug use are discussed. Negative adolescent outcomes, such as delinquency and drug use, are seen as arising within the family and later exacerbated by the influence of peers. If family interventions are to be effective, the authors assert, peer associations, social skills, parent monitoring, and parent drug use must be addressed. The authors suggest that the processes leading to adolescent drug use can potentially be identified and helped earlier than adolescence.

"Managing Adolescent Behaviors at School: Implications for Families," by Thomas J. Glynn and Marianne Haenlein, provides a review of school-based drug use prevention programs and discusses how families can contribute significantly to the success of these programs. Various types of drug use prevention programs are identified and evaluated—resistance to pro-smoking pressures approaches, social influences and modified social influences methods, cognitive-behavioral technique, and personal health and general skills approaches. The inclusion of such family skills as communication, decision making, and values clarification, the authors point out, can significantly enhance the effectiveness of intervention programs. A discussion of future research and activities that might involve families in school-based prevention programs is also included.

"Peer Relationships, Social Competence and Substance Abuse Prevention: Implications for the Family," by Gilbert J. Botvin and Stephanie Tortu deals with the onset and early stages of substance abuse from the perspective of peer relations and psychosocial development. Particular attention is paid to the importance of personal and social competence and the development of healthy peer relationships and their implication for families. Intervention strategies that enhance the acquisition of general personal and social skills are discussed as well as those that increase resistance to negative social influences that support substance use. By modeling and reinforcing nonsubstance use behaviors and adequate personal and social skills, the authors assert, the family can both foster the acquisition of positive behaviors and facilitate the development of healthy peer relationships.

I express appreciation to Carla Vera for her superior contribution to this volume. At each stage of development, she enhanced this project with her characteristic efficiency, productivity and good will.

Robert H. Coombs, PhD

I. ADOLESCENT DRUG USE: A FAMILY PROBLEM

The Institutionalization of Drug Use in America: Hazardous Adolescence, Challenging Parenthood

Robert H. Coombs, PhD
Morris J. Paulson, PhD
Risa Palley, BA

In contemporary America, multibillion dollar industries have created a situation where child raising is hazardous. "Even if you are a good parent," a mother lamented, "there is no guarantee that you can succeed in keeping your kids away from drugs."

The abuse of drugs by American youth has caused widespread concern. "It is sad and sobering," a California official acknowledged, "that crime and drug use is no longer the exception among high school students. It is the norm" (Van de Kamp, 1986).

This article first discusses the incidence and trends in adolescent substance use and highlights some of the resulting problems. Next, it explores the institutionalized conditions that entice youngsters to use substances and then argues the need for a federal family policy.

Robert H. Coombs is Professor of Biobehavioral Sciences, UCLA School of Medicine and Director, Office of Education, UCLA Neuropsychiatric Institute and Hospital, 760 Westwood Plaza, Room B7-349, Los Angeles, CA 90024. Morris J. Paulson is Professor of Child Psychology, UCLA Neuropsychiatric Institute and Hospital. Risa Palley is a graduate student at the University of California, Los Angeles.

The authors thank Kathryn Coombs for her assistance in the preparation of this paper.

INCIDENCE AND TRENDS

A national survey of high school seniors conducted by the Institute for Social Research at the University of Michigan (Johnston, O'Malley and Bachman, 1986, p. 20) prompted investigators to conclude,

> This nation's high school students and other young adults still show a level of involvement with illicit drugs which is greater than can be found in any other industrialized nation in the world. Even by historical standards in this country, these rates still remain extremely high.

By their mid-20s, 75-80% of American young adults have tried an illegal drug, including about 50-55% who have tried some illicit drug other than, or usually in addition to, marijuana. Among high school seniors these proportions are 61% and 40% respectively. During 1985 one in every twenty high school seniors smoked marijuana daily. About the same number drank alcohol daily, and some 37% had five or more drinks in a row at least once in the two weeks prior to this study (Johnson et al., 1986).

About 30% of these students had smoked cigarettes in the prior month and 20% were daily smokers. Many of the light smokers convert to heavy smoking after high school; 26% of those ages 19-27 smoke daily and 21% smoke half a pack or more per day (Johnston et al., 1986). Seventeen percent of high school seniors had tried cocaine and this number increases to 40% by age 27.

Alcohol, the most popular drug in America, is widely abused by adolescents. According to figures from the National Institute of Alcohol Abuse and Alcoholism, about 3.3 million youngsters are problem drinkers (Noble, 1978). A national study of high school students (Hubbard et al., 1983) found that 30% identified themselves as "heavy drinkers."

The Institute of Medicine (National Academy of Sciences, Research Opportunities, 1980) reported that "Young adolescents of junior high school age drink more than was true a generation ago; a larger percentage of them drink, and are having their first drinking experience earlier; and they drink larger quantities and report more frequent intoxications."

A California statewide survey of more than 7,000 intermediate and senior high school students selected at random from 87 California secondary schools (Skager, 1986) found that half of the eleventh graders had consumed alcoholic beverages and half had experimented with other drugs. A comparison of seventh, ninth and eleventh graders showed a steady escalation in drug and alcohol use. Among the seventh graders 58% had tried alcohol, and of this group 16% had been drunk at least once. By the ninth grade (mostly 14-year olds), 78% had experimented with alcohol, and 47% had become intoxicated. By the eleventh grade, 85% had tried alcohol and 65% had been drunk on at least one occasion.

According to the Skager survey (1986), experimentation with other drugs also escalates with age. Among his 12-year olds, 11% had experimented with illicit substances, and 8% had been "high" at least once. A sharp increase occurred among the 14-year olds where 36% had tried drugs and 30% been intoxicated at least once. Higher still is drug use and intoxication among the eleventh graders; 51% had experimented and 45% been high at least once. In this older age group (mostly 16-year olds), 42% had used marijuana, 18% cocaine and 15% amphetamines; one in every 13 students smoked marijuana daily.

More than 16 million Americans use marijuana at least once a month; 25% are between the ages of 12 and 17 (4.1 million), 51% are between 18 and 25 (8.3 million) and 24% are over age 25 (3.8 million) (Strategy Council on Drug Abuse, 1979).

Among Skager's (1986) California subjects, daily marijuana use occurred among 5% of the ninth graders and 7% of the eleventh graders. Projected to a statewide population, an estimated 60,000 California adolescents are involved in daily marijuana use.

Use of cocaine, one of the most addictive substances known to man, has risen dramatically in popularity during the past decade. Johnson et al. (1985, p. 2) reported a 300% national increase in cocaine use during the past decade. "Cocaine use was up among virtually all the subgroups examined: among both males and females, college-bound and non college-bound, rural and urban areas, and all regions of the country except the South."

During the 1980s, the price of cocaine has dropped and its strength tripled. Once an expensive drug, it is now available for as little as $5 to $15 in a hardened paste, typically 70% pure cocaine, called "crack" or "rock." In contrast with the powdered form, this preprocessed smokeable form of cocaine is cheaper, more concentrated substance induces a much more intense and extremely addictive "high."

Polydrug use, another alarming phenomenon, occurs when two or more substances are used at the same time. Because drugs may interact synergistically, the result can be more harmful than the simple additive effects of any two drugs. As exemplified by the tragic case of Karen Quinlan, permanent loss of consciousness or even death may result. The percentage of eleventh graders (16-year olds) in California who report polydrug use at least once a month, projected to a statewide population, represents almost 30,000 students (Skager, 1986).

Summarizing our society's precarious situation with regard to adolescent drug use, Lester Wolff, a former Chairman of the House Committee on Narcotics Abuse and Control, said that the problem has exploded "from epidemic to pandemic proportions." It has grown so large, he says, that "neither this nation nor any other nation in history—has ever before faced a problem that is so insidious and so dangerous" (Wolff, 1985).

THE HUMAN COST

The reports on adolescent drug use read like a litany of death and impairment. A sampling of grim statistics provides a glimpse of the personal and familial devastation that can result from chemical dependence.

Life expectancy in the United States has steadily risen over the last 75 years for all age groups except those between the ages of 15 and 24. Within this age group, the death rate has increased, not decreased (CompCare, 1981). During a recent year (1985), 53,000 adolescent lives were lost, about the same number killed in Viet Nam over a five year period (Glenn, 1986). These deaths, together with high rates of accident, injury, and disappearance are often related to substance abuse.

The possibility of overdose is an ever present risk. The Drug Abuse Warning Network (DAWN), a government-sponsored information system, found that the illicit use of barbiturates alone was involved in about 25,000 hospital emergency room visits and 5,000 drug-related deaths in one year (Baschner and Friedman, 1979). Reporting on Emergency Room admissions among 6-17-year olds in three major California metropolitan areas (San Francisco, Los Angeles, and San Diego), 1337 youths were admitted for drug-related problems during one year (California State Department of Alcohol and Drug Programs, 1983).

The statistics on death and injury resulting from drunk driving are also appalling. Alcohol-related highway deaths are the number one killer of 15-24 year olds (National Center for Health Statistics, 1980). Approximately 10,000 young people of this age are killed each year in alcohol-related accidents of all kinds including drownings, suicides, violent injuries, homicides and injuries from fire (National Institute on Alcohol Abuse and Alcoholism, 1983).

Although drivers between the ages of 16-24 represent only 20% of the licensed drivers and less than 20% of total miles driven, they account for 42% of all fatal alcohol-related auto accidents (U.S. Department of Transportation, 1984). The lethal mixture of drinking and driving destroys the lives of more than 8,000 young Americans every year and maims and cripples countless more. Drunk driving plays a role in 10% of all deaths in the U.S. and is the principal cause of death through accident among those aged 15-24 (National Institute on Alcohol Abuse and Alcoholism, 1984). These statistics led officials to call alcohol "the most lethal form of substance abuse among our youth, the leading cause of death among young people" (California Commission, 1986).

The long-term psychological effects of substance abuse are also disturbing. Because drugs substitute chemically induced feelings for natural ones, they act as a social and emotional retardant, shielding youth from normal problem-solving experiences, and impairing judgement, discrimination and information processing abilities. Mood fluctuations, anxiety, hostility and depression often follow prolonged use. Any of these disabilities can lead to failure in school, and severely disrupt interpersonal relationships at home and elsewhere (Smart, 1976; Milman et al., 1983).

Adolescents who abuse drugs, Milman (1983) observes, miss "vital, active engagement in the process of growing up—a failure to experience suffering, to come to grips with anxiety, to tolerate ambiguity and frustration and postponement." Without these experiences, she notes, youngsters "emerge from adolescence without having experienced it, without having addressed its tasks, without being able to carry into adulthood the legacy of conflicts resolved, obstacles overcome, fears conquered, social skills mastered, values defined, and relationships established" (Milman, 1983, p. 53).

Adolescents who use substances are at risk for a variety of health problems, a few of which are gastritis, gastrointestinal hemorrhage, malnutrition, impaired reflexes, lowered immunity to infections, and possible interference with reproductive development (Cohen, 1981; National Academy of Sciences, Research Opportunities, 1980). Marijuana, reportedly ten times more potent than it was a decade ago (Meyer, 1985), may cause hormonal damage, permanent short-term memory impairment and serious learning disabilities due to its effect on the central nervous system.

Juvenile crime, another pathological indicator of substance abuse, is reportedly higher now than at any time in American history. In 1984, the California Department of Justice reported that 66,000 Californians under age 20 were arrested for felony and misdemeanor violations involving alcohol (drunk driving, drunkenness and violations of liquor laws) and 46,000 were arrested for drug law violations (California Department of Justice, 1985). Among these youngsters, the recidivism rate is reportedly over 70% (Sorrentino, 1979). A San Diego District Attorney maintains that "a very high percentage of the country's burglaries, vandalism, car thefts and robberies are committed by adolescent drug users seeking to support their addictions." Discussions abound concerning the need for more jails, prisons, and other detention facilities to "warehouse" juveniles and young adults.

These dismal statistics cannot convey the tragic human dimensions of the problems created by substance abuse. In just a few moments with the parents of chemically dependent adolescents, one immediately senses their frustration, despair and interpersonal turmoil as they try to manage their children, and their children's problems. Society's perilous situation with regard to adolescence is summarized by Judith Reidinger, Executive Director of the National Drug Abuse Foundation as follows: "Adolescent drug abuse may be leading a whole generation of handicapped young people unable to function effectively in an increasingly demanding world. We must help to preserve our most valuable resource—our youth" (ADAMHA News, 1980).

INSTITUTIONALIZED INCENTIVES TO USE SUBSTANCES

A variety of potent societal forces compete against parental influence for the minds of American youth. The easy availability of substances, the paraphernalia industry, the ongoing advertising of alcohol and over-the-counter drugs, and the media glamorization of drug life-styles all provide powerful incentives for youngsters to use substances.

The Illicit Drug Industry: Easy Availability

A few decades ago, drugs were generally unavailable to adolescents. Alcoholic beverages were accessible, but drinking was frowned upon and community sanctions exerted when conduct norms were unheeded.

Times have changed. In our contemporary society, youth have easy access to alcohol and illicit drugs and the use of these substances, modeled by cultural heroes, is now acceptable.

The economic principle of supply and demand underlies drug availability. The demand, provided primarily by adolescents and young adults, is generated at schools which serve as major distribution centers. In a recent magazine survey, 57% of drug using respondents reported schools as the place where most of their drugs are obtained (California Commission, 1986).

Though prohibited by law, adolescents find it relatively easy to purchase alcoholic beverages. When police in one California city initiated a decoy system in community stores, minors were able to buy alcohol in 60-65% of these establishments (California Commission, 1986).

Currently the demand for illegal drugs is so high, and the profit margin so lucrative, that suppliers thrive, despite the risk of criminal justice penalties. The cocaine trade alone is reported to be a $30 billion industry; if ranked among Fortune 500 businesses, it would be listed seventh (Entertainment Industries Council Report, 1985).

Drug profiteers do not always fit the stereotype of sinister underground criminals. White-collar professionals, rather than underworld "thugs," are often involved. In a 1985 Los Angeles crackdown, for example, authorities filed actions against 34 individuals, including some two dozen physicians, nurses and other clinicians involved in selling false prescriptions to drug suppliers (Jalon, 1986).

With relatively little effort, an amateur chemist can develop and sell "designer drugs," slight variations of illicit substances like heroin. Months may pass before officials are alerted and the chemical ingredients analyzed and declared illegal. For less than $1,000, one reporter legally purchased all the ingredients necessary to produce a batch of methamphetamine with a street value of $40-$60,000 (Meyer, 1985). In only a two month period, a young white-collar worker reportedly supplemented his $40,000 annual income by $25,000 through cocaine dealing (Meyer, 1985). Some middle-class suburbanites cultivate marijuana plants in their backyards to satisfy their own needs, and sell the rest for a profit of several thousand dollars.

The illicit drug trade has developed into a sophisticated industry. With lucrative profits, major distributors can easily afford advanced technology to transport and disseminate products. Even teenage street gangs now utilize electronic surveillance devices to avoid detection.

The traditional "war on drugs" strategy has relied on law enforcement and the criminal justice system to monitor and control drug problems. Yet, despite steady increases in funding and manpower—more agents making more arrests—these officials seem to be losing ground. Drug busts amounting to millions of dollars are regularly reported in the media but these arrests only symbolize the enormity of the illicit drug industry. "We're bigger, better and more efficient," one criminal justice official observed, "but the problem just seems to grow at an astronomical rate" (Meyer, 1985).

Only a small percentage of the narcotics smuggled into the United States is intercepted by law enforcement officials. A 1987 study by the Office of Technology Assessment, presented to the Senate Permanent Subcommittee on Investigations, concluded that, although Customs and Coast Guard officers have seized increasing quantities of drugs over the past five years, spending more than $800 million on interdiction efforts in one year (1986), illegal drug imports are increasing. The Customs Service was allotted $25 million in the Anti-Drug Abuse Act of 1986 to set up a "command, control, communications and intelligence system" to facilitate federal interdiction efforts, but little more than the appearance of drug interdiction has resulted. Federal funds to stop illegal drugs from entering the United States increased from $400 million in 1981 to $820 in 1986, yet the value of incoming drugs continues to escalate. In only two years, 1984 to 1986, incoming heroin increased from about four to six tons and cocaine has more than doubled – from 60 tons to 130 tons (House Select Committee on Narcotics Abuse and Control, 1987). These increases caused one official to observe that federal efforts to stop the flow of drugs into the United States are "as effective as digging a hole in the ocean" (Johnson, 1987).

The Drug Paraphernalia Industry: Trendy Drug Items

Paraphernalia refers to the items used in using, preparing, packaging and storing drugs. This industry had its start in the mid-1960s when marijuana smokers gravitated to novelty stores that provided such items as rolling papers, bongs, roach clips and pipes. Enterprising craftspeople and cigarette jobbers began to supply paraphernalia to the "alternative" stores that sold "counterculture" items such as embroidered clothing, leather sandals, "hippie" beads, etc. Since demand greatly exceeded supply, a high markup of these items guaranteed high profits (Wynne et al., 1980).

In the early 1970s these items were manufactured and advertised for the first time nationally to attract marijuana smokers. Since 1974, three trade publications and ten consumer-oriented magazines emerged, reflecting the explosive growth of this industry (Wynne et al., 1980).

During the late 1970s the paraphernalia industry aggressively expanded their market by reinvesting profits in high technology product research and development. The greatest industry growth was during 1976 and 1977 when record stores and novelty gift shops added paraphernalia items to their standard inventory. As paraphernalia grew more visible and acceptable, some stores in suburban shopping malls created paraphernalia sections to reap the high profits (Wynne et al., 1980).

At the urging of concerned citizens, the industry soon came under attack by local, state and federal authorities. In order to legally defend industry members, and to promote more responsible and responsive sales and advertising methods, several regional associations and one national trade association formed (Wynne et al., 1980).

Currently the paraphernalia industry reports between 15,000 and 25,000 retail outlets, mostly in California and metropolitan New York, with estimated annual sales between $50 million and several billions. Record stores account for about one-third of all retail paraphernalia sales. Less than 1% of the retail business conducted via mail order (Wynne et al., 1980).

Drug paraphernalia has been described as "the ultimate glamorization" of drug use (U.S. House Subcommittee on Crime, 1986). Open sale and advertising communicates an image of drugs as acceptable, even respectable and commonplace. Adolescents who frequent these "head shops" are titillated by the fancy tools and accessories that are promoted as desirable, trendy and "hip."

Much of the opposition to this mushrooming industry has been at the grassroots level in many communities. This antiparaphernalia movement has stirred federal, state and local officials to action. Community groups have lobbied for legislation to restrict the manufacture, sale and possession of drug-related paraphernalia, and undertaken local activities such as newspaper editorials, and the boycotting of stores that sell paraphernalia (Wynne et al., 1980).

In response to these activities, the White House Domestic Policy Staff requested in 1979 that the Drug Enforcement Administration (DEA) and the Justice Department consider federal legislation to prohibit the manufacture, sale and possession of drug paraphernalia. The response was that the problem is best handled, not through federal legislation, but by state and local governments and the private sector (Wynne et al., 1980).

To assist states, the DEA prepared a Model Drug Paraphernalia Act which features these basic provisions:

1. defines the term "drug paraphernalia";
2. stipulates factors that courts-of-law and other authorities should consider in determining whether an object comes within the definition;
3. makes the manufacture, advertising, delivery, and use of drug paraphernalia a criminal offense;
4. makes a special offense the delivery of drug paraphernalia to a minor; and
5. defines prohibited conduct concerning the manufacture, advertisement, delivery and use of drug paraphernalia and specifies what "criminal state of mind" must accompany such conduct. (Wynne et al., 1980)

As of 1986, 38 states had adopted a Model Anti-Paraphernalia Act. However, few localities devote any significant effort to enforcing these state laws. Raids on "head shops" are often dismissed in court; defense attorneys argue that these laws are too vague, too broad and that they require store owners to be clairvoyant in identifying customer intent. To protect themselves legally, store owners now display signs like these: "Any reference to illegal usage will result in a refusal of service" or, "Customers must sign statements declaring they will not use purchases with illegal drugs" (Stewart, 1984; Banks, 1983; Jalon, 1986).

A massive mail order industry has developed with substantial profits. This prompted federal hearings and a subsequent bill, "The Mail Order Drug Paraphernalia Control Act" (HR 1625) (U.S. House of Representatives, 1986). Despite increasing public concern and efforts by criminal justice officials to control paraphernalia, little change has occurred. These items are widely available for those who want to obtain them.

The Advertising Industry: Seductive Messages

An adolescent's environment is saturated with media messages that effectively promote the use of alcohol and over-the-counter drugs, and suggest tolerance toward the use of illegal substances.

In one year, the average child watches more than 20,000 commercials during the more than 1,300 to 1,400 hours of television viewing. Advertisers spend more than $700 million a year on television and other media to make sure that their marketing messages reach large numbers of children (American Academy of Pediatrics, 1986).

According to one estimate, children are exposed to over 5,000 beer and wine commercials on television each year and at least 2,500 liquor ads in major magazines (CompCare, 1983). A child will see alcohol consumed on television an average of 75,000 times before he or she is of legal drinking age (Radecki, 1986).

The pervasiveness of alcohol advertising is illustrated by advertising statistics of one beer company, Anheuser-Busch, the tenth-largest advertiser in the United States (Broder, 1987). Anheuser-Busch is reported to have a 1985 advertising and promotion budget of $523 million, with sales totalling $8.4 billion, yet this company represents only 38% of the U.S. beer market (Broder, 1987).

Television exposes children to adult behaviors in ways that suggest that these behaviors are normal and risk free. Alcohol and drugs are often portrayed in inviting terms implying that "everyone does it." Endorsements by noted athletes, entertainers and other celebrities are particularly effective in promoting the idea that alcohol and medication are necessary parts of everyday living. One observer noted that "Years of exposure to alcohol ads creates an image in children's minds that life without alcohol is like a bird without wings."

Advertisements promote the concept that popularity, friendship, adventure, achievement, sex appeal, and true love are enhanced by substance use. Other enticing messages suggest exclusive status in elite friendship groups whose substance using members are associated with wealth, high status, and social sophistication. Such seductive messages are especially alluring to adolescents during a developmental life period marked by profound social insecurities and self-doubts.

Research evidence indicates that adolescents and young adults who are exposed to alcohol ads on television and in magazines, compared to those less exposed, perceive drinking as more acceptable, attractive, and rewarding. The heavily exposed youngsters in one study drank liquor more often—31% vs. 15%—than their less exposed associates (Atkin and Block, 1981).

Though various governmental and community groups have pressured the industry to balance advertising messages by providing accurate information about the harmful effects of alcohol and other drugs, little effective self-regulation has actually occurred. Advertising agencies continue to market alcoholic beverages as if they were as wholesome as vegetable soup.

In a national poll conducted by *Business Week* magazine (February, 1985), 57% of the respondents favored banning alcohol advertising from the broadcast media. Clearly, responsible self-regulation by the advertising industry is long overdue, yet little progress has been made.

According to Federal law, the Secretary of the Treasury is entitled to prohibit advertisements for distilled spirits, wine, or malt beverages made by mail or interstate or foreign commerce that are "false, misleading, obscene, or indecent." Advertisements are also subject to regulation by the Federal Trade Commission and the Bureau of Alcohol, Tobacco and Fire Arms (BATF). But these regulatory agencies have been inept in reducing the intriguing and misleading advertisements that encourage youngsters to use these health endangering products. BATF's record on controlling alcohol advertisement is dismal. Alcohol advertising, Wallack (1984) says, is "clearly misleading, yet the public's representative (BATF) has been and continues to be the handmaiden of the industry it should be regulating and it is unlikely that any change in this relationship will be forthcoming."

The Pharmaceutical Industry: Medicalization of the Human Condition

Remarkable advances in science and technology during the past half century have given medical science an increased capacity to relieve pain, treat diseases and prolong life. Accustomed to "miracle drugs," most Americans have an uncritical acceptance of drug therapy. "Much of our population," a pharmacist observed, "is conditioned to think that the first moment of mental, physical or emotional discomfort is a signal for instant pharmaceutical treatment" (Spierer, 1986). "I haven't got time for the pain!" are the lyrics from a popular song used in a television ad for a pain reliever.

According to Robert Seidenberg (1971), the Pharmaceutical Industry has thoroughly exploited this "feel better fast" attitude in its advertisement campaigns. His ten-year survey of pharmaceutical advertisements led him to conclude:

> Through picture and text, the psychiatrist as well as other physicians are being "advised" to prescribe "mind-drugs" for an ever expanding variety of conditions, old and newly conceived, in addition to their use as "needed" adjuncts to relieve "anxiety" accompanying practically every medical illness and surgical procedure. (Seidenberg, 1971)

In his statement, "Advertising and Drug Acculturation," presented before the U.S. Senate Committee on Monopoly of Small Business Committee, Seidenberg (1971) pointed to physicians as the key market for drug advertisers, the "gatekeepers of the legal drug industry." Physicians, he says are wooed and propagandized by pharmaceutical advertisers through several mailings a day, and frequent visits by pharmaceutical representatives who provide free samples.

"I probably receive 30 to 40 throw away medical journals free," one internist remarked. "There's a lot of drug company money out there" (Golden, 1987). Such promotional efforts have significantly popularized drug therapy and reinforced the concept that a physician's role is to prescribe drugs. Many physicians have been persuaded to think first of chemical solutions to problems—sedatives for sleeplessness, rather than social or psychological help, laxatives for constipation rather than diet change. Seidenberg estimated that, in order to promote psychotropic drugs, more than $10,000 a year is spent by the drug industry for each psychiatrist in the United States.

In his book, *The New Industrial State* John Kenneth Galbraith (1971) contends that in early American capitalism, the "accepted economic sequence" was that a company first determined the products needed and wanted by the public, and then, based on that information, produced those products. The purpose of advertising was to inform the public about the products it wanted.

However, with the rise of twentieth century industrial capitalism, this economic sequence has changed. Now giant corporations develop products on a long-term basis, utilizing future projections of the market. After determining which products represent maximum profitability over a period of time, mass media advertising campaigns then stimulate public feelings of need for those products. The pharmaceutical industry is a prime example. During the 1950s and 1960s, this industry created and stimulated feelings of need for drugs. These marketing efforts, with ever expanding advertising budgets, produced geometric sales.

Prescription drugs are now a multibillion dollar industry. The public has been convinced that human problems such as anxiety, misbehavior, obesity, insomnia, overpopulation, sadness, rage, marital difficulty, and school adjustment all require medical attention. Once a problem is considered as a "disease," it is easy to think of drugs as a cure (Bernstein and Lennard, 1973).

If miracle drugs like sulfa and penicillin can eradicate devastating disease, new "wonder drugs" may alleviate the problems of daily life. Bernstein and Leonard (1973) refer to this reasoning as the "medicalization of the human condition."

> Though the accomplishment of life ever-lasting, healthy and happy, may be impossible, the fantasy is not, and the main result of such predictions by science has been to convince the public that human suffering is a medical disease. People have become less and less willing to accept pain and anguish as natural concomitants of living, and have come to expect medicine to put an end to all personal suffering. (Bernstein and Leonard, 1973)

Is it any coincidence that the national upswing in adolescent drug use has followed a period of intensive advertising to convince the public that a chemical cure exists for every conceivable maladjustment? Is it any surprise that drug use, once considered primarily an "underworld" phenomenon, is now an acceptable, even glamorized aspect of American life?

Summarizing this pro-drug orientation, one official concluded,

> This society assumes that there's better living through chemistry—whether it is the multi-billion dollar pharmaceutical industry, the international liquor companies, or the underground distribution of illicit substances. This society looks for pain eradication, relief, gusto, and a lift through substances. (California Commission, 1986)

The Mass Media: Glamorization of the Drug Lifestyle

A media explosion occurred after television appeared on the American scene in the late 1940s. This technological invention dramatically altered the recreational habits of Americans and became a major source of information, attitudes and values. Surveys in the early 1950s indicated that by graduation, high school students had spent 11,000 to 15,000 hours viewing television (Manchester, 1974). Nearly four decades later, these figures doubled. More than 20,000 hours of accumulative television viewing now occur before high school graduation, compared to about 12,000 hours spent in school (Resnik, 1985).

In order to attract viewers, script writers and producers provide high-action episodes that often glamorize drugs, crime, and street life. In 1970, the first author (Coombs) spent several months as a researcher in a Synanon-like program associating with hard-core addicts sent there by the courts in lieu of prison. This proved to be a cultural shock, and involved exposure to an entirely new vocabulary of street jargon. Within a few years, this vocabulary, popularized by the media, became commonplace among middle-class youth. Television, cinema and rock music gave this specialized argot common usage.

An ongoing mental diet of pro-drug messages during the formative years of personality development no doubt takes its toll, as reflected by this comment from a 20-year-old addict. "Parents have this vision of what school is like when they attended it. They remember how kids who smoked pot were the social rejects. But today, the minority is the majority. If you don't do drugs, you are out of it. You ain't cool. You ain't with it. You ain't nothing on the social scene" (Meyer, 1985).

In other words, alcohol and other drugs are now status symbols among many youngsters. "It is real easy to make friends if you get high," one youth commented. "No one cares about your views on the Middle East; all you talk about is drugs, drugs, drugs" (Beyette, 1983).

An editor of *Parade Magazine* who published a July 1985 story entitled, "Does Hollywood Sell Drugs to Kids?" testified before a Congressional Committee that with only a modest investment of time and effort, he identified and viewed 57 major motion pictures that contained pro-drug messages. Only nine were found with negative messages. Several of the films aimed at the teenage and young adult audience suggested that marijuana and heavy drinking are necessary components for having a good time. "Getting blitzed on pot or booze is treated in these films as a sort of inevitable right of teenage passage," he testified (Satchell, 1985).

Until recently media representatives have resisted self-regulatory efforts, arguing that censorship stifles creativity. In 1985, however, the Entertainment Industries Council (EIC) marshalled the combined resources of the media industries (recording companies, the motion picture industry and television) to reverse the trend that glamorizes drug and alcohol lifestyles. Joining with the National Institute on Drug Abuse, the EIC sponsored a 1986 conference in Los Angeles on cocaine abuse and the media. Poignant testimonies were given by media executives and celebrities about loved ones whose lives had been lost or permanently scarred by chemical dependency. "Those of us in the entertainment industry believe," a media executive remarked, "that there is a great opportunity before us to educate young people to make a decision—to make a right decision—ideally not to be involved in drugs and alcohol abuse" (Dyk, 1986).

In 1984, the media donated well over three-quarters of a billion dollars of free time to public service campaigns. But an A. C. Neilsen Company study found that these "no-use" messages did not reach the younger audiences. Of the 98 public service announcements pertaining to drug and alcohol abuse aired by CBS during January 1985, the gross audience impressions (number of times viewed by audience members) were as follows: adults, 422 million; teens (ages 12-17), 10.4 million; and children (ages 2-11), 68 million. Similar studies of NBC's 585 public service announcements also found that children and youth are least likely to see them.

Although encouraging media plans are apparently underway to reverse the negative trend that glamorizes drug lifestyles, it is questionable whether the damage can be reversed. Can an entire generation change who have matured in an environment saturated with messages that glamorize substances?

FAMILY STRENGTHENING TO PREVENT SUBSTANCE USE

Parents compete against formidable odds when they try to prevent their offspring from using alcohol and other drugs. With well organized, billion dollar industries intentionally or inadvertently promoting these substances, what hope do parents have? What influence can they have in the face of such overwhelming obstacles?

Governmental efforts to prevent drug abuse, which overlook the role of families, are usually ineffective, and sometimes counterproductive. The immense industries that evolved to deal with drug problems have done relatively little to help parents. Although an increasing number of specialists have been enlisted to combat drug use, problems have multiplied rather than diminished. A growing army of criminal justice personnel has not impeded the escalation of drug-related problems. Prisons and jails mushroom to make room for increasing numbers of young people whose personal lives have become entangled with drugs. These institutions often function as "graduate schools" that sharpen criminal skills, expand the network of "connections," and generally reinforce drug lifestyles (Coombs, 1981).

Traditional interventions utilize punitive approaches that ignore the potential of parents to alter their adolescents' behaviors (Coombs, 1984). Such measures are often stigmatizing, lengthy, after-the-fact treatments that are rarely successful (Coombs, 1981). These methods fail to take into account the fact that families are the most potent source of social control, the catalyst for emotional well-being and the keystone of societal civility. Intervention programs aimed at youth, rather than the interacting family, are likely to be futile (California Department of Alcohol and Drug Programs,

1983). The potential of family strengthening approaches for preventing and resolving youth problems has scarcely been tapped.

During recent years, considerable research literature has accumulated to support the view that family strengthening approaches such as family therapy and parent training constitute the most effective intervention techniques. Family strengthening interventions that utilize a constructional or educational approach, rather than the stigmatizing criminal justice or medical models, offer great promise. Based on the reconstructive philosophy of the social learning model, family interventions instigate and consequate within the youth's own family and peer networks. Figure 1 compares the family strengthening approach with traditional ones (Coombs, 1984).

The potential success of family interventions is summarized by Bronfenbrenner (1977) as follows,

> When we apply our best minds to the problems of caring for children, I think we will have the deflating experience of rediscovering the wheel. We will find that families, after all, are really very efficient. We don't need a new social vehicle. All we have to do is create new conditions to enable families to do what they do better than anybody else. (Bronfenbrenner, 1977)

The Need for a Federal Family Policy

At no other time in history has the need for parent training and other forms of family strengthening been more apparent. At stake is the health and well-being of American youth. If youngsters' lives are to be enriched rather than impaired, national resources must be marshalled to strengthen families. Corporate profit-making schemes that promote and glamorize substance use are most effectively counteracted by solidifying families and enhancing parental effectiveness. Parents offer the greatest potential for preventing drug use among American youth.

Because the United States has no family policy, many governmental and privately sponsored endeavors undermine families and put adolescents at risk. A few high profile politicians have underscored this need, but little progress has ensued.

In 1976, for example, Presidential candidate Jimmy Carter re-

COMPARISON OF TRADITIONAL APPROACHES WITH FAMILY LEARNING APPROACH

	Traditional Approaches	*Family Learning Approach*
Underlying assumption	Deficient (sick and/or deviant) personalities become substance abusers.	Normal youth become substance abusers.
Treatment approach	Remedial (psychotherapy, detention, or alternative medication).	Preventive skill development via education and training.
Extent of anti-drug counseling	Maximal, which may unwittingly stimulate curiosity, drug sophistication and experimentation.	Minimal, emphasis on developing prosocial behaviors.
Treatment focus	On the individual.	On the family in social context.
Impact on family	Fragment the family through incarceration, etc.	Solidify the family through keeping the members together and strengthening family skills.
Impact on individual	Stigma (participants are "patients," "law-breakers," juvenile offenders," etc.).	Education/personality growth through skill attainment; participants are "students."
Resulting self-concepts	Identify with street subculture.	Identify with "straights."
Resulting life-style and attitude	Dopers are cool; straight is lame.	Straight's okay.
Outreach cost benefits	Continuing governmental subsidy; reliance on professional services.	Parents are potentially not only more concerned and aware, their impact can be more long-lasting and effective; moreover, they charge no fee.

FIGURE 1

marked: "It is clear that the national government should have a strong pro-family policy, but the fact is that our government has no family policy, and that is the same as an anti-family policy" (Woessner, 1978). His running mate, Walter F. Mondale, echoed this view: "We need to begin examining the impact of changing social conditions on the family. We need to begin shaping a society that doesn't just tolerate family life, or pretend to be neutral toward it. We need instead a society that nourishes it, and helps it grow strong'' (Mondale, 1977).

Elaborating on this theme, U.S. Senator Orin Hatch identified families as "the original custodians and providers of health, education and welfare." "Families are," he says, "the bedrock of our country and we must recognize that what strengthens the family strengthens the society" (Department of Health, Education, and Welfare, 1980). Urging that family issues be raised to a national level, Hatch proposes an examination of the impact on the family of every piece of legislation before it becomes law (*Family Therapy News*, 1986).

Charles McC. Mathias, Jr. noted, "Just about every social, economic and ideological unit in the country has a lobby and a respondent government policy except our most basic unit, the family" (*Congressional Record*, 1986). In fact, as Lazar (1978) observed, many national programs act in a destructive fashion with respect to families.

In an article entitled, "A Family Policy for the Nation" (1986), U.S. Senator Daniel Patrick Moynihan observed, "American social policy until now has been directed toward the individual. The individual—and the various circumstances relating to him—has been our primary unit of measurement: men, women and children are all lumped together." In a July 1986 hearing before the U.S. Senate Rules and Administration Committee Moynihan said: "The family situation America faces today is without historical precedent. We do not know what is going on." Speaking in support of a resolution to create a Senate Special Committee on Families, Youth and Children, he urged, "It is time that the U.S. Senate—whose members are rightly alarmed by the enormous problems facing American families and children—make an institutional commitment to the study of these issues and to an examination of possible remedies."

Moynihan argued that the United States is probably the first society in history in which children are distinctively worse off than adults, and that, "A nation that fails to put its' children first, finishes last" (Moynihan, 1985).

A Statewide Family-Centered Approach to Drug Prevention

The prevention of alcohol and drug misuse requires a coordinated, multifaceted approach that strengthens families in all racial, ethnic and sociocultural environments, and rewards youngsters of all ages and developmental circumstances for lifestyles that exclude the unwholesome use of substances. A viable prevention plan must effectively link in coordinated effort the actions of elected officials, service providers, the media, volunteer organizations, governmental agencies, churches, neighborhoods, families and youths. Rather than isolated and competitive programs, a comprehensive approach requires a concerted effort that benefits all parents and their children.

An example of a family-oriented approach is offered by the California Commission on the Prevention of Drug and Alcohol Abuse. Initiated by State Attorney General John K. Van De Kamp in 1986, this comprehensive plan interrelates significant segments of society to produce an environment conducive to viable families and healthy adolescents. Coordinated antidrug efforts involve the mass media, private industry, religious and voluntary organizations, schools, health care providers and law enforcement and regulatory agencies. Figure 2 displays the conceptual model that underlies this prevention plan (California Commission, 1986).

After a series of public hearings where expert witnesses presented their views and their recommendations for prevention, a document was published (Van De Kamp, 1986) to outline specific goals for this coordinated plan.

Two major financial and organizational elements underlie the plan. First, the commission proposes an unprecedented and sweeping ballot initiative to create a $600 million-a-year state "Children's Superfund" to finance a massive new state drug and alcohol abuse prevention effort. This Children's Superfund, totally self-financed by taxes on alcohol and cigarettes, is earmarked solely for the prevention of drug and alcohol abuse. These new taxes, long overdue, will raise taxes on alcohol and cigarettes only to the level at which they would be today had they been indexed for inflation; neither tax has been increased in the state for 18 years. Second, the

A Conceptual Model for Preventive Approaches to Alcohol and Drug Abuse

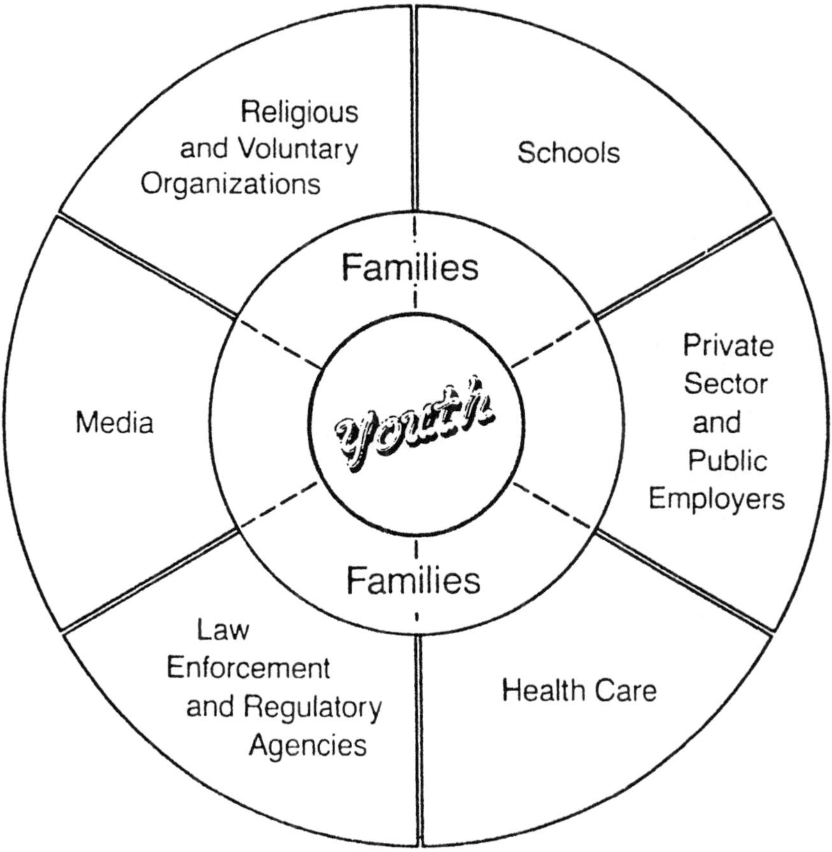

FIGURE 2

proposal envisions the creation of the California Master Plan for the Prevention of Drug and Alcohol Abuse Among Our Children. The state master plan, developed with community input, will provide the basic framework for a coordinated statewide program. It defines the respective roles of the state and the communities in relation to each other and in terms of the overall program. A State Prevention Council, supported by a State Resources Center, will coordinate state level activities. A Community Master Plan will provide the framework for planning and coordinating publicly funded programs within local communities.

Below, a few of the Commission recommendations are briefly outlined:

The Mass Media: (1) A media campaign, organized by a Governor's Media Task Force to bring together the best talent in radio, television, video, cinema, print, and advertising agencies to make significant contributions that deglamorize substances and promote healthy lifestyles; (2) Encouragement of advertising executives to develop and monitor self-regulating policies that discourage marketing messages that directly or indirectly contribute to drug and alcohol use.

Religious and Voluntary Organizations: (1) The establishment of local Prevention Councils to promote and coordinate innovative programs, and to strengthen neighborhoods conducive to healthy family life, especially in neighborhoods comprised of impacted families with low-income, underserved minority populations; (2) The organization and coordination of parent-training sessions and parent-support groups within local schools, churches and health care agencies; (3) The ongoing training of clergy, teachers and lay leaders in effective prevention strategies and health education.

Health Care Providers: (1) The establishment of licensing requirements for physicians, nurses, psychologists, social workers and family counselors to ensure adequate training in the use of strategies pertaining to drug-related problems among children and adolescents; (2) Health warning labels on containers and advertisements for alcoholic beverages.

Schools: (1) As a requirement for graduation, high school students must demonstrate a knowledge of the effects and consequences of alcohol and drug use; (2) To be eligible for credential renewal, teachers should demonstrate competence in drug and alcohol prevention strategies; (3) The initiation and support of peer leadership training programs, peer counseling and support groups to develop and reinforce positive social norms; (4) Provide adult education programs that enhance parenting skills and techniques that prevent drug-related problems; (5) Legal immunity for teachers who intervene with students suspected of possessing or using drugs or alcohol; (6) Incentive programs to encourage teachers to work with high-risk youths and to become more effective in providing prevention programs; (7) Student assistance programs to provide appropriate help to students with physical, emotional, legal, medical, familial and social problems related to drug use.

Private Sector and Public Employees: (1) The sponsorship by employers of health promotions programs that benefit entire families. A decrease in absenteeism, a reduction in sick leave, and improved productivity occur when things go well for employees at home. Personnel policies that reduce stress and enhance coping include day-care services for children within close proximity to the work site, flex job scheduling, job sharing and maternity leaves. On-site health promotion and training for employees and families, opportunities for meaningful community involvement for workers and their families (such as recreational, athletic, health fairs, etc.) and employee assistance programs that enhance healthy family life; (2) Employee assistance programs to assist employees who are enmeshed in alcohol- and drug-related problems. Although job termination may be required in some cases, a referral for needed help may save a valuable employee, prevent other employers from inheriting an impaired employee, and most importantly, provide youngsters with the necessary support and professional help; (3) Partnership with schools and community-action groups to help discourage school dropouts by offering jobs to those who do not plan on college, if grades and attendance are maintained. In Boston, for example, more than 10,000 high risk students have been placed in summer jobs and permanent jobs, thanks to guarantees made by business leaders (*Los Angeles Times*, Editorial, 1987).

In sum, this plan is no panacea for all drug-related problems. But it exemplifies the kind of governmental supported programs, guided by a clear family policy, that must be undertaken to counteract institutionalized societal forces that aid and encourage alcohol and drug use.

If youngsters are to be spared the self-destruction sequela of drug abuse, every effort must be made to strengthen families and to reduce the pro-drug messages that glamorize and promote the inappropriate use of substances. Societal control can be most effectively achieved, not by expanding regulatory and criminal justice agencies, but by thoughtful efforts that strengthen families and increase the potential of parents to effectively manage their own children.

REFERENCES

Atkin, C. & Block, M. (1981). *Content and Effects of Alcohol Advertising*. Bureau of Alcohol, Tobacco and Firearms, U.S. Government, Washington, DC, Report of a Michigan State University Study.

Banks, Sandy. (1983, February 20). Careful head shops still raided. *Los Angeles Times*, Section V, Part 9, p. 1.

Bernstein, Arnold & Lennard, H.L. (1973). Drugs, doctors and junkies. *Society, 10*(May-June), pp. 14-25.

Beschner, George M. & Friedman, Alfred S. (1979). *Youth Drug Abuse: Problems, Issues and Treatment*. Lexington, MA: D.C. Heath and Company.

Beyette, Beverly. (1983, September 18). Teenager's no. 1 drug: Alcohol. *Los Angeles Times*, pp. 1, 22-25.

Broder, John M. (1987, March 26). Head of Anheuser-Busch's beer subsidiary resigns as financial scandal spreads. *Los Angeles Times*, p. 1.

Byrne, Susan. (1977, May). Nobody home: The erosion of the American family. *Psychology Today*, pp. 40-47.

California Department of Alcohol and Drug Programs. (1983). *Youth = Alcohol and Drug Abuse, Consolidation of Available Data*. Sacramento: Author.

Clark, Wayne. (1985, December 12). Testimony given to San Francisco hearing, *Attorney General's Commission on the Prevention of Drug and Alcohol Abuse*, p. 28.

Cohen, S.J. (1981). *The Substance Abuse Problems*. New York: The Haworth Press.

Community and Legal Responses to Drug Paraphernalia. (1980). DHEW, Public Service, ADAMHA (ADM) 80-963.

CompCare. (1983). *Facts About Teenage Problem Drinking and Drug Abuse*, Newport Beach, CA: Author. Based on an interview with representatives of U.S. Bureau of Vital Statistics Branch, April 15, 1983.

Coombs, Robert H. (1981). Back on the streets: Therapeutic communities' impact upon drug users. *American Journal of Drug and Alcohol Abuse, 8*(2), pp. 185-201.

Coombs, Robert H. (1981). Drug abuse as a career. *Journal of Drug Issues, 11*(4), pp. 369-387.

Coombs, Robert H., Santana, F.O. & Fawzy, F.I. (1984). Parent training to prevent adolescent drug use: An educational model. *Journal of Drug Issues, 14*(2), pp. 393-402.

Crime and Delinquency in California – 1984. (1985, June). California Department of Justice, Bureau of Criminal Statistics Special Services, pp. 126-133.

Dyk, Brian. (1986, January 29). Testimony to the Los Angeles hearing, *Attorney General's Commission on the Prevention of Drug and Alcohol Abuse*, p. 25.

Editorial. (1987, March 26). A promising incentive. *Los Angeles Times*, p. 4.

Entertainment Industries Council, Inc. (1985, Fall/Winter). EIC co-sponsors cocaine conference in Los Angeles. pp. 4-5.

Fatal Accident Reporting System, 1982. (1984). U.S. Department of Transportation, DOT No. HS-806-566.

Federal Strategy for Drug Abuse and Drug Traffic Prevention – 1979. (1980). Cited in NIDA Service Research Report, "Community and Legal Responses to Drug Paraphernalia," DHEW Publication No. (ADM) 80-963.

Gailbraith, John Kenneth. (1971). *The New Industrial State*, (2nd ed.). Boston: Houghton-Mifflin.

Glenn, H.S. (1986, September/October). Affluence and the family. *Focus on Family and Chemical Dependency*, pp. 6-7, 32, 46.

Golden, William E. (1987, March 19). "Information Overload: Coping With the Medical Literature," oral presentation given at the American Medical Association 37th Annual Convention, New Orleans, Louisiana.

Hatch, Orin. (1986). *Family Therapy News*, p. 5.

Hubbard, Robert L., Cavanaugh, E.R., Rachal, J.V., Schleñger, W.E. & Ginsburg, H.M. (1983). Alcohol Use and Problems Among Adolescent Clients in Drug Treatment Programs. *Alcohol Health and Research World*, 7(4), pp. 10-18.

Institute of Medicine, National Academy of Sciences, (1980). *Report of a Study: Alcoholism, Alcohol Abuse and Related Problems*. Opportunities for Research. National Academy Press, Washington, D.C., Pub. No. IOM-80-04.

Jalon, Allan. (1986, January 27). 'Head shops' try to head off convictions. *Los Angeles Times*, p. 6.

Jalon, Allan. (1986, June 8). Deep inside the pill trade. *Los Angeles Times*, pp. 10-15; 23-26.

Johnson, Sterling. (1987, March 19). Drug war turned 'sad state of affairs,' *USA Today*.

Johnston, Lloyd D., Bachman, J.G. & O'Malley, P.M. (1986). *Monitoring the Future, 1975-1985: Questionnaire Responses From the Nation's High School Seniors*. Ann Arbor, MI: Institute for Social Research, The University of Michigan.

Johnston, Lloyd D., O'Malley, P.M. & Bachman, J.G. (1986). *Drug Use Among American High School and College Students and Other Young Adults: National Trends Through 1985*. DHHS Publication No. (ADM) 86-1450. p. 20.

Lazar, Irving. (1978). *Formulating National Policies on Child and Family Development, Year 1*. Ithaca, NY: Cornell University, Department of Community Service.

Legislation Relating to Mail Order Drug Paraphernalia, H.R. 1625. (1986,

May 8). Hearing Before the Subcommittee on Crime of the Committee on the Judiciary, U.S. House of Representatives.

Manchester, William. (1974). *The Glory and the Dream*. Boston: Little Brown and Company.

Meyer, J. Stryker. (1985, November). *Drugs in the '80s: A San Diego Union Special Report*, pp. 1-24.

Milman, Doris H., Bennett, A.A. & Hanson, M. (1983). Psychological effects of alcohol in children and adolescents. *Alcohol, Health and Research World*, NIAAA 7(4), pp. 50-53.

Mondale, Walter F. (1977, May). The family in trouble. *Psychology Today*, p. 39.

Moskowitz, Daniel B. & Pave, I. (1985, February 25). The sobering of America: A push to put drinking in its place. *Business Week*, pp. 112-113.

Moynihan, Daniel Patrick. (1985, May 22). *Congressional Record*, Volume 31, No. 68., p. 1.

Moynihan, Daniel Patrick. (1986, February 3). Report: Proceedings and Debates, *Congressional Record*, 99th Congress, 2nd Session, Volume 132, No. 8.

Moynihan, Daniel Patrick. (1986, March 22). A family policy for the nation, 1965-1986. *America*, pp. 221-223.

News and Information Services, University of Michigan, "Youth Drug Use Little Improved in Class of '85 Survey Shows," (1985, November 6). p. 2. Based upon Johnson, et al. (1986), *Drug Use Among American High School Students, College Students and Other Young Adults: National Trends Through 1985*. DHHS Publication No. (ADM) 86-1450.

Noble, Ernest P. (1978). *Third Special Report to the U.S. Congress on Alcohol and Health*, Technical Support Document, DHEW Publication No. (ADM) 79-832.

Radecki, Thomas, Chairman of the National Coalition on Television Violence, 1983. Alcoholism and other alcohol-related problems among children and youth. (August, 1986). Cited by the National Council on Alcoholism, Inc.

Reidinger, Judith, Executive Director of the National Drug Abuse Foundation, (1980, March 21). *Alcohol Drug Abuse and Mental Health Administration (ADAMHA) News*, Vol. VI, No. 6, p. 7.

Report on the National Conference for Youth on Drinking and Driving, (1984, April 27-30). Washington DC: U.S. Department of Health, and Human Services, NIAAA.

Resnik, Hank. (1985). *Television and Families: Impact and Interaction*. National Council for Families and Television, Volume 8, No. 3, pp. 2-7.

Satchell, Michael. (1985, October 24). Statement before the United States Permanent Subcommittee on Investigation, Washington, DC.

Seidenberg, Robert. (1976). Mass media inducement: Enticements to begin. In R.H. Coombs, L. Fry and P. Lewis (eds.) *Socialization in Drug Abuse*. Cambridge: Schenkman Publishing Company, Inc.

Skager, Rodney. (1986, May). A statewide survey of drug and alcohol use among

California's students in grades 7, 9 and 11. Winter 1985-86. In *Attorney General's Commission on the Prevention of Drug and Alcohol Abuse.*

Smark, Reginald G. (1976). *The New Drinkers: Teenage Use and Abuse of Alcohol.* Toronto, Canada: Addiction Research Foundation Program, Rep. Serial No. 4.

Sorrentino, A. (1979). *How to Organize the Neighborhood for Delinquency Prevention.* New York: Human Science Press.

Sperling, Dan. (1985, October 8). Teen cocaine dependency use on rise. *USA Today*, in *Attorney General's Commission on the Prevention of Drug and Alcohol Abuse*, p. 53.

Spierer, Diane. (1986, January 9). Testimony to San Diego hearing, *Attorney General's Commission on the Prevention of Drug and Alcohol Abuse*, p. 72.

Stewart, Robert W. (1984, January 5). Year old law yields few convictions. *Los Angeles Times*, p. 1.

Television and the Family. (1986). Elk Grove, IL: American Academy of Pediatrics.

Testimony, President of the National Federation of Parents for Drug Free Youth, (1986). Before the U.S. House Subcommittee on Crime.

U.S. Congress, Office of Technology Assessment data. (1987, March 19). Cited by House Select Committee on Narcotics Abuse and Control.

U.S. DHHS National Center for Health Statistics. (1980, November). Public Health Service, Publication No. (PHS)81-1232.

U.S. DHHS; NIAAA, Public Health Service. (1983). Questions and answers: Teenager alcohol use and abuse. *Prevention Plus: Involving Schools, Parents and the Community in Alcohol and Drug Education.* Rockville, MD: Publication no. CADM 841256.

Van de Kamp, John K. (1986, May). *Attorney General's Commission on the Prevention of Drug and Alcohol Abuse.* Executive Summary, Statement of the Commission.

Wallack, Lawrence. (1984). Prevention Research Group of the Institute of Epidemiology and Behavioral Medicine, San Francisco: Medical Research Institute.

Woessner, Bob. (1978, May 7). The family: Family scope undefined. *Green Bay Press-Gazette.*

Wolff, Lester. (1985, November 17). U.S. House of Representatives Select Committee on Narcotic Abuse and Control.

Wynne, R.D., Blasinsky, M., Cook, P. et al. (1980). *Community and Legal Responses to Drug Paraphernalia*, NIDA, Services Research Report, DHEW Publication Number (ADM) 80-963.

Youth, Alcohol and Drug Abuse. (1983, November). Department of Alcohol and Drug Programs, State of California, Health and Welfare Agency, ADP 83-10, p. 29.

Zweig, Connie. (1986, November 28). Doctors use acupuncture to help addicts kick habit. *Los Angeles Times*, pp. 1, 4.

Family Theory and Research on Adolescent Drug Use: A Review

Thomas J. Glynn, PhD
Marianne Haenlein, PhD

While numerous research investigations have explored problems relating to drug abuse, emphasis on the role of the family in these investigations is relatively new. Traditionally, drug abuse was viewed within a medical framework and the majority of research and treatment efforts focused on the individual (Clayton, 1979; Freedman & Finnegan, 1976). Over the past decade, however, research efforts have looked beyond the drug-using individual to determine the role of the family in the initiation and maintenance of drug use. As a result of these efforts, several family factors have been identified that appear to influence drug use (e.g., Glynn, 1984; Seldin, 1972; Stanton, 1979a). In addition, a number of theoretical and methodological problems within the literature have been identified that have limited the conclusions that may be drawn from these investigations. To better understand these conclusions and to identify the most promising areas of future research, we will start by reviewing these theoretical and methodological issues.

THEORETICAL AND METHODOLOGICAL ISSUES

At the theoretical level, understanding the relationship between the family and drug use has been limited by a relatively recent em-

Thomas J. Glynn is Program Director for Smoking Research, Office of the Director, Division of Cancer Prevention and Control, National Cancer Institute, Blair Building, Room 432, 9000 Rockville Pike, Bethesda, MD 20892-4200. Marianne Haenlein is Deputy Project Manager, Prospect Associates, Ltd., 1801 Rockville Pike, Suite 500, Rockville, MD 20852.

pirical foundation and a paucity of theoretically guided research (e.g., Braucht, Brakarsh, Follingstad, & Berry, 1973; Glynn, 1984; Long & Scherl, 1984). Empirical investigations have addressed a broad range of issues, including the influence of structural characteristics of the family, such as birth order (e.g., Greenwald, Carter, & Stein, 1973; Rathus, Richner-Rathus, & Siegel, 1977; Schultz & Wilson, 1973) and family size (Binion, 1979; Schultz & Wilson, 1973), as well as dynamic characteristics of the family, such as the parent-child relationship (e.g., Blechman, 1982; Stanton, 1979a) and parenting style (e.g., Blum and Associates, 1972; Baumrind, 1975). Additionally, different stages of drug use, including initiation, maintenance, cessation, and prevention (e.g., Kandel, 1974, 1978; Glynn, 1981), and type of drug used, such as tobacco, marijuana, heroin, and stimulants (e.g., Glynn, 1982), have been explored.

Given the relatively recent investigation of issues related to drug use and the family and the broad range of topics investigated, it is not surprising that our understanding of the factors that influence drug use only begins to scratch the surface of these issues. This situation is exemplified by investigations of the effect of birth order on adolescent drug use. Investigations not only have yielded conflicting results but have utilized varying samples and methods as well (Glynn, 1984). The resulting problem is the uncertainty about both the origin of these discrepant results and the nature of the effect of birth order on adolescent drug use. In this way, the empirical foundation in this area, while broad, lacks the depth of understanding within each topic area that will come with continued research.

In addition to this relatively weak empirical foundation, no single theoretical perspective has guided the majority of these investigations. Research has addressed the issue of drug use and the family from perspectives ranging from psychosocial (e.g., Kandel, 1978) to psychodynamic theory (e.g., Hendin, Pollinger, Ulman, & Carr, 1981). Based on different theoretical perspectives, investigations of the relationship of the family to drug use have each asked different questions, thus making integration of the resulting data difficult. In addition, each perspective has been criticized as incomplete (Huba, Wingard, & Bentler, 1980). Even more serious, these attempts to identify family-related factors that influence drug use in isolation of other factors have in many cases resulted in overly simplistic causal assumptions. Many family-oriented theoreticians have viewed the factors influencing drug use as functioning along linear causal lines (i.e., A causes B or A and B cause C) rather than as occurring as a complex set of feedback mechanisms operating within an open system (i.e., A causes B, B causes C, C causes A) (Baltes, 1979; Stanton et al., 1978).

At the methodological level, generalizations about the relationship between the family and drug use have been limited by methods of subject selection, operational definitions, and measurement and procedural confoundings. Subjects often have been recruited from psychiatric and delinquent populations, with the result that conclusions from these studies cannot readily be extended beyond these special populations (Blechman, 1982; Hamburg, Kraemer, & Jahnke, 1975). Further, generalizations are restricted because many of the subjects investigated were heavy drug users. In this case, conclusions are limited not only because these individuals reflect the extreme end of the continuum of drug use and may therefore represent an inherently different group but because the established behavioral patterns of addiction would be expected to alter fundamentally the nature of interactions within the family environment, as has been consistently demonstrated by Stanton and his colleagues (e.g., 1978, 1982).

In addition to the methodological problems emanating from the selection of subjects from nonrepresentative populations, efforts to integrate investigations exploring drug use and the family have been hampered by the fact that little attention has been paid to the operational definition of drug use in terms of both the amount, as mentioned above, and the type of drug being used. Many investigations make no distinction between categories of drugs, and although the majority of early investigations focused on more potent drugs of abuse such as opiates (Clayton, 1979; Glynn, 1984), results are often generalized to all drug categories. This practice is not without some theoretical rationale. It has been argued that all drug categories, regardless of pharmacologic differences, may be linked by their dependence-producing effects. These drugs all serve as reinforcers, maintain behavior directed toward drug acquisition, and lead to the sacrifice of other reinforcers (Kalant et al., 1978). Convincing arguments for the unifying addictive features of drugs ranging from tobacco to opiates have been made (Henningfield, Griffiths, & Insinski, 1981). However, in view of the evidence of different influences on and patterns of use for different types of drugs (Stanton, 1978), appropriate concern should be given to generalizations about the influence of family factors across categories of drugs used. Using this same logic, it seems appropriate to recommend caution in terms of generalizations across varying doses and frequencies of drug use as well.

Concern about various measurement and procedural confoundings in these early investigations also has been raised. Self-report questionnaires have been used extensively as an index of drug use, and some investigators have expressed concern over inaccuracies of reports of both the type and amount of drug use resulting from individual biases (Hamburg et al., 1975). Such biases would be particularly problematic for cross-sectional investigations of drug abusers of different ages because of the confounding of age and history. Because different age groups have experienced different histories, they will likely hold different views about both the type and amount of drug use. For example, attitudes about cigarette use are markedly different in the 1980s compared with the 1960s. Increased awareness in the 1980s of the deleterious effects of tobacco use might be reflected in a respondent's bias to underreport tobacco use. Even more problematic for investigations on drug use and family factors is that response bias might be directly correlated with important family factors, such as divorce. For example, adolescents from divorced families might overreport drug use as a way of calling attention to their problems. Thus reports of higher incidence of drug use in adolescents of divorced families, based on self-report questionnaires alone, may not necessarily reflect any effect of divorce per se on drug use. It is possible that divorce is correlated more with self-report of drug use than actual drug use. In either case, unambiguous interpretation of the relationship between divorce and drug use is difficult to achieve. Obviously, confidentiality and other methodological procedures must be used to prevent ambiguous results that emanate from methodological confoundings relating to response bias.

Another methodological problem that has served to limit conclusions from investigations of drug use and the family concerns the use of retrospective data. Even when such data can be verified beyond subjects' recollections, the attribution of a causal relationship between prior family events and drug use is problematic in the absence of information about other individuals encountering the same family event but not resorting to drug use (Salmon & Salmon, 1977). Thus retrospective data only provide one-half of the information that is necessary for predicting future drug use.

Finally, a very important concern has been expressed about the fruitfulness of approaching a complex multivariate problem with simplistic bivariate experimental designs and analyses (Blechman, 1982). This concern, a statistical one at first glance, is in fact a methodological reflection of the more fundamental theoretical issue discussed earlier. That is, as a result of attempts to identify individual family-related factors that influence drug use in isolation of other factors, overly simplistic causal assumptions have been made. Appropriate to the level of these assumptions, bivariate statistics were used. However, drug use and its relation within the family are characterized by complex interactions occurring over many years and involving individuals at many life stages. It seems more appropriate that an etiologic model incorporate multicausal and dynamic influences, and as a result, the appropriate statistical procedures must assess multivariate relationships.

In summary, it is apparent that significant theoretical and methodological problems have impeded progress in the research of family factors that influence drug use. However, given the range of issues addressed, the diversity of theoretical perspectives used, and the variety of methodological problems present within this short history of family-related drug use research, it is no wonder that the data base developed thus far, while providing a firm foundation by which to direct future research, does not provide an unambiguous delineation of which and in what way family factors influence drug use from initiation to cessation. It does, however, provide the foundation not only for theoretically and methodologically superior research but for the identification of promising topics for future investigations.

The remainder of this paper will review the literature on drug use and the family to identify broad family factors that are thought to influence drug use and propose areas of future research designed to identify more specifically the nature of these factors and the way in which they influence drug use. Against this background of theoretical and methodological issues, we adopt a systems-lifespan orientation to studying the family and adolescent drug use (e.g., Baltes, 1979; Baltes & Brim, 1980; Baltes, Reese, & Lipsitt, 1980; Glynn, 1982, 1984; Klagsbrun & Davis, 1977; Stanton, 1979b). Drug use is viewed as a functional behavior set within the context of both the user's and the family members' past histories and future expectations. Members' histories and expectations change constantly as they move through different life stages, and their patterns of interaction and personal coping strategies change as well. Thus to understand better the initiation and maintenance of drug use within the family system, our goal is to identify the patterns of interaction and coping that appear to contribute to the initiation, reinforcement, and maintenance of drug use within the family system. For this reason, the literature on drug use and the family will be organized around the dynamic structures of the parent-child relationship and the parent as teacher, including both parental style and parental modeling.

PARENT-CHILD RELATIONSHIP

Considerable attention has been paid to the nature of the parent-child relationship as an aspect of the family that is likely to influence adolescent drug use (e.g., Coleman, 1981a; Gorsuch & Butler, 1976). Research has focused on identifying consistent features of the individual roles within the mother-father-child triad as well as identifying specific developmental stages and life events within this unit that appear to influence drug use. The near unanimous conclusion is that a positive relationship between the child and his or her parents can serve as a deterrent to the use of drugs (e.g., Auerswald, 1980; Brook, Whiteman, Gordon, & Brook, 1984, 1985; Gorsuch & Butler, 1976; Kandel, 1973, 1974, 1978, 1982; Reilly, 1975; Stanton & Todd, 1982; Stanton et al., 1978). Although the presence or absence of either or both parents has been associated with increased smoking (Nolte, Smith, & O'Rourke, 1983) and use of alcohol and marijuana (Stern, Northman, & Van Slyck, 1984; Brook, Whiteman, & Gordon, 1985), Gorsuch and

Butler (1976) have even suggested that, in predicting a child's drug use, "the presence or absence of parents is less crucial than the nature of the parental relationship" (p. 124).

The relationship between mother, father, and child is, of course, fraught with many potential pitfalls. However, investigations of families with a drug-abusing member have identified some consistent patterns. The most common theme is that of a dominant mother who is overindulgent, overprotective, and manipulative. The father, on the other hand, is typically far more subordinate, being viewed as weak, inept, and uninvolved (e.g., Zimmering, Toolan, Safrin, & Wortis, 1951; Attardo, 1965; Torda, 1968; Seldin, 1972; Eldred & Washington, 1976; Schwartzman, 1975; Salmon & Salmon, 1977; Schneider, Kojak, & Ressdorf, 1977; Stanton, 1979a, 1979b; Kaufman, 1981). While the father's passive role in this pattern projects greater distance from and less affection to the child (Brook, Gordon, & Brook, 1980; Brook, Whiteman, Brook, & Gordon, 1981; Brook, Whiteman, & Gordon, 1981; Schneider et al., 1977), the mother's more active role, to the point of overinvolvement, does not necessarily bring with it greater affection (Brook et al., 1980; Brook, Whiteman, Brook, & Gordon, 1981; Brook, Whiteman, & Gordon, 1981). Thus children in this pattern may feel caught between extremes of over- and underinvolvement but in neither case perceive the parental acceptance and love that they need.

Although less consistent, other patterns—particularly of paternal interaction—have been identified. For example, some investigators have documented patterns of paternal overindulgence and manipulation (Alexander & Dibb, 1975, 1977; Kaufman & Kaufman, 1979). Kirschenbaum, Leonoff, & Maliano (1974) described fathers of drug users who assumed a more traditional role of providing material support, engaging in stereotyped masculine activities, and maintaining an appearance of control, independence, and emotional maturity. Even within these different observed roles of fathers, just as in the different roles observed between the typical mother and father described above, there is a pattern of either high or low overt involvement. Based on observations that neither underinvolvement nor overinvolvement necessarily conveys affection, it is possible that the perception of the absence of parental love and acceptance, more than the specific extremes of over- and underinvolvement, is the more critical factor contributing to adolescent drug use.

Accompanying these roles within the mother-father-child triad are ineffective and symptomatic communication problems (Cannon, 1976; Jurich, Polson, Jurich, & Bates, 1985; Kandel, 1978; Reilly, 1976; Wittenborn, Smith, & Wittenborn, 1970). Not only is the interaction between the drug user and his or her parents typical of the classic generation gap, but communication between parents is often poor as well. Again, the theme of a perceived absence of love and acceptance emerges. Interactions are described as affectless, without intimacy, and negative (Kirschenbaum et al., 1974; D'Onofrio, Thier, Schnor, Buchanan, & Omelich, 1982; Norem-Hebeisen, Johnson, Anderson, & Johnson, 1984; Reilly, 1975, 1976). Even more disturbing is the fact that attempts to enhance communication are often sabotaged by denial of the existence of any problems (Huberty, 1975; Kaufman, 1981). Not only is recognition of the child's drug use difficult for parents, but in recognizing their child's problems, parents must often face their own problems (Stanton, 1978, 1980). The escalation of the complexity of the problem does not stop there; parents are not the only individuals within the family to interact with the drug-using adolescent. The role of siblings, although not extensively investigated, also has been shown to be a factor in the adolescent's drug use (e.g., Cleveland, 1981; Coleman, 1979).

While minor variations have been reported in overt interaction within the family in terms of both individual roles and communication, there is considerable agreement that these aberrant patterns of interaction are reflections of more serious underlying family conflict (Reilly, 1976) and that a significant portion of this family conflict may be attributed to emotional isolation (Cotroneo & Krasner, 1976; Bratter, 1975; Eldred & Brown, 1974; Huberty & Malmquist, 1978; Huberty & Huberty, 1983; Rathus et al., 1977; Stanton, 1979a). Even within a supporting, loving environment, the establishment of independence during adolescence is difficult. However, within an emotionally isolated family, an ongoing approach-avoidance situation is created for the adolescent, making the struggle even greater. The adolescent is struggling to gain the emotional love and support of a family in which he or she feels powerless (DeForest, Robert, & Hays, 1974) while simultaneously attempting to establish his or her independence from the family unit. As a result, some investigators suggest that the child may become fixed at the stage of individuation and remains in conflict over establishing independence (Alexander & Dibb, 1975; Attardo, 1965; Freedman & Finnegan, 1976; Kaufman, 1981; Kirschenbaum et al., 1974; Madanes, Dukes, & Harbin, 1980; Noone & Reddig, 1976).

Although there is agreement that drug-using adolescents feel conflict over establishing their independence, agreement does not exist over the precise role that drugs play in this conflict. On the one hand, Spotts and Shontz (1980, 1985) postulate that chronic drug use compensates for ego deficiencies and fills gaps in personal structure, thereby enabling the adolescent to achieve individuation. Stanton et al. (1978, 1980), on the other hand, propose that drug use creates a dramatic family situation that focuses attention on the individual, thereby drawing family members closer together and avoiding individuation. One theory views drug use as a tool for attaining independence and separating from the family, while the other views drug use as a tool for drawing the family closer together.

The precipitating factors involved in emotional isolation within the family also has been a topic of interest. It has been postulated that failure to establish attachments and provide sufficient nurturing early in a child's development contributes to later feelings of isolation (Arnini, Salasnek, & Burke, 1976; Braucht et al., 1973; Vaglum, 1985). More popular is the belief that the conflict between feelings of emotional isolation and establishment of independence emanates from specific stress events. These events include physical and emotional abuse (Baer & Corrado, 1974; Binion, 1979); divorce, especially during adolescence (Kolb, Gunderson, & Nail, 1974); changes in financial status or paternal occupation (Duncan, 1978); and death or loss of a significant other (Coleman, 1980a, 1980b; Coleman & Stanton, 1978; Duncan, 1978). Researchers have been interested in determining which precursors or set of precursors play a more significant role in initiating adolescent drug use; no consistent subset has emerged. A more promising approach is that of Bry (1983), who suggests that the number of predisposing factors, which include stress events, rather than any particular set of factors may be an important dimension for predicting drug use.

PARENTS AS TEACHERS

Patterns of interaction and coping that appear to maintain drug-using behavior over time are reinforced and maintained not only by the dynamics of the parent-child relationship outlined above but also by the parent as an active teacher and model of such patterns. Certainly not unrelated to the patterns of interaction and communication already described, discipline problems in families of drug users are often the rule (Jurich et al., 1985). Discipline problems arise not only from the type of discipline used (Jurich et al., 1985) but from the consistency with which it is implemented (Wittenborn et al., 1970).

Three types of discipline have been described—laissez-faire, authoritarian, and democratic (Jurich et al., 1985; Baumrind, 1971). Laissez-faire is characterized by ultimate freedom: the child sets his or her own rules and limits with little parental guidance. Authoritarian discipline is at the other end of the spectrum: parents alone determine all rules and limits for the child. Democratic discipline is jointly implemented by the parents and child. It is the democratic style that appears to have the most positive effect on the prevention of serious drug problems among adolescents (Braucht et al., 1973). Both laissez-faire (Blum and Associates, 1972; Hunt, 1974; Krug & Henry, 1974) and authoritarian (Baumrind, 1971, 1975; Norem-Hebeisen et al., 1984) parenting styles have been closely associated with adolescent drug use. This observation is particularly evident at the extremes of laissez-faire and authoritarian styles where both neglect (Mayer & Black, 1977) and abuse (Baer & Corrado, 1974; Binion, 1979) have been linked with adolescent drug use. These findings of a significant effect of the style of parental discipline on adolescent drug use are quite consistent with the evidence discussed earlier regarding the parent-child relationship and family communication patterns. Each of these factors reflects an aspect of the dynamic relationships within the family.

PARENTAL MODELING

Although no less powerful an influence, the last family factor to be discussed, that of parental modeling, differs in that it reflects a more "passive" component of family interaction. The degree to which parents themselves use drugs consistently has been shown to influence their children's decisions regarding drug use (Barnes, 1977; Brook, Whiteman, Brook, and Gordon, 1981; Forster, 1984; Gorsuch & Butler, 1976; Huba & Bentler, 1980; Huba et al., 1980; McDermott, 1984; Mellinger, 1971; Smart & Fejer, 1972). Parental modeling of cigarette smoking (Dobbs & Marsh, 1983; Rittenhouse & Miller, 1984; Wilcox & Gillies, 1984) or the use of alcohol (Rittenhouse & Miller, 1984) or other drugs as a "psychological crutch" (Jurich et al., 1985) condones these behaviors regardless of any verbal messages to the contrary. Mixed messages such as parental drug use and instructions for the adolescent to abstain from drug use can be confusing and may further define drug use as an "adult" behavior and a mechanism by which the adolescent may demonstrate his or her adulthood. As Salmon and Salmon (1977) conclude, "This background provides poor role models to the young person who as a result has difficulty in his/her own roles . . . if he/she achieves those roles at all." Perhaps most important is the influence of parental modeling in combination with the influences of the individual roles within the mother-father-child triad, established communication patterns, and parental style that create the backdrop for adolescent drug use.

FUTURE RESEARCH

Because the literature on drug use and the family was reviewed with the goal of identifying both theoretical and methodological problems as well as general family factors that are thought to influence drug use, it seems appropriate to suggest areas of research that would show the most promise for significantly advancing our understanding of the relationship between adolescent drug use and the family. First, in relation to the drugs themselves, increased attention should be paid to potentially unique abuse characteristics of different classes of drugs and to varying amounts of use. Second, in relation to the parent-child relationship, research should focus on delineating more clearly the role of a perceived lack of love and support in drug use. Additionally, resolution of the conflicting models of the role of drug use in adolescent individuation would contribute significantly to our understanding of drug use. Third, in relation to the larger family system, considerable work is needed in the area of evaluating the influence of the relationship between parents and the relationship with siblings on adolescent drug use. Finally, in relation to theoretical and methodological issues, future efforts should attempt to incorporate the lessons of past methodological problems and, perhaps more importantly, should focus on empirically evaluating specific hypotheses set within sound theoretical frameworks.

When Kurt Lewin reminded us that there is nothing as useful as a good theory he assumed, of course, that theory is always developed in pursuit of a goal. The goal in much of the theory development and basic research in the family/adolescent substance use area, however, has not always been clear—either within the field or in its declarations of intent to others—and therefore has not advanced as far as it might with its wealth of talented investigators. A reasonable future expectation, therefore, might be that these theoretical and research efforts be designed and implemented with a single, clear goal in mind—the development of generalizable, cost-effective, durable, and readily adoptable intervention programs that will provide the means for a reduction in the incidence and prevalence of adolescent substance use.

REFERENCES

Alexander, B.K., & Dibb, G.S. (1975). Opiate addicts and their parents. *Family Process, 14*, 499-514.

Alexander, B.K., & Dibb, G.S. (1977). Interpersonal perception in addict families. *Family Process, 16*(1), 17-38.

Arnini, F., Salasnek, S., & Burke, E. (1976). Adolescent drug abuse: Etiological and treatment considerations. *Adolescence, 11*, 281-299.

Attardo, N. (1965). Psychodynamic factors in the mother-child relationship in adolescent drug addiction: A comparison of mothers of schizophrenics and mothers of normal adolescent sons. *Psychotherapy and Psychosomatics, 13*(4), 249-255.

Auerswald, E.H. (1980). Drug use and families—In the context of twentieth century science. In B.G. Ellis (Ed.), *Drug abuse from the family perspective* (DHHS Publication No. ADM 80-910, pp. 117-126). Washington, DC: U.S. Government Printing Office.

Baer, D.J., & Corrado, J.J. (1974). Heroin addict relationships with parents during childhood and early adolescent years. *Journal of Genetic Psychology, 124*, 99-103.

Baltes, P.B. (1979). Life-span developmental psychology: Some converging observations on history and theory. In P.B. Baltes & O.G. Brim (Eds.), *Lifespan development and behavior* (Vol. 2, pp. 256-281). New York: Academic Press.

Baltes, P.B., & Brim, O.G., Jr. (Eds.). (1980). *Lifespan development and behavior* (Vol. 2). New York: Academic Press.

Baltes, P.B., Reese, H.W., & Lipsitt, L.P. (1980). Life-span developmental psychology. *Annual Review of Psychology, 31*, 65-110.

Barnes, G.M. (1977). The development of adolescent drinking behavior: An evaluation review of the impact of the socialization process within the family. *Adolescence, 12*, 571-591.

Baumrind, D. (1971). Current patterns of parental authority. *Developmental Psychology Monographs*, 4, (Whole No. 1).

Baumrind, D. (1975). Early socialization and adolescent competence. In S.E. Dragastin & G.H. Elder (Eds.), *Adolescence in the life cycle: Psychological changes and social context*. Washington, DC: Hemisphere.

Binion, V.J. (1979). A descriptive comparison of the families of origin of women heroin users and nonusers. In National Institute on Drug Abuse (Ed.), *Addicted women: Family dynamics, self perceptions, and support systems* (DHEW Publication No. ADM 80-762). Washington, DC: U.S. Government Printing Office.

Blechman, E.A. (1982). Conventional wisdom about familial contributions to substance abuse. *American Journal of Drug and Alcohol Abuse, 9*, 35-53.

Blum, R.H. and Associates. (1972). *Horatio Alger's children*. San Francisco.

Bratter, T.E. (1975). Wealthy families and their drug abusing adolescents. *Journal of Family Counseling, 3*, 62-76.

Braucht, G.N., Brakarsh, D., Follingstad, D., & Berry, K.L. (1973). Deviant drug use in adolescence: A review of psychosocial correlates. *Psychological Bulletin, 79*, 92-106.

Brook, J.S., Gordon, A.S., & Brook, D.W. (1980). Perceived paternal relationships, adolescent personality, and female marijuana use. *Journal of Psychology, 105*, 277-285.

Brook, J.S., Whiteman, M., Brook, D.W., & Gordon, A.S. (1981). Paternal determinants of male adolescent marijuana use. *Developmental Psychology, 17*, 841-847.

Brook, J.S., Whiteman, M., & Gordon, A.S. (1981). The role of the father in his son's marijuana use. *Journal of Genetic Psychology, 138*, 81-86.

Brook, J.S., Whiteman, M., & Gordon, A.S. (1985). Father absence, perceived family characteristics and stage of drug use in adolescence. *British Journal of Developmental Psychology, 2*, 87-94.

Brook, J.S., Whiteman, M., Gordon, A.S., & Brook, D.W. (1984). Paternal determinants of female adolescent's marijuana use. *Developmental Psychology, 20*, 1032-1043.

Brook, J.S., Whiteman, M., Gordon, A.S., & Brook, D.W. (1985). Father's influence on his daughter's marijuana use viewed in a mother and peer context. *Advances in Alcohol and Substance Abuse, 4*, 165-190.

Bry, B.H. (1983). Empirical foundations of family-based approaches to adolescent substance abuse. In T. Glynn, C. Leukefeld, and J. Ludford (Eds.), *National Institute on Drug Abuse Research Monograph Series Number 47* (DHHS Publication No. ADM 83-1280). Washington, DC: U.S. Government Printing Office.

Cannon, S.R. (1976). *Social functioning patterns in families of offspring receiving treatment for drug abuse*. Roslyn Heights, NY: Libra Publishers.

Clayton, R.R. (1979). The family and federal drug abuse policies—programs: Toward making the invisible family visible. *Journal of Marriage and the Family, 41*, 637-647.

Cleveland, M. (1981). Families and adolescent drug abuse: Structural analysis of children's roles. *Family Process, 20*, 195-304.

Coleman, S.B. (1979). Siblings in session. In E. Kaufman and P. Kaufman (Eds.), *Family therapy of drug and alcohol abuse*. New York: Gardner.

Coleman, S.B. (1980a). Incomplete mourning in the family trajectory: A circular journal to drug abuse. In B.G. Ellis (Ed.), *Drug abuse from the family perspective* (DHHS Publication no. ADM 80-910). Washington, DC: U.S. Government Printing Office.

Coleman, S.B. (1980b). Incomplete mourning and addict/family transactions: A theory for understanding heroin abuse. In D.J. Lettieri, M. Sayres, & H.W. Pearson (Eds.), *Theories on drug abuse* (National Institute on Drug Abuse Research Monograph Series No. 30). Washington, DC: U.S. Government Printing Office.

Coleman, S.B. (1981). An endangered species: The family as addict or member of an addict family. In T.J. Glynn (Ed.), *Drugs and the family* (DHHS Publication No. ADM 81-1151). Washington, DC: U.S. Government Printing Office.

Coleman, S.B., & Stanton, M.D. (1978). The role of death in the addict family. *Journal of Marriage and Family Counseling, 4*, 79-91.

Cotroneo, M., & Krasner, B.R. (1976). Addiction, alienation, and parenting. *Nursing Clinics of North America, 11*(3), 517-525.

Deforest, J.S., Robert, T.K., & Hays, J.R. (1974). Drug abuse: A family affair? *Journal of Drug issues, 4*, 130-134.

Dobbs, J., & Marsh, A. (1983). Smoking among secondary school children (OPCS Survey) London: HMSO.

D'Onofrio, C.N., Thier, M.D., Schnor, A.E., Buchanan, D.R., & Omelich, C.L. (1982). The dynamics of adolescent smoking behavior. *World Smoking and Health, 7*, 18-24.

Duncan, D.F. (1978). Family stress and the initiation of adolescent drug abuse: A retrospective study. *Corr Soc Psychiatry Appl Behav Ther, 24*, 111-114.

Eldred, C.A., & Brown, B.S. (1974). Heroin addict clients' description of their families of origin. *International Journal of the Addictions, 9*, 315-320.

Eldred, C.A., & Washington, M.N. (1976). Interpersonal relationships in heroin use by men and women and their role in treatment outcome. *International Journal of the Addictions, 11*, 117-130.

Forster, B. (1984). Upper middle class adolescent drug use: Patterns and factors. *Advances in Alcohol and Substance Abuse, 4(2)*, 27-36.

Freedman, T.G., & Finnegan, L.P. (1976). Triads and the drug-dependent mother. *Social Work, 21*, 402-404.

Glynn, T.J. (1981). From family to peer: A review of transitions of influence among drug-using youth. *Journal of Youth and Adolescence, 10*, 363-384.

Glynn, T.J. (1982). Families and drugs: A life-span research approach. *American Journal of Drug and Alcohol Abuse, 9*, 396-411.

Glynn, T.J. (1984). Adolescent drug use and the family environment: A review. *Journal of Drug Issues, 2*, 271-295.

Gorsuch, R.L., & Butler, M.C. (1976). Initial drug abuse: A review of predisposing psychological factors. *Psychological Bulletin, 83*, 120-137.

Greenwald, S.R., Carter, J.S., & Stein, E.M. (1973). Differences between background, attitude, functioning, and mood of drug addicts. Alcoholics and orthopedic patients. *International Journal of the Addictions, 8*, 865-874.

Hamburg, B.A., Kraemer, H.C., & Jahnke, W.A. (1975). A hierarchy of drug use in adolescence: Behavioral attitudinal correlates of substantial drug use. *American Journal of Psychiatry, 132*, 1155-1163.

Hendin, H., Pollinger, A., Ulman, R., & Carr, A.C. (1981). Adolescent marijuana abusers and their families. *National Institute on Drug Abuse Research Monograph Series No. 40* (DHHS Publication No. ADM 81-1168). Washington, DC: U.S. Government Printing Office.

Huba, G.J., & Bentler, P.M. (1980). The role of peer and adult models for drug taking at different stages in adolescence. *Journal of Youth and Adolescence, 9*, 449-465.

Huba, G.J., Wingard, J.A., & Bentler, P.M. (1980). Framework for an interactive theory of drug use. In D.J. Lettieri, M. Sayers, and H.W. Pearson (Eds.), *National Institute on Drug Abuse Research Monograph Series No. 30* (DHHS Publication No. ADM 84-967). Washington, DC: U.S. Government Printing Office.

Huberty, D.J. (1975). Treating the adolescent drug abuser: A family affair. *Contemporary Drug Problems, 4*(2), 179-194.

Huberty, D.J., & Huberty, C.E. (1983). Drug abuse. In M.R. Textor (Ed.), *Helping families with special problems*. New York: Jason Aronson.

Huberty, D.J., & Malmquist, J.D. (1978). Adolescent chemical dependency. *Perspectives in Psychiatric Care, 16*, 21-27.

Hunt, D.G. (1974). Parental permissiveness as perceived by the offspring and the degree of marijuana usage among offspring. *Human Relations, 27*, 267-285.

Jurich, A.P., Polson, C.J., Jurich, J.A., & Bates, R.A. (1985). Family factors in the lives of drug users and abusers. *Adolescence, 20*(77), 143-159.

Kalant, H., Engel, J.A., Goldberg, L., Griffiths, R.R., Jaffe, J.H., Krasnegor, N.A., Mello, N.K., Mendelson, J.H., Thompson, T., & Van Ree, J.M. (1978). Behavioral aspects of addiction: Group report. In J. Fishman (Ed.), *The bases of addiction* (pp. 463-496). Berlin: Dahlem Konferenzen.

Kandel, D. (1973). Adolescent marijuana use: Role of parents and peers. *Science, 181*, 1067-1070.

Kandel, D. (1974). Inter- and intragenerational influences on adolescent marijuana use. *Journal of Social Issues, 30*(2), 107-135.

Kandel, D. (1978). Convergences in prospective longitudinal surveys of drug use in normal populations. In D. Kandel (Ed.), *Longitudinal research on drug use: Empirical findings and methodological issues*. Washington, DC: Hemisphere-Wiley.

Kandel, D. (1982). Epidemiological and psychosocial perspectives on adolescent drug use. *Journal of the American Academy of Child Psychiatry, 21*, 328-347.

Kaufman, E. (1981). Family structures of narcotic addicts. *International Journal of the Addictions, 16*, 273-282.

Kaufman, E., & Kaufman, P.V. (Eds.). (1977). *Family therapy of drug and alcohol abuse.* New York: Gardner.

Kirschenbaum, M., Leonoff, G., & Maliano, A. (1974). Characteristic patterns in drug abuse families. *Family Therapy, 1*, 43-62.

Klagsbrun, M., & Davis, D.I. (1977). Substance abuse and family interaction. *Family Process, 16*, 149-173.

Kolb, D., Gunderson, E.E.K., & Nail, R.L. (1974). Pre-service drug abuse: Family and social history characteristics. *Journal of Community Psychology, 2*, 278-282.

Krug, S.E., & Henry, T.J. (1974). Personality, motivation, and adolescent drug use patterns. *Journal of Counseling Psychology, 21*, 440-445.

Long, V.F., & Scherl, D.J. (1984). Developmental antecedents of compulsive drug use: A report on the literature. *Journal of Psychoactive Drugs, 16*, 169-182.

Madanes, C., Dukes, J., & Harbin, H. (1980). Family ties of heroin addicts. *Archives of General Psychiatry, 37*, 889-894.

Mayer, J., & Black, R. (1977). Child abuse and neglect in families with an alcohol or opiate addicted parent. *Child Abuse and Neglect, 1*, 85-98.

McDermott, D. (1984). The relationship of parental drug use and parents' attitude concerning adolescent drug use to adolescent drug use. *Adolescence, 19*, 89-97.

Mellinger, G.H. (1971). Psychotherapeutic drug use among adults: A model of young drug users? *Journal of Drug Issues, 1*, 274-285.

Nolte, A.E., Smith, B.J., & O'Rourke, T. (1983). The relationship between health risk attitudes and behaviors and parental presence. *Journal of School Health, 53*, 234-240.

Noone, R.J., & Reddig, R.L. (1976). Case studies in the family treatment of drug abuse. *Family Process, 15*(2), 325-332.

Norem-Hebeisen, A., Johnson, D.W., Anderson, D., & Johnson R. (1984). Predictors and concomitants of changes in drug use patterns among teenagers. *Journal of Social Psychology, 124*, 43-50.

Rathus, S.A., Richner-Rathus, L., & Siegel, L.J. (1977). Behavioral and familial correlates of episodic heroin abuse among suburban adolescents. *International Journal of the Addictions, 12*, 625-632.

Reilly, D.M. (1976). Family factors in the etiology and treatment of youthful drug abuse. *Family Therapy, 2*, 149-171.

Rittenhouse, J.D., & Miller, J.D. (1984). Social learning and teenage drug use: An analysis of family dyads. *Health Psychology, 3*, 329-345.

Salmon, R., & Salmon, S. (1977). The causes of heroin addiction—A review of the literature. Part II. *International Journal of the Addictions, 12*(7), 937-951.

Schneider, R.J., Kojak, G., & Ressdorf, H. (1977). Father-distance and drug abuse in young men. *Journal of Nervous and Mental Disease, 165*, 269-274.

Schultz, D.A., & Wilson, R.A. (1973). Some traditional family variables and their correlations with drug use among high school students. *Journal of Marriage and the Family, 35*, 628-631.

Schwartzman, J. (1975). The addict, abstinence, and the family. *American Journal of Psychiatry, 132*, 154-157.

Seldin, N.E. (1972). The family of the addict: A review of the literature. *International Journal of the Addictions, 7*, 97-107.

Smart, R.G., & Fejer, D. (1972). Drug use among adolescents and their parents: Closing the generation gap in mood modification. *Journal of Abnormal Psychology, 79*, 153-160.

Spotts, J.V., & Shontz, F.C. (1980). A life theme theory of chronic drug abuse. In D.J. Lettieri, M. Sayers, & H.W. Perason (Eds.), *Theories on drug abuse: Selected contemporary perspectives* (DHHS Publication No. ADM 80-967). Washington, DC: U.S. Government Printing Office.

Spotts, J.V., & Shontz, F.C. (1985). A theory of adolescent substance abuse. In J.S. Brook & D.W. Brook (Eds.), *Alcohol and substance abuse in adolescence:* Vol. 4 (pp. 117-138). The Haworth Press.

Stanton, M.D. (1978). The family and drug misuse: A bibliography. *American Journal of Drug and Alcohol Abuse, 5*, 151-170.

Stanton, M.D. (1979a). Family treatment approaches to drug abuse problems: A review. *Family Process, 18*(3), 251-280.

Stanton, M.D. (1979b). Drugs and the family. *Marriage and Family Review, 2*(2), 1-10.

Stanton, M.D. (1980). A family theory of drug abuse. In D.J. Lettieri, M. Sayers, & H.W. Pearson, (Eds.), *Theories on drug abuse: Selected contemporary perspectives*. National Institutes on Drug Abuse Research Monograph Series Number 30. Washington DC: U.S. Government Printing Office.

Stanton, M.D., & Todd, T.C. (1982). *The family therapy of drug abuse and addiction*. New York: Guilford Press.

Stanton, M.D., Todd, T.C., Heart, B., Kirschner, S., Kleiman, J.I., Mowatt, D.T., Riley, P., Scott, S.M., & Van Deusen, J.M. (1978). Heroin addiction as a family phenomenon: A new conceptual model. *American Journal of Drug and Alcohol Abuse, 5*, 125-150.

Stern, M., Northman, J.E., & Van Slyck, M.R. (1984). Father absence and adolescent "problem behaviors": Alcohol consumption, drug use, and sexual activity. *Adolescence, 19*, 301-312.

Torda, C. (1968). Comments on the character structure and psychodynamic processes of heroin addicts. *Perceptual and Motor Skills, 27*, 143-146.

Vaglum, P. (1985). Young drug abusers' problems of attachment to the family. *Journal of the Oslo City Hospitals, 35*, 69-76.

Wittenborn, J.R., Smith, J.R., & Wittenborn, S. (Eds.). (1970). *Communication and drug abuse*. Springfield, IL: Charles C Thomas.

Zimmering, P., Toolan, J., Safrin, R., & Wortis, S.B. (1951). Heroin addiction in adolescent boys. *Journal of Nervous and Mental Disease, 114*, 19-34.

II. FAMILY STYLES, STAGES AND VARIETIES

Contrasting Family Patterns of Adolescent Drug Users and Nonusers

Robert H. Coombs, PhD
Morris J. Paulson, PhD

Perhaps the most intrinsically perilous segment of life's journey is that between childhood and adulthood. For those who fall prey to alcohol and drug problems, this time can be painful, costly, and in some cases, deadly.

Despite the magnitude of the problem, and an increasing spotlight of publicity, our verifiable knowledge of how and why youngsters become and remain substance abusers is remarkably scant. Though stereotypes and hypotheses abound, relatively little systematic theory presently exists to illuminate factual information or formulate effective interventions.

Traditional interventions have been based on entrenched models that regard substance abusers as inherently deficient people whose primary motivation for using alcohol and other drugs is to seek relief from personal problems. The failure of this model to explain much of the data, or to generate effective solutions, hasn't reduced the frequency with which it's invoked.

This deficient-person model which has dominated professional and lay thinking for decades, almost invariably derives from clinical observations or retrospective studies of those at the maintenance

Robert H. Coombs is Professor of Biobehavioral Sciences, UCLA School of Medicine and Director, Office of Education, UCLA Neuropsychiatric Institute and Hospital, 760 Westwood Plaza, Room B7-349, Los Angeles, CA 90024. Morris J. Paulson is Professor of Child Psychology, UCLA Neuropsychiatric Institute and Hospital.

or discontinuation stages of drug involvement, most often those confined in jails, mental hospitals, or residing in other treatment settings. In such studies there have been few comparisons with non-users, let alone matched samples, and very few ethnographic studies in noninstitutional settings. To a surprising degree, researchers have neglected the study of noninstitutionalized substance users. The logistics are more complicated, the subjects less cooperative, and the data often fit poorly with preconceived ideas derived from the deficient-person model.

We assume that substance abuse is a learned phenomenon, not simply a product of socioemotional pathology. This is not to deny the obvious, that personal and social problems accrue to those who become chemically dependent or that such problems can and do contribute to further substance abuse. But the quest here is to ascertain how and why substance abuse begins and escalates. We begin with the assumption that drug and alcohol abuse begins with normal youth, not just a pathological subset of the youthful population beset with problems from which they wish to escape. Initiation occurs among youths from all segments and strata of society.

During adolescence, drug and alcohol use is almost always a social experience, rarely a solitary one (Blumer et al., 1967). From our perspective, it is learned behavior, performed to gain peer approval and other social rewards. The role of the family in fostering or mitigating against these processes is explored in this chapter.

THE STUDY POPULATION

Our information comes from the first year of a multiyear study of two contrasting groups of adolescents—those who use substances and those who refrain from them, and from their parents (Coombs, in press).

The study population consists of 262 youths, between the ages of 13 and 17, with comparison groups matched as closely as possible for sex, age and ethnicity (see Table 1). After obtaining informed consent from all participants, structured interviews were conducted with each adolescent. We also interviewed one parent or guardian.

A substance "user" is defined as one who, during the month preceding the initial interview, used any of the following sub-

TABLE 1

ADOLESCENT SUBSTANCE USE BY SEX, AGE, AND ETHNICITY

	USERS (n=145)		NON USERS (n=117)		TOTAL	
Sex						
Male	74	(51.0%)	60	(51.3%)	134	(51.1%)
Female	71	(49.0%)	57	(48.7%)	128	(48.9%)
Age						
13 years	23	(15.9%)	30	(25.6%)	53	(20.2%)
14 years	29	(20.0%)	24	(20.5%)	53	(20.2%)
15 years	27	(18.6%)	20	(17.1%)	47	(17.9%)
16 years	37	(25.5%)	21	(17.9%)	58	(22.1%)
17 years	29	(20.0%)	22	(18.8%)	51	(19.5%)
Ethnicity						
Anglo-American	77	(53.1%)	54	(46.2%)	131	(50.0%)
Hispanic-American	68	(46.9%)	63	(53.8%)	131	(50.0%)

stances: alcoholic beverages, illegal drugs, prescription drugs illegally obtained, inhalants and solvents, etc. for the purpose of altering mood, affect or state of consciousness.

The study population was drawn from an area approximately an hour's drive from downtown Los Angeles. We selected these communities because drug availability and social reinforcement for drug use are reportedly high and economically depressed minorities reside there in large numbers.

Because this study deals with illegal behavior, locating cooperative subjects and obtaining valid information were challenging. As noted earlier, the technical difficulties of fieldwork have been one of the major impediments to obtaining information from populations in noninstitutional settings.

High-risk youth who "hang-out" on the streets were contacted, mainly at Boys' Clubs (one third of whose members are female). With the full consent and approval of Club officials, salaried research assistants who were well known and trusted in the informal network of the streets spent time at the youth centers playing ball and participating in other activities. At an appropriate time these assistants explained the purpose of the study to the youths and elicited their cooperation.

Our goal was to achieve a study population that included at least forty were adolescents of each age, 13 though 17, about half of whom were currently using substances and half abstaining.

Unlike most drug researchers of adolescents, we wanted to avoid data derived from captive subjects in schools and other institutional settings. The resulting study population is a purposive rather than a random sample of the community. In its major characteristics, however, the study group quite closely matched the general population, as measured by census data. Ethnicity is the only parameter in which the group studied differed significantly from the community population, which is about 19 percent Hispanic and 78 percent Anglo. By design, approximately one-half of the study population was Hispanic-American, the other half Anglo-American. Most families reported themselves to be either middle-class (46 percent) or working-class (35 percent).

Each youngster and one of his or her parents (or guardians) were interviewed, usually in their home. Each interview was conducted separately, with assurance that all data was held in strict confidence. Our study utilized many of the measurement scales compiled by the National Institute on Drug Abuse (Nehemkis et al., 1976; Abelson et al., 1977; Johnston et al., 1979). This enabled us to use standardized scales and measures as much as possible.

PROFILE OF THE USER AND NONUSER POPULATIONS

As Table 2 shows, nearly all those in the study population defined as users were involved with either alcohol or marijuana/hashish, with other substance use spread thinly among a wide variety of intoxicants. Of the 70 adolescents who used substances other than alcohol, 68 (97 percent) reported marijuana/hashish as the most frequently used drug.

Of the drinkers, three-fourths drank on five or fewer days a month; 15 percent drank on six to ten days, and six percent on 11-20 days. Only three people reported drinking on more than 20 days.

TABLE 2

INCIDENCE OF SUBSTANCES CONSUMED BY USERS (n=145)

	Have Tried		Use Monthly	
	n	%	n	%
Substances:				
Alcohol	143	98.6	136	93.8
Marijuana-Hashish	70	48.3	56	38.6
PCP	18	12.4	3	2.1
Amphetamines	14	9.7	5	3.4
Cocaine	13	9.0	5	3.4
Paint	12	8.3	3	2.1
Barbiturates	10	6.9	1	0.7
Quaaludes	8	5.5	4	2.8
LSD	5	3.4	1	0.7
Gasoline	5	3.4	0	0.0
Psilocybin	3	2.1	0	0.0
Peyote	2	1.4	0	0.0
Heroin	0	0.0	0	0.0
Other	0	0.0	0	0.0

On the days they imbibed, most reported having only one or two drinks, with beer the beverage of choice.

Nearly half the users had tried marijuana or hashish, and 39 percent reported that they smoke at least once a month. Some users had tried other substances, such as PCP (12 percent), amphetamines (10 percent), cocaine (9 percent), paint fumes (8 percent) or barbiturates (7 percent), but only a few use these substances regularly (see Table 2).

Of those who use, 74 percent gave as the reason either to be happy, to make things more fun, or because it feels good.

Not all of those classified as nonusers are pure abstainers. Nearly half (48 percent) reported that they had never consumed alcoholic beverages. The others (52 percent) said they previously had a drink, but not within the last month. Eighty-four percent of the nonusers had no previous experience with other substances; of those who had used (mostly marijuana), all but two had quit. Clearly, "users" and "nonusers" as defined in this study are not polar opposites.

A major goal of this study is to examine the familial patterns that differentiate between adolescent users and nonusers, to search for similarities or differences which might explain the familial underpinnings that vary among comparison groups.

FAMILY STATUS

The hypothesis that socioeconomic deprivation contributes to delinquency and drug use is based on the popular notion that parental separation and economic hardship represent deficiencies for which drugs and crime are compensation. Corollary to this reasoning is that broken homes and families of lower socioeconomic status produce a disproportionate share of substance-using youths. But there is less evidence to support this view than might be supposed (Fawzy, Coombs, Simons and Bowman-Terrell, 1986).

The view that substance abuse stems from broken homes and economic hardship is not supported by our results (Coombs, Wellisch and Fawzy, 1985). When compared with their nonusing peers, adolescents in our study who regularly use alcohol and/or other substances are no more likely to come from single-parent homes than from traditional families; nor are their parents of lower socioeconomic status.

In fact, a smaller, though statistically insignificant proportion of users came from families with less than $15,000 annual income and, at the very lowest income level, the percentage of nonusers was slightly higher. This contradicts a popular view that poverty is an underlying cause of substance abuse.

Other measures also fail to show substance users as products of low-status homes. Adolescent users are as likely to come from middle-class (white-collar) families as from working-class (blue-collar) homes. Similarly when working-class families are stratified by skill level (skilled, unskilled and laborer) no significant differences are found in the proportion of users and nonusers.

In our study population, 17 percent came from single-parent families. Youngsters from these homes were no more involved with substances than those from intact families. Apparently a mother's impact on her children is constant regardless of whether the father is present or absent. However, as the following discussion indicates, a father's positive involvement can be a significant deterrent to an adolescent's drug related behavior.

PARENT-YOUTH INTERACTION

Getting Along

Patterns of interaction between adolescents and their parents were also explored. Using a number of measures, we found that a positive parent-youth relationship deterred adolescent substance use (Coombs and Landsverk, 1988). Others have reported similar results (Auerswald, 1980; Brook, Whiteman, Gordon and Brook, 1984, 1985; Kandel, 1982; Stanton and Todd, 1982).

When asked about the importance of getting along with parents, 83 percent of the nonusers and 65 percent of the users said it is "very important" ($p < .01$). This finding is consistent with research by others (Jessor and Jessor, 1977; Mercer et al., 1978; Kandel et al., 1978) and supports the view that young people who admire and respect their parents are significantly less likely to use substances.

When the parent's role is considered, results show that fathers and mothers who develop and maintain warm relationships with their youngsters experience the greatest success in inhibiting drug involvement. This finding is also consistent with findings from other studies (Streit et al., 1974; Rathus et al., 1977; Brook et al., 1980, 1981).

Nonusers are significantly more likely to feel "extremely or quite close" to their father (72 percent versus 47 percent of users; $p < .001$). The difference is less pronounced when closeness to mother is considered (88 percent versus 73 percent of users; $p < .05$).

A number of other family factors also demarcate users from their nonusing counterparts. Abstainers, compared to users, are significantly more interested in being like their fathers (68 percent versus 49 percent; $p < .05$). A similar plurality exists for emulation of mothers (77 percent versus 53 percent; $p < .01$). When it comes to trust, 64 percent of the abstainers feel trusted by their mothers, while only 48 percent of the users feel that way ($p < .01$).

Parental praise also differentiate users and nonusers. Abstainers report receiving more praise and encouragement than users. The difference is most striking when considering the behavior of fathers. Almost half the abstainers report receiving frequent fatherly praise while only 26 percent of the users say the same ($p < .01$).

Parental encouragement comes in many forms, such as helping with personal problems. When asked how often personal problems are discussed with father and mother, evidence is again found that an involved father has high potential for discouraging substance use behavior. Those whose fathers never or hardly ever discuss personal problems are more likely to use substances than abstain (78 percent versus 60 percent, $p < .01$). While mothers are generally more active than fathers in helping young people with personal problems, there is no statistically significant difference between users and nonusers with regard to mother's help with personal problems.

Parental involvement in vocational and educational planning, yields similar results and confirms the conclusion that parental involvement plays an important role in influencing the substance use pattern of their offspring.

Rule Making

Results show that parents who enact clear, consistent limit-setting rules stand the best chance of deterring their children from substance use. This conclusion emerges from examination of a number of different measures.

In general, parents of users, especially mothers, are described by their children as less strict than those of nonusers. When it came to "laying down the law" on specific types of behavior, abstainer's parents more often develop and enforce rules.

Interestingly, the strongest contrast between the two groups focuses on doing homework. Whereas 69 percent of nonuser's parents insist on the completion of homework, only 46 percent of the users' parents invoke a similar rule ($p < .001$). Rules about the amount of dating, time spent watching television and consumption of alcoholic beverages also differentiate significantly between comparison groups. Almost all parents (91 percent) have rules against using drugs; there are no statistically significant differences between comparison groups.

Abstainers' parents may be stricter and have more rules, but they are not more punitive. Among comparison groups, a near equal number reported that punishment "always" or "usually" follows undesirable behavior. These results square with the findings of other researchers (Chein et al., 1964; Reilly, 1975; Alexander and Dibb, 1977; Graven and Schaef, 1978) that the parents of users tend to ignore appropriate behaviors but respond to the negative ones, thus creating a punitive family environment. Though the parents of users and abstainers are about equally prone to punish for infractions, many significant differences occur in the frequency with which praise, encouragement and reinforcement of positive behavior are given, with the scales of generosity tipping in favor of abstainer's parents.

Parent-Peer Loyalties

There is no lack of researchers who note the importance of peers in influencing drug-using behavior (Jessor and Jessor, 1977; Margulies et al., 1977). But our results indicate that the need for peer acceptance is equally important for users and nonusers. More than three-quarters of both groups indicate that being accepted and liked by friends is of great importance. That is, users are not more "peer oriented" than nonusing adolescents. The desire for peer approval exists among all adolescents regardless of one's orientation to substances.

The contrast between comparison groups is not in desire for peer approval but in friend selection and choice of peer activities. Our results show that users associate with friends who use substances, while nonuser's friends tend to refrain from them. When asked, "Have any of your friends ever used marijuana or hashish?" significantly higher number of users reply affirmatively ($p < .001$). The same pattern is found when asked about other drugs.

Drug users attend parties almost three times more often than nonusers. One third (31.4 percent) of the users attend such functions "once a week or more," compared with only 12.8 percent of the abstainers.

In spite of this strong desire to be liked and approved by peers, most youths (68 percent of the nonusers and 55 percent of the users) report that parents have a greater influence on their behavior than friends. Drug users, compared to nonusers, are somewhat less family oriented. They talk with friends about their problems more often (47 percent compared to 30 percent), regard their friends as more understanding (52 percent compared to 33 percent) and are less likely to value parental ideas (49 percent compared to 70 percent).

The extent of differential parental influence among users and abstainers is most evident in specific situations, such as when a parent strongly objects to a child's choice of friends. In such cases, substance users are much more likely to ignore a parent's complaint, with only 48 percent reporting they would reduce their involvement or stop completely, compared to 75 percent of the nonusers. Twice as many users (52 percent) as nonusers (25 percent) say they would disregard parental objections and continue to see their friends ($p < .0001$).

PARENTAL AND SIBLING LIFE-STYLES

A final aspect of familial influence is that of life-style modeled by parents and siblings. Specifically, we sought information about family involvement with religion and substances.

Parental Religiosity

According to our results, the religious behavior of parents plays an important role in influencing teenagers. Religious importance for a youngster's mother significantly differentiates between abstainers and users (85 percent versus 75 percent, $p < .05$), but a father's valuing of religion differentiates more significantly. Nearly three-quarters (70 percent) of the abstainers' fathers indicated religion as "very important," while only 55 percent of the users' fathers felt that way ($p < .001$).

In the matter of church attendance, seven out of ten (68 percent) of the nonuser's mothers went to church weekly or monthly, compared to 52 percent of the user's mothers ($p < .01$). Father's attendance was also significantly related to adolescent use of substances ($p < .05$).

Parental and Sibling Use of Substances

In general, our results show that adolescents are more likely to remain substance-free when parents and siblings also refrain from these substances. These results are similar to previous studies which document generational continuity in alcohol and drug use (Coombs and Dickson, 1981; Fawzy, Coombs and Gerber, 1983), with the second generation not only using, but using a greater variety of substances than their parents (Tec, 1970; Smart and Fejer, 1972; Annis, 1974; Lawrence and Velleman, 1974).

More of the users' fathers drink hard liquor (70 percent versus 59 percent of the abstainers' fathers) and they drink significantly more often ($p < .05$). A similar pattern exists for beer and wine consumption, with the fathers of nonusers abstaining at a higher rate (20 percent versus 12 percent for users' fathers), or drinking less than once a week (34 percent versus 27 percent).

Similar results held for the drinking habits of mothers, with 67 percent of the nonusers saying their mothers never drink hard liquor, while only 49 percent of the users say the same.

This relationship between parental behavior and offspring behavior held up consistently for a variety of other substances, including use of cigarettes, marijuana/hashish, and coffee. For example, 85 percent of mothers, and 64 percent of fathers who smoke more than one pack of cigarettes each day have a substance using adolescent.

Marijuana and hashish were the most popular illegal drugs used by parents. Of the 21 teenagers who are aware of their father's use of these drugs, 17 (81 percent) were users. Similarly, of the 18 mothers known to have used marijuana and hashish, 14 (78 percent) of the reporting offspring were users.

Even more striking than the relationship between adolescent and parental substance use is that between youths and their siblings. Significant differences between user and abstainer groups exists for seven of 12 substances: marijuana ($p < .01$), LSD ($p < .01$), PCP ($p < .02$), amphetamines ($p < .001$), barbiturates ($p < .02$), Quaaludes ($p < .03$), and cocaine ($p < .01$).

These results support the saying "Like father (and mother, and brother and sister) like son/daughter."

CONCLUSIONS

What emerges from these data is a clear indication that modes of family life significantly impact the course of adolescent substance use or nonuse.

Our results are contrary to two commonly accepted beliefs about family patterns and teenage substance use. Children from lower sociometric circumstances are not more likely to be substance users, nor are children of one-parent families. Considering the rapidly increasing number of single-parent families these results are of great practical significance.

This study consistently shows that parent-youth relationships influence a developing youngster's use of alcohol and other drugs. Compared to adolescents who drink and use other drugs, nonusers generally feel closer to both parents, consider it important to get along with them, and want to be like them when they grow up. Typically their parents provide more praise and encouragement, develop feelings of trust with them and help them with personal problems. Perceived as more strict, nonusers' parents more typically set more limits with regard to homework, dating, television viewing, curfew and use of alcohol. Yet, they are not more punitive. Instead, control is enhanced through praise and encouragement. This apparently fosters emotionally close relationships that encourage youth to seek parental advice and guidance. Youngsters who feel loved and trusted by parents, whom they emulate, are not likely to embarrass them with unacceptable behavior.

Nondrug using life-styles occur most often when parents model these behaviors themselves. Our results show that parents who are religious and abstain from the use of substances less often have youngsters who drink and use drugs. Youth are more likely to use substances if their parents model these behaviors.

In short, parental abstinence from substances may be the first line of defense against youthful initiation and escalation, and parental efforts to maintain a quality relationship with their children may be the best hedge against greater involvement with substances.

REFERENCES

Abelson, H., P. Fisburne, and I. Cisin. (1977). National Survey on Drug Abuse, 1977. Volume I. Main Findings. Rockville, Maryland: National Institute on Drug Abuse.

Alexander, B.K. and G.S. Dibbs, 1977. "Interpersonal perception in addict families." *Family Process* 16(1).

Annis, H.M. 1974. "Patterns of intrafamilial drug use." *British Journal of the Addictions* 69: 361-369.

Auerswald, E.H. 1980. "Drug use and families – in the context of twentieth century science." In B.G. Ellis (ed.), *Drug abuse from the family perspective* (DHHS Publication No. ADM 80-910, pp. 117-126). Washington, D.C.: U.S. Government Printing Office.

Blumer, Herbert, Alan Sutter, Roger Smith, and Samir Ahmed. 1967. *The World of Youthful Drug Use*. Berkeley, California: University of California Press, 48-60.

Brook, J.S., A.S. Gordon, and D.W. Brook. 1980. "Perceived paternal relationships, adolescent personality, and female marijuana use." *Journal of Psychology* 105, 277-285.

Brook, J.S., M. Whiteman, D.W. Brook, and A.S. Gordon. 1981. "Paternal determinants of male adolescent marijuana use." *Developmental Psychology* 17, 841-847.

Brook, J.S., M. Whiteman, A.S. Gordon, and D.W. Brook. 1984. "Paternal determinants of female adolescent's marijuana use." *Developmental Psychology* 20, 1032-1043.

Brook, J.S., M. Whiteman, A.S. Gordon, and D.W. Brook. 1985. Father's influence on his daughter's marijuana use viewed in a mother and peer context. *Advances in Alcohol and Substance Abuse* 4, 165-190.

Chein, I., D.L. Gerard, R.S. Lee, and E. Rosenfeld. 1964. *The Road to H: Narcotics, Delinquency, and Social Policy*. New York: Basic Books, Inc.

Coombs, R.H. and K.M. Dickson. 1981. "Generational continuity in the use of alcohol and other substances: A literature review." *Abstracts and Reviews in Alcohol and Drinking* 2(4 April): 1-7.

Coombs, R.H. (1981). The Social Context of Adolescent Substance Use: A Comparison of Abstainers and Users. Monograph ADP (A-003-2) 81-2, California Department of Alcohol and Drug Programs, Sacramento, California, 317 pp.

Coombs, R.H., D.K. Wellisch, and F.I. Fawzy 1986. "Drinking patterns and drinking problems of female adolescents: A comparison of abstainers, past users, and current users." *American Journal of Drug and Alcohol Abuse*, 11: 3/4, 315-348.

Coombs, R.H. and J. Landsverk (1988). "Parenting styles and substance use during use." *Journal of Marriage and the Family*, 50 (May). Childhood and Adolescence".

Fawzy, F.I., R.H. Coombs, and B.E. Gerber. 1983. "Generational continuity in the use of alcohol and drugs: The impact of parental substance use on adolescent substance use." *Psychiatry Digest*, International Synopsis. (Abstract)

Fawzy, F.I., R.H. Coombs, J.M. Simons, and M. Bowman-Terrell (1987). "Family composition, socioeconomic status and adolescent drug use." *Addictive Behaviors: An International Journal*, 12:1, 79-83.

Graven, D.B. and R.D. Schaef. 1978. "Family life and levels of involvement in an adolescent heroin epidemic." *The International Journal of Addictions* 13(5).

Jessor, R. and S.L. Jessor. 1977. *Problem Behavior and Psychosocial Development: A Longitudinal Study of Youth*. New York: Academic Press.

Johnston, L.D., J.G. Bachman, and P.M. O'Malley. 1979. *1979 Highlights – Drugs and the Nation's High School Students: Five Year National Trends*. Rockville, Maryland: National Institute on Drug Abuse.

Kandel, D.B., R.C. Kessler, and R.Z. Margulies. 1978. "Antecedents of adolescent initiation into stages of drug use: A developmental analysis." *Journal of Youth and Adolescence* 7(1).

Kandel, D. 1982. Epidemiological and psychosocial perspectives on adolescent drug use. *Journal of the American Academy of Child Psychiatry* 21, 328-347.

Lawrence, T.S. and D.J. Velleman. 1974. "Correlates of student drug use in a suburban high school." *Psychiatry* 37.

Margulies, R., R.C. Kessler, and D. Kandel. 1977. "A longitudinal study of onset of drinking among high school students." *Quarterly Journal of Studies on Alcoholism* 38, 897-912.

Mercer, G.W., J.D. Hundleby, and R.A. Carpenter. 1978. "Adolescent drug use and attitudes toward the family." *Canadian Journal of Behavioral Science* 10(1).

Nehemkis, A., M.A. Macari, and D.J. Lettieri. 1976. *Drug Abuse Instrument Handbook*. Rockville, Maryland: National Institute on Drug Abuse.

Rathus, S., L. Eichner-Rathus, and L. Siegel. 1977. "Behavioral and familial correlates of episodic heroin abuse among suburban adolescents." *International Journal of the Addictions* 12(5): 625-632.

Reilly, D.M. 1975. "Family factors in the etiology and treatment of youthful drug abusers." *Family Therapy* 2: 149-171.

Smart, R.G. and D. Fejer. 1972. "Drug use among adolescents and their parents: Closing the generation gap in mood-modification." *Journal of Abnormal Psychology* 79(2): 153-160.

Stanton, M.D. and T.C. Todd. 1982. *The Family Therapy of Drug Abuse and Addiction*. New York: Guilford Press.

Streit, E., D.L. Halsted, and P.J. Pascale. 1974. "Differences among youthful users and nonusers of drugs based on their perceptions of parental behavior." *The International Journal of the Addictions* 9(5): 749-755.

Tec, N. 1970. "Family and differential involvement with marijuana: A study of suburban teenagers." *Journal of Marriage and the Family* 32(4): 656-664.

Developmental Stages in Drug Use: Changing Family Involvements

Robert H. Coombs, PhD
Kathryn Coombs, MA

Comparable to the development of any conventional career, drug use consists of a series of stages (Coombs, Fry and Lewis, 1976; Coombs, 1981a). The further one travels along this career course, the deeper the personal investment, the greater the commitment and, consequently, the decreased likelihood of considering alternative careers.

A drug user does not travel the course alone. However unwillingly, his family plays an important part in his career development. This chapter traces the sequence of the drug career—initiation, escalation, maintenance, discontinuation, and renewal—with special reference to family involvement at each stage.

Others have previously discussed the developmental stages in the escalation of drug use. Delineating the developmental sequence of drug use by substance, Kandel and Faust (1975) report that adolescents tend to use drugs progressively in the following order: (1) beer or wine; (2) hard liquor or tobacco; (3) marijuana; and (4) other illicit drugs. Utilizing a more conceptual approach, Nelson (1978) defines drug use symptomatically in four stages: (1) experimental use, (2) more regular use, (3) daily preoccupation, and (4) dependency. Other approaches have been offered by Alksne et al. (1967) and Sadava (1977).

Robert H. Coombs is Professor of Biobehavioral Sciences, UCLA School of Medicine and Director, Office of Education, UCLA Neurological Institute and Hospital, 760 Westwood Plaza, Room B7-349, Los Angeles, CA 90024. Kathryn Coombs is a graduate student in English at California State University, Northridge.

INITIATION: LAUNCHING THE CAREER

To understand drug initiation, two realities must be recognized. First, experimentation typically begins during adolescence. Second, young people rarely use drugs alone; initiation is almost always a social rather than a solitary happening.

Two of our own research projects support these conclusions. The first, a retrospective study of 309 hard-core addicts in the Los Angeles area, found ages 15 and 16 as most typical for initiation to hard drugs (Coombs, 1981b). The other study, a longitudinal analysis of 245 drug users, age 9 through 17, who were contrasted with an equal number of nonusers, further identified the adolescent initiation age by documenting the paucity of users under age 12, even when the definition of "drug use" was reduced to "cigarette smoking." Yet, in these same neighborhoods, it was also difficult to locate abstainers among those over the age of 16 (Coombs, 1981a).

The second reality—that young people rarely begin and continue drug use alone—is made clear by the youths' descriptions of their initiation circumstances, how they were first offered drugs by acquaintances as gestures of warmth and friendliness. Some youngsters ask to be allowed to try drugs in the company of their more sophisticated companions. A friendly gathering is nearly always the setting for early use.

It is, of course, no accident that adolescence marks the beginning of what may lead, quite unexpectedly, to full-fledged drug careers. Adolescence is a period of transition from childhood to adulthood, a time when developmental needs are urgently felt by youth but rarely understood by parents; these needs often predispose adolescents to drug experimentation.

The Need for Independence

In our society there are no clear rites of passage to mark the transition from childhood to adulthood, no clear ceremonies or formal designations to confer upon youth the adult status and role, with its privileges and responsibilities. Instead, children must gradually win for themselves the desired privileges of the adult status. As Baumrind (1985, p. 44) puts it, "Today the gap between puberty and psychosocial maturity is wider than ever before, resulting in a prolonged status of being in limbo, conducive to all kinds of social experimentation."

Gaining freedom and autonomy rarely come easily for aspiring adults. Usually youth must struggle to gain independence from parental control, especially when parents, lacking better techniques, utilize force as the dominant method of child management. Baumrind (1985, p. 45) says that,

> the child's compliance with peer values takes on a radically *transformed* significance when such compliance acquires the implication of emancipation from parental constraint. Patterns of behavior which had previously been employed in an unreflective manner in peer interactions . . . may begin to be employed strategically in relations with parents to serve the end of emancipation. The process of negotiating new role definitions with parents may be marked by conflict and instability.

Force, of course, is an effective means of control when parents are bigger than their children and in close enough proximity to enforce their edicts. But when adolescent children become strong and spend little time at home, parental control can quickly diminish.

Lacking rapport and mutual understanding with their children and obviously losing control, parents typically respond with criticism and punitive measures. Youth react by spending more and more time away from home with peers where they can find what is lacking at home—freedom, independence, and acceptance. This alliance with peers, combined with the widening rift with family members, increases the potential of drug use, especially when parents, frustrated with their teenage children, simply give up, letting them have free rein.

The Need for Adventure

Many teens involve themselves in drug experimentation out of curiosity, or in search of adventure. Adventure and excitement have been universal attractions for adolescents through the ages. Most adults can recall youthful pranks and games involving risk, running, and hiding. Youth who live in economically depressed areas seem to need distractions of this type to shield them from the discouraging realities and problems of congested city life; toughness, dare deviltry, and risk-taking become ideals and measures of manhood. In his book, *The Urban Villages*, Gan (1962) portrays street life in such a neighborhood as being "dominated by the adventurous episode . . . an opportunity for thrills and a chance to face and overcome challenge." This feverish appetite for street thrills has also been noted by other observers (Feldman, 1973).

This addict explains that his childhood idols were the neighborhood dope fiends and hustlers:

> I thought a dope fiend, man, was the coolest dude, because, well I can't remember seeing one feeling bad or sick, or being really desperate, you know. The only thing I can remember was when they're loaded, and when they're standin' there, talkin' that talk, and I thought—MAN!

Adolescents from prosperous neighborhoods also find adventure and excitement, usually of their own making. Drug use, being illegal and potentially harmful, offers considerable risk and can therefore be a challenge. And, if handled properly, drug experimentation can bring considerable recognition from peers.

Being chased by police seems an extension of the games children play (cops and robbers, hide-and-seek, etc.) and offers considerable excitement. "It's really fun to get people all riled up," a youthful user confessed. Small wonder, then, that increasing police surveillance and efforts to propagandize youth about the risks of drug use can be counterproductive, for they reinforce rather than diminish youthful experimentation with substances.

Clearly, deviation from the law is seen as glamorous, thrilling, and daring by the individual and his peer group. The first arrest by this youth, for example, is described as exciting and rewarding. He couldn't wait to parade his adventure before his peers. "That's part of the whole joyous feeling," he said. "I just knew all my friends would say, 'Hey, man, what did you get busted for?' 'All right!' 'Did they beat you up?' 'What happened?' I had heard guys talk to other guys about being arrested."

The fact that traditionally there have been more male addicts (and other social deviants) than female may suggest that adventure-seeking and risk taking are more urgent needs for boys than girls. To achieve the adult role, boys must "prove" their manhood, but traditionally there has been little need for adolescent girls to prove they have "guts" and are not "chicken." Challenging activities may separate the men from the boys, but there has been little mention of such activities distinguishing women from girls. One never says to a girl, "Buck up and get in there and be a real woman." Neither does the military promise to "make a woman out you." To males we say, "Try to be a man," but to girls the message is, "Be a woman" (Coombs, 1968).

The reason for this contrast probably reflects social structural factors in the traditional home. Generally, sex typing for girls is fraught with fewer difficulties because as young children they are so consistently exposed to adults of the same sex—mothers and female teachers. By contrast, boys spent most of their time during the formative years with those of the opposite sex. As Lynn (1966) has noted, the mother serves as a model for a girl much as a detailed map does for a traveler. As a model for a boy, however, a father who is gone most of the time is analogous to a map showing major outlines but lacking most of the detail. Consequently, the clearest idea that young boys have of appropriate masculine behavior is to be different from females. If girls are clean, obedient, cautious, and expressive, boys feel they should be the opposite—rugged, disobedient, aggressive, and unsentimental. If boys do not distinguish themselves clearly from females, they are stigmatized as being "sissies," "mama's boys," or "wimps," but there seem to be no equivalent denigrating labels for girls.

However, as the traditional woman's role changes, girls seem destined to higher involvement in adventurous activities such as drug use. Baumrind and Moselle (1985, p. 44) explain,

> The social role of women has been permanently altered with two possible consequences for drug use: first, to the extent that maternal presence in the home is an essential part of the traditional upbringing, the countervailing force exerted by traditional upbringing will be less prominent; and second, young women are likely to engage in increasingly greater risk-taking

> and adult-disapproved behavior, making them as likely candidates as their male peers for drug use. . . .

The Need for Peer Approval

For teenagers of both sexes, drug initiation is most often a social decision. Much has been written about adolescence as "the peer stage," a period of life where self-consciousness is keen and the need for peer acceptance dominant. The worst pain an adolescent can experience is to be socially disregarded or ostracized. This, no doubt, accounts for the rigid conformity to youth styles and manners. In social gatherings, it is a rare adolescent who can refrain from liquor and drugs when others are imbibing. At this stage, one must fit in and not stand out as different.

Youth experiment with substances, not because of their inherent value, but because they want to be "cool," to fit in with the group. This youth's experience, cited by Chein et al. (1964), is illustrative:

> I was at a party. Everybody was having a good time. I wanted to be one of the crowd. I thought, "If it didn't hurt them, it wouldn't hurt me." That started the ball rolling. They were sniffing it that time. Two or three pulled out a few caps; said, "Here, if you want to, try." I accepted. They weren't trying to addict me; they just gave it to me.

Kandel et al. (1978) showed that the three most important factors for initiation into marijuana are first, marijuana use by a youth's friends; second, a youth's friends having attitudes and values conducive to use; and third, availability of the drug.

Initiation is not necessarily premeditated, as this addict recalls: "The friends I hung around with, we all started together. We just decided one day, let's try and sniff glue and see what happens."

Teenagers who *seek* initiation often do so out of curiosity, as this addict recalls:

> I remember hearing an older guy talking to another dude and telling him how much he was cracking up, talking about how they had smoked some weed. And right away I noticed that he liked it. They were laughing and talking and really having a

> good time. And my curiosity was really on it's P's and Q's right there. I was wanting to see what was going on.

A six year statewide study in Illinois (Schwartz, 1977) found that a teenager's friends, not his parents, race, or social standing, determine whether he will break the law or not. "Parents and institutions can have an influence on the peer-group norms," the report indicates, "but once the peer standards are established, they become the overriding influence." Small wonder peer pressure is referred to as "the Pied Piper of adolescence."

At the initiation stage, family interactions can significantly affect drug outcomes. As Kandel explains (1978, p. 75),

> Parents and peers may have an indirect effect on adolescent behavior. For example, adolescents from a loving home may be less likely to become delinquent, not because of the direct influence of the parental bond, but because youths from such homes will tend to associate with certain kinds of friends less prone to delinquent activities. It is these friends, in turn, who directly influence the adolescent.

Home life at the time of initiation is often described by those who escalate into higher levels of drug use as socially and emotionally unrewarding. Parents who give little time and attention to their children may find their influence increasingly diminished. When asked about her home life as a child, an addict responded, "I didn't like it. Ever since I was 12 years old my mother let me do whatever I wanted. It was like not really having anyone care about me. She never really disciplined me."

Another addict recalls:

> They never really showed me much love and affection. My father never used to take me anywhere. I would be in Little League or something and everybody's parents would come and watch, but mine never came. I didn't want to face it. I would hide it somehow, you know, and I'd make excuses for it. I was always on the run, and doing things with my friends. I would hide behind my drums out in the garage—isolated. I never came in except to eat and sleep.

In short, the typical family pattern at the time of initiation seems to be one of little discipline or meaningful interaction between parents and children. The father often seems to be a vague presence in the home and the teenagers themselves spend little time at home. Parents are viewed as providers of food and shelter with emotional support and attention coming from peers.

ESCALATION: UP THE CAREER LADDER

The transition from initiation to full acceptance in the drug career is neither rapid nor automatic. It is an apprenticeship period, a time of proving oneself, of gaining experience and being accepted by established drug users. It involves learning and proving one's loyalty to the expected values and behaviors of the drug world. It is also a time of experimenting with a variety of drugs, of cutting ties with "straight" associates, and spending more and more time on the streets. It is a period of becoming increasingly preoccupied with drugs and involved with others who use them. In short, the escalation stage is a period of learning and development, of challenge and struggle and, from the perspective of the user, of achievement. "It is a time," one said, "of beginning to view yourself as a dope fiend and finding pleasure in taking hold and advancing."

The critical question is: Why do some youth escalate into full drug careers while others do not? Apparently, there is a fine line between experimentation and the time when drugs start to become the main aspect of one's life.

At this stage, Kandel found (1978, pp. 88-9) the parent-child relationship to be an important predictor. While closeness to parent isn't one of the more important factors determining marijuana initiation, she says it does influence escalation into the use of other illicit drugs. Adolescents who report the greatest closeness to their parents are least likely to begin using harder drugs. Of the two parental components, warmth and control, warmth is more important than control, although some control is relevant.

Popular opinion has long held that youths who escalate into regular use do it primarily to avoid pain—first, the discomfort of emotional problems that seem less serious when one is drugged and, second, the physical pain and sickness created by drug withdrawal.

According to this view, one escalates into deeper levels of drug involvement in order to avoid these discomforts (Lindesmith, 1947). While drugs are being used intermittently, tolerance does not develop, but once regular use has begun, tolerance to and physical dependence upon the drug result. When one's source of supply is interrupted, withdrawal symptoms follow—nausea, vomiting, and diarrhea. Once the drug is readministered, the symptoms subside.

Initially, during the "honeymoon stage" drug taking is associated with euphoria; with the onset of the abstinence syndrome, however, usage continues in order to avoid acute withdrawal symptoms—at least, that is the popular view. Because this concept holds that no right-thinking person would allow himself to get into such a sorry state, the notion of the drug pusher has emerged—ruthless characters of the underworld who exit from dark shadows to tempt innocent youth and enslave them for their own mercenary benefits.

Research has shown these notions to be mythical (Atkyns and Hanneman, 1974). McAuliffe and Gordon (1974) found evidence that addicts are primarily motivated by the quest for euphoria; their drug-related activities may be better explained as the search for "highs," rather than the avoidance of withdrawal symptoms. Similarly, in *The Road to H*, Chein et al. (1964) report that heroin initiates sought out established addicts and asked to be included in their drug-using activities; nowhere was there proselyting, coercion, or seduction. "If you have good drugs, you don't need to be a pusher," a former dealer explained. "The drugs will sell themselves. It's just like selling candy; people are attracted to you."

More importantly, youth are motivated by social rewards as well as the drug's euphoric effects. "Ask any drug user if his whole life has been miserable," an addict challenged, "and he will say that is not the case; he will tell you that drugs fit him well and that he likes the whole thing. When you get into drugs you have a good time. There are lots of rewards on the way up—involvement in a social group, status and acceptance by others, and a lot of recognition. If you are successful, people start to admire you just like they do in any group."

Another user reflects:

> At that time I was really heavy, a fat kid, and I felt really self conscious. Anything I could do to make them like me I would do. I would get high with them, and laugh and joke with them and shit like that. I was a people pleaser. It was important to me for them to like me.

But as Blumer and colleagues (1967) point out, these social rewards are neither automatically nor easily attained; they must be earned.

> In order to understand how youngsters are led to use drugs, one must first recognize how the juveniles themselves limit the types of people they will introduce to drugs. Although "mellow dudes," "pot-heads," and "players" have easy access to the marketplace, any recent initiate who arrives on the scene, willing to try drugs, must fulfill a number of requirements. Furthermore, a certain trust must be established before the initiate will be "turned on." To "turn someone on" means to introduce them to a drug, usually marijuana. To turn someone on is an expression of friendship, trust, and acceptance.
>
> The user has got to establish himself with some sort of acceptance," an addict said, "some kind of visibility and identity; he's got to go through certain experiences." Because drugs are illegal, such a person must first be adept at finding them; although this is rarely a problem for an established addict with viable connections, it can be difficult for a newcomer. "He's going to have to front some money to score some drugs because when he is new and hasn't established himself, he has to go through a middleman or a common friend. The dealer, always expecting a 'bust' (arrest), is leery of unproven people.

In this situation, many things can go wrong. One can get "burned" when given bad dope or when a middleman takes a too-large cut for his services. If, as an unestablished person, one retaliates or tries to put pressure upon others, resulting problems may make it difficult to succeed.

Feelings of accomplishment result from having endured hard times and winning the acceptance and admiration of peers. "When you are on top of things," a user said, "you are surrounded by admiring people who aspire to be like you, other drug users and those who have a fascination with the street life."

Interestingly, one of the surest ways to enhance one's status and reputation is to spend time in jail. Here the addict develops new skills, new connections, and, most importantly, establishes a reputation. "If you see a guy in jail," one said, "then you know he's on the same side as you are. Unless he has gone through a few hard knocks like that, he's going to have a hard time being accepted because he hasn't paid his dues like the others." And, in the view of a female addict, "You can't be a real man without spending some time in the joint."

> All my friends had been in jail, and I never had; I had never been busted for anything. They would always talk about jail this and that, and I felt left out and couldn't get into a conversation with them. So I wanted to go to jail. I didn't consciously think of it that way until I got there. Then I thought, "Okay, I know what it's like now, let me out." But it didn't work like that. But when I got out I could sit down and talk to them, and say bla-bla this and bla-bla that. Whatever they were talking about I could be a part of.

Prison experiences seem to serve the same function for addicts as college and training schools do for those with conventional careers. That penitentiaries serve as parallel educational systems is made clear by this addict's comment: "I went to two universities, Soledad and San Quentin. Soledad is sort of like a gladiator school. There are lots of refinements of skill and knowledge that you can acquire only through experience and training by others in a jail setting."

Youth sent to detention facilities are, in their own words, "fed a bunch of jive and then let loose back on the streets to practice what they have learned there." They exchange "war stories" much as locker-room athletes do—how they got "busted," how they were set up by "the Man," and what happened. "You just can't talk about it unless you've been exposed to it before. It all seems like an adventurous life. Man, this cat has really lived!"

In short, to move up in the drug world, as in any career, the initiate must demonstrate qualities important there; he must appear cool, reliable, and responsible. In addition, he must be adept at handling potentially dangerous situations. If he qualifies over time, the road into the distribution system may open for him, drugs will be more plentiful and cheaper, he can attain the life-style he aspires to and, while he is on top, he will be surrounded by admirers and those who wish to emulate him. Having gained a hard-earned reputation, he becomes "hooked," not only physically, but socially and psychologically as well.

During the escalation stage, a drug user's family follows its own escalation process comparable to grief phases. Parents are at first unaware of the problem, especially since their interpersonal relationships are usually distant. Then, as unmistakable evidence crops up, their reaction is often denial. One teenage boy, for example, brought home an expensive stereo set and installed it in his room. Not until months later, did his parents ask where it came from and then accepted his story that it was borrowed. Amused, the boy added, "I wonder if they would have gone for it if I had 'borrowed' a Porsche?" Another youngster stated, "I don't know if they knew or if they just didn't want to accept the fact that their son might be using joys." But parents cannot successfully avoid the issue when their son or daughter is "busted." Arrest is often the first undeniable evidence facing parents of an escalating drug user.

Once a parent is aware of his son or daughter's drug activities, he usually reacts to save face. When arrested for minor offenses, parents typically bail them out as quietly as possible. Others send them away to treatment-oriented schools or rehabilitation centers.

After the initial period of shock and denial wears off fathers become involved in parental monitoring, often for the first time. In hope that employment will bring about a change for the better, some fathers employ their offspring. In such a way, they hope to keep an eye on them while protecting their hard-earned family reputations.

However, by the time parents react, their adolescent children are usually well on their way to full-fledged drug careers. Because the social reinforcers for a drug-using life-style are everywhere about them "tightening their grip," parents have a formidable task trying to change their youngster's projected course.

MAINTENANCE: ATTENDING TO BUSINESS

Drug careers eventually reach a point where they become "mature," fully ripened. At this point, they must be maintained. Here, a drug user's activities focus almost exclusively on the acquisition and use of drugs. One is fully committed to such pursuit. "Users devote their entire lives to that way of living," an addict explained. "Getting drugs is a daily obsession, a total devotion."

Prior to this stage, it was "lots of fun" trying different drugs, meeting new friends, exchanging information, and sharing experiences. At these premaintenance stages, the rewards of getting "high" were mostly social rather than physiological. Such initiates are comparable to fully developed users as frolicking cubs are to a mother bear who, in order to survive, must steadily grub out an existence. That is, at the maintenance stage, the pursuit of drugs is serious business, not "fun and games." "There is a survival consciousness about it," a heroin addict pointed out.

> You've got to fight to get to the top; and when you are there, you've got to maintain yourself in all areas—making sure that you have enough money to purchase your next supply of drugs, that you have a place to stay and can keep up with whatever material possessions you own, that those people who are fronting drugs or dealing for you are doing what they are supposed to. But whether you are on top or at the bottom, you are acutely aware that you have to maintain your existence at whatever point you are at.

For most people, survival connotes food, shelter, and clothing. For the drug user, however, survival involves drugs first, then other things; obtaining drugs takes precedence over everything else. "If a user has ten dollars in his pocket and is hungry and waiting for his connection, he is not going to buy a hamburger," one user observed. "He is going to go without until his connection shows up with the drugs. If he has a choice between buying drugs and paying the rent, he is going to buy the drugs and worry about where he will stay later because those things always take second priority. Drugs are always first in importance."

At the initiation stage, a youth has a choice of going to a hamburger stand with one group of friends or using drugs with another. Because he still has social ties in both worlds, it's a heads-or-tails situation; he can choose between activities, both of which may seem rewarding.

At the escalation stage, most of one's friends are using drugs, but tenuous ties are still maintained to the straight world; a survival consciousness has not yet developed. If funds are low, he does not have to choose between eating or using drugs; he can do both, usually by borrowing from friends. At this stage, friends look after one another; but at the maintenance stage, a user cannot count on borrowing money because, in all likelihood, the other users he knows are in the same predicament.

Friendship groups have the potential of fulfilling two important functions – instrumental functions (helping to attain utilitarian goals such as obtaining money or drugs) and expressive functions (providing socio-emotional rewards such as acceptance and interpersonal support). At the initiation and escalation stages, friends typically fulfill both functions. But at the maintenance stage, as among conventional careerists, associates fulfill mostly instrumental rather than expressive functions. At this stage, group membership is fluid and individuals move from one group to another according to their survival instincts. And because they are periodically pressured by the police and undercover narcotic agents, considerable suspicion exists within these groups. "There is," one observed, "a lot of uptightness and lack of trust about who is a snitch."

Most of the drug user's activities occur on the streets, that is, in relatively small geographic areas inhabited by other drug careerists – a "copping area." Social life in these areas revolves almost exclusively around who has drugs. A typical day is filled with seeing many other users at various stages of getting or using drugs and talking about who has the best drugs. "Only one thing is important," one addict explained, "getting drugs!" Typically, a user will hang around with one group until his connections are exhausted or the situation gets "hot" from police activities. Then he moves on to another copping area. "All the people I know," an addict confessed, "are either related to the drug business or have some sort of leverage that will help me."

Another addict described his networking activities as follows:

> Knowing and meeting the people is important. Eventually I built up a whole network. I knew 12 other hippie types, psychedelic, weed and speed dealers, and we all had each other's phone numbers. It was like a big game. I spent 4 hours a day on the phone calling this guy and that guy, and would get 60 hits of this for 20 hits of that, and bring me three bags of weed. I worked over a hundred hours a week at that.

While success is smiling on the addict, he may be indistinguishable from a successful businessman. He may drive an expensive car, have prosperous living quarters, and assistants working for him. Like a shrewd businessman, a dealer must be clever, prudent, and cautious. He must understand how to minimize costs and maximize profits.

Most importantly, a dealer must have a good business reputation so that others will feel comfortable in dealing with him. "The dealer is a middleman, sort of a manager who is on consignment from others," one explained. "Not only must he have good connections with his sources, but also he must know the people he is selling to, who to trust and who to avoid." While maintaining his own habit, a dealer has got to be adept at street survival, for no one is going to "front" him drugs if he has a reputation for being easily "busted." He must be a person who is trustworthy and responsible, one with a proven record.

But because of challenging conditions, it is not always easy to remain on top; few maintain the dealer role for any length of time. On the streets, roles can switch swiftly so that a person who is dealing one week may be buying from a former customer the following week.

When drugs are available, addicts often establish a "run," a consecutive daily use of drugs akin to an alcoholic binge. Because the body can manage continuous daily usage of heroin, those who use this drug often maintain their runs for a year or longer. "It's not like a user can go for a week using drugs and then lay off for a few days because he is strung out," an addict said. "Even five or six hours without this drug can mean the beginning of withdrawal symptoms."

What is withdrawal like? In the words of an addict, "When you have trouble getting heroin, you start feeling a backache, sort of stiff, and your bones start aching; your vertebrae just sort of ache. You feel cold, but it's not like you can cover up and get warm. All the time you know there is only one thing that is really the matter with you – your body craves the heroin." Interestingly, just obtaining a new supply of heroin may give enough reassurance to relieve bodily distress signals. According to one addict, there may be no way to "fix" immediately after securing heroin, but symptoms may begin to subside with the knowledge that the drug is safely hidden in a pocket; with the immediate threat taken care of, it is possible for an addict to continue about his street business with his reassurance in his pocket, not in his vein.

More severe and dramatic is the "crash" of barbiturate and amphetamine users. Convulsions often accompany withdrawal of "red freaks" (barbiturate users). The "speed freak's" run is by necessity of short duration. High-dose amphetamine users can seldom continue a run for more than ten days before exhaustion overtakes them and their tolerance renders the drug ineffective at any dosage level. "You go through cycles of intense highs where it is always sunrise," one said. "You stay up days and nights with all of your body functions going at maximum." Then, when the body cannot take any more, the user "crashes." As an addict put it, "He's out; his body just collapses. The worst part is toward the end of the run when you are ready to crash, and then later when you have to get up and get your body going again." Then the cycle is renewed with more methadone, more pills.

Since a heroin habit can be maintained for an extended period of time, the vicissitudes of daily living can be most challenging. If addicts haven't "fixed" late at night, morning may be a cruel awakening with the knowledge that last night's reprieve has expired and they are forced to hit the streets, borrow, steal—whatever is necessary—to come up with the necessary cash.

> My routine for a typical day would be staying in bed until I figured out a way to get some money such as burglarizing, or giving short change. For a long time I'd work with my father in his business and I'd make some really good money. I'd sit around the office feeling sick for a couple hours till lunch time and then I'd go straight to the connection. When I came back to work, I would go to the bathroom and fix; I had an outfit in my drawer. That would last until about 5 o'clock. Through the day I would keep fixing.

Although some addicts have legal sources of income (Caplovitz, 1978), more of them try to keep afloat on welfare payments or by borrowing from parents. In our study of 309 addicts (Coombs, 1981a), nine out of ten indicate these sources. But an equal number report such illegal means as shoplifting, stealing expensive items from cars, and burglarizing homes, stores, and offices.

Small drug purchases to tide themselves over are sometimes made possible by exchanging goods and services. Johnson and Prebel (1979) found that addicts in East Harlem often got by for short periods of time by "steering" (recommending a dealer to a buyer), "touting" (finding customers for a dealer), "copping" (acting as "go-between" for dealer and buyer who never meet), or trading services such as providing free lodging for another user.

In contrast to earlier years, drug users at the maintenance stage rarely live at home with parents. Instead, the relationship is usually one of "floating in and out" of the parental home (more "in" during the initiation stage and more "out" during the maintenance stage).

Drug-related activities almost inevitably create conflict and strain between drug-using youth and their families. As one addict explained, "Parents are in a bind and don't know what to do. On the one hand they don't want to put up with the behavior, yet they realize that it is their son or daughter and hope that things might change." Yet as the drug user's career progresses, his parent's realistic hopes for change fade.

During the maintenance stage, the drug user's family, like his friends, fulfills instrumental functions. It is unfortunate that the user's family relinquishes its expressive functions for instrumental ones long before friends do. At a time when friends are providing social and emotional support, during initiation and escalation, the family and home have already been relegated to instrumental status: "I would be home just to eat and sleep. . . . "

Small wonder, then, that these same parents are used by their drug-using children at later stages of the drug career. One young user who was frequently arrested explained:

> Whenever I get released, I always play it to my people (his parents) so I won't have to wait another 60 or 90 days for them to find a placement for me. So I'd always go home for a few hours and then go right back on the streets again.

Users also manipulate their parents for financial resources. Some parents become so frustrated, and so sure that their son or daughter will use, that they provide money to purchase drugs as an alternative to crime. One addict recalled, "A lot of times they'll buy the stuff for me so I won't get busted because they know I am going to it regardless. So they'd rather just give me the money."

When parents are unwilling to provide cash, their addicted offspring will "burn them" with more blatant techniques of exploitation. "I'd burglarize their house and when they found out that I did it, I told them they could buy the stuff back." So, though ignored as children, these offspring are now the center of family attention.

When all else fails on the streets, the drug careerist tends to fall back on parents. His chief survival skill is manipulation, and his parents, alternately hopeful and despairing, are readily manipulated.

DISCONTINUATION AND RENEWAL: TERMINATING THE CAREER?

Drug careers may be terminated abruptly through a drug overdose or temporarily due to incarceration or forced participation in court-committed treatment programs. Rarely do drug users end their careers voluntarily and take up a new way of life. This is not only because of the realities of their addiction—that is, craving highs and eschewing withdrawal symptoms—but because they have undergone so many difficult experiences that they have a big stake, an emotional investment, in drug-related activities. One explained,

> For him to drop out when he is succeeding would be to suffer all the loss of rewards, all of the goals he has worked so hard to get to. He has a lot of investment and has had to go through a lot of painful experiences, each one of which has entrenched him further. After a while, he has burned most of his bridges with the straight world and has become locked into this way of life.

For these reasons, ex-addicts are about as plentiful as ex-physicians. One addict queried,

> If you are successful, why change? Why change careers when you have invested so much time and energy getting there? You are absolutely wasting your time talking to someone about quitting when he has devoted a lot of his life to it and things are still going good for him. You have to catch him at a time when he has hit bottom and is discouraged.

The drug user who is succeeding lives a life of adventure; there is a romantic flavor to the feeling of accomplishment in outwitting the police and of being smarter than "lames," those whose lives revolve around monotonous "rat race" type jobs. When a user is discouraged, though, his life can become as monotonous as it is for the "lames." "It's the same hassles day in and day out, just fighting to get by; it's a daily grind."

Any addict will affirm that only those who fail in the drug world will consider a lifestyle change. Good candidates for treatment programs are those who have "burned out"—the exhausted, those drained of their resources and with "burned" connections, those who are frequently sick and without property or social standing among other users. Upon arrest, one such user commented "Well, I was kind of glad, because I was so strung out. I figured, you know, the only way I'm going to stop is if I get busted, you know, that's the only thing I had in my mind."

Unlike their successful associates, such individuals are not welcomed or supported by other users, especially if they are suspected of "snitching" or otherwise deviating from street mores. One said,

> To be content, a user has to keep moving up and maintaining dignity among his peers. Society doesn't want anything to do with you and tosses you in jail; if your own kind reject you too, you had better start looking for a way to get out, 'cause you have failed.

Detox centers play an important role in helping users who have hit bottom – described by a former addict as "decrepit-looking people who are nutritionally starved because they have simply foregone food; they needed all their money for expensive drugs." It is an opportunity to rest, to eat regularly, to reduce the cost of one's habit and then to return to the streets renewed. These centers become "revolving doors" when the same users, by various manipulations, enter and re-enter the detox facilities.

Incarceration forces users to abstain from drugs, providing of course that drug traffic is controlled within prison walls. Although users try to maintain a tough image ("It ain't no meatball; I can handle it"), nobody likes to serve time in a penitentiary. An experienced addict, one who is "cool," reveals no anxiety when arrested, nor does he resist arrest or rebuke police. "It's more of trying to go along and cooperate the best you can, so you won't be hassled," an addict pointed out. "You know that's the most expedient way to be released. A lot of times it's just routine; the police have been through it before and so have you. Sometimes they even know you by your first name. It's all in the day's work." Chances are good that the user will be released on OR (own recognizance) the next day after arraignment. "It's not unusual to be picked up one night and be out on the streets scoring the next day, having just suffered minimal overnight discomfort."

Those who incur prison sentences are usually booked for a whole battery of charges because, as one addict pointed out, "Any day on the streets the user is going to commit a variety of crimes. If you could follow him around, you would see that it's hard to spend just one hour without breaking the law one way or another (under the influence, having an outfit on you, etc.)."

A stiff prison sentence does not end a user's career; it only temporarily suspends drug use. Eventually, the user will be released and then typically will return to drugs. The prison expression, "Out the gate by eight, in the spoon by noon," conveys this reality. "It's not the end," an addict commented, "it's just part of the game. You have to stop using for a while – or if you can get it in there, that is even further evidence of your ability to beat the system."

Incarceration typically reinforces the drug career by providing an opportunity for less experienced users to "learn a little bit more." It also increases the social distance between users and straight society, for it defines users as criminals and societal officials ("the Man") as persecuting opponents. "When you are in jail, you realize that the enemy has got you," one said.

Labeling a drug user as criminal reinforces deviant behavior, for as a person thinks of himself, so does he act. This truism has been documented in a wide variety of human situations (Coombs and Davies, 1966). Interestingly, those users who avoid the criminal label can, in many ways, live a productive life. One needs only to look at American housewives, many of whom are habituated to psychotropic drugs, to realize that the criminal user is only the "tip of the iceberg" (Parry et al., 1976).

In recent years, criminal justice officials, hoping to rehabilitate users, have increasingly given young users the option of spending time in treatment programs in lieu of prison. To meet this need, treatment programs have mushroomed. Participating in such a program is regarded by users as "easy time", and information circulates on the streets about the various treatment options. It is to the user's advantage to learn as much as possible about them and how to get in. "It's an easy way to avoid jail," one pointed out. "It is also a way to regain your strength, sort of slow down, take a temporary reprieve before you get back out there and have the same sort of fun that you once had, try to recapture those rewards."

Another addict described fellow participants in a detox program:

> A lot of people are there for different reasons. Some are there just to kick and go back out. Some are there because things just got too hot for them on the street. Some dudes sneak out the window, split to town and then come back saying "Man, how would you like to go halfers on a 25?"

Program officials, trying to put their best foot forward, frequently publish dramatic results of rehabilitation success. Some therapeutic communities have claimed to be effective with 80 percent to 90 percent of those who have completed their programs. What they don't publicize is that very few users finish these programs and that the majority "split" within the first month. An independent study of Phoenix House in New York City, for example, found that only 79 (3.7 percent) out of 2,110 admissions completed the program (Waldorf and Daily, 1975).

Our own longitudinal research with 309 hard-core addicts from the Los Angeles area found that more than two-thirds entered state-supported, self-help therapeutic communities under pressure from the courts (Coombs, 1981b). Only a small fraction indicated they were there to change themselves, and most left before graduation. As one user pointed out, "Those who have the most marketable skills in terms of things going for them on the streets are the ones who split first. The ones who stay until graduation don't have so much to give up in the real world."

When tracked down after 12 to 18 months on the streets and interviewed again by ex-addicts, only nine of the entire cohort had abstained from harmful substances, and none had been court referrals; all had come to the treatment program as "burnouts," weary of the "hassles" of street life and seeking a change of lifestyle (Coombs, 1981b).

Since discontinuation and renewal is an ongoing cycle, the family attitude is variable. When a user first participates in a detoxification program, especially voluntarily, his family has high hopes. By his second or third round in such centers, they are understandably less optimistic. Although resigned to his addiction, parents rarely give up hope completely. One female addict, in detoxification after two incarcerations said, "I know all I have to do is call my dad.

He'll feel sorry for me and say, 'O.K., you've been away a month, come on home.' But I know that when I get there, I'll start the whole bullshit all over again."

Because of all the attention, addicts sometimes perceive their parental relationships as improving. A female addict explains: "Before I was unhappy at home; I didn't feel that I could talk to my mother at all. *Now* I have a good relationship with her. She just didn't know how to express herself and neither did I."

Another addict remembers:

> Well, my parents were having their disagreements. And my father and I were never really that close. He just worked all the time and was never around. We never sat down and talked with each other. Well, now he's showing a lot of concern for me. He's helped me with money, and he's talked to me, and given me a lot of understanding. He tells me lots of things to look at about myself, you know. I just say "yeah, yeah"; letting it go in one ear and out the other.

Even though ignoring his father's advice, he was obviously pleased by the attention, especially as contrasted by the lack of it in earlier years.

SUMMARY

The family life of a drug user is inextricably intertwined with his increasing habit. At the initiation stage parental relationships influence how much time a youth will spend at home or with peers. Youngsters who have not developed close bonds with parents, or are in conflict with them, are not likely to be at home much. Parental uninvolvement during childhood can result in minimal control when children reach adolescence.

The family's influence is especially apparent at the escalation stage. Youths who are emotionally closer to their parents are less likely to escalate into illicit drug use. Those with weak family ties are more prone to seek greater involvement in the drug world. With little family loyalty to hold him back, and a great deal of social reinforcement to use drugs, one can easily escalate into deeper involvement.

When parents become aware of their adolescent's increasing involvement in the drug world, great attention of a negative form usually ensues. This is counterproductive if it pushes the youth further from the home. When "hassled" at home, youth seek ego rewards elsewhere, typically from peers who may be experiencing similar problems. Youngsters who receive little positive reward at home and considerable positive reinforcement from drug using peers easily reject adult-imposed standards about drugs. Thus, a career of substance abuse may escalate as parental impact declines and socialization on the streets accelerates (Coombs, 1981a).

Clearly, the most opportune time to alter the evolution of drug use and resulting family stress is to intervene as early as possible, optimally before adolescence begins. The task, it seems, is to make home a rewarding place so that a youngster's self-esteem is grounded in rewarding interactions with parents and others. When the parental home becomes an unrewarding environment, youth spend their discretionary time elsewhere, often on the streets with friends who are experiencing similar difficulties. In these settings, where parental monitoring is absent, youth can quickly evolve from drug sampling to patterned use, and adopt the values of behavioral styles associated with drug use.

Typically, the drug addict's family seems to have a long-standing role as fulfiller of instrumental rather than expressive functions. This role becomes apparent during the escalation stages until a young addict reaches daily preoccupation (the maintenance stage), at which point his family is typically manipulated for money and other instrumental goals.

A lifestyle that involves the compulsive use of substances, does not spring full blown into existence over night. Like conventional careers and lifestyles, it develops gradually. The further one travels along the course of the drug career, the deeper the personal investment, the greater the commitment and consequently the decreased likelihood of considering alternative lifestyles. Decades of unsuccessful remediation efforts attest to the difficulty of changing a person who has evolved to the maintenance stage.

If families are to be spared the enormous stress related to a youngster's drug use behaviors, effective prevention efforts must be developed. These should involve families in significant learning opportunities that improve the quality of parenting skills.

REFERENCES

Alksne, H., Lieberman, L., & Brill, L. (1967). A conceptual model of the life cycle of addiction. *International Journal of Addictions, 2*, 221-240.

Atkyns, R.L. & Hannemann, G.J. (1974). Illicit drug distribution and dealer communication behavior. *Journal of Health and Social Behavior 15*, 36-43.

Baumrind, D. & Moselle, K.A. (1985). A developmental perspective on adolescent drug abuse (pp. 41-67). In *Alcohol and Substance Abuse in Adolescence*. Brook, Lettieri, Brook and Stimmel, (eds.), *Advances in Alcohol and Substance Abuse 4*(3/4), New York: The Haworth Press.

Blumer, H., Sutter, A., Smith, R. et al. (1967). *The World of Youthful Drug Use*. Berkeley: University of California Press, 48-60.

Brook, J. S., Whiteman, M., & Scovell, Gordon A. (1983). Stages of drug use in adolescence: Personality, peer and family correlates. *Developmental Psychology 19*(2), 269-277.

Caplovitz, D. (1978). *The Working Addict*. White Plains: M.E. Sharpe.

Chein, Isador, Gerard, D.L., Lee, R.S. & Rosenfeld, E. (1964). *The Road to It: Narcotics, Delinquency and Social Policy*. New York: Basic Books.

Coombs, R.H. & Davies, B. (1966). Self-Conception and the Relationship Between High School and College Scholastic Achievement. *Sociology and Social Research 50*:4 (July), 460-471.

Coombs, R.H., Fry, L.J. & Lewis, P.G. (eds.). (1976). Socialization in Drug Abuse. Cambridge, Massachusetts: Schenkman Publishing Co.

Coombs, R.H. (1981b). Back on the Streets: Therapeutic Communities Impact upon Drug Users. *American Journal of Drug and Alcohol Abuse 8*:2 (Autumn), 185-201.

Coombs, R.H. (1981). Drug abuse as a career. *Journal of Drug Issues 11*(4), 369-387.

Feldman, H.W. (1973). Street Status and Drug Wars. *Society*, 10 (May/June), 32-38.

Frykholm, B. (1985). The drug career. *The Journal of Drug Issues 15*(3),333-346.

Garry, E.J. (ed.) (19). *A Reason for Tears*. Fort Lee, New Jersey: H.E.L.P. of America.

Johnson, B. & Preble, E. (1979). Some addicts swap goods and services for drugs. ADHAMA News.

Kandel, D.B. (1980). Developmental stages in adolescent drug involvement. In *Theories on Drug Abuse: Selected Contemporary Perspectives*. Lettieri, Sayers, Pearson (eds.), National Institute of Drug Abuse Research Monograph 30.

Kandel, D.B. (1975). Stages in adolescent involvement in drug use. *Science 190*, 912-914.

Kandel, D.B. (1985). On processes of peer influence in adolescent drug use: A developmental perspective (pp. 139-163). In *Alcohol and Substance Abuse in Adolescence*. Brook, Lettieri, Brook and Stimmel, (eds.), *Advances in Alcohol and Substance Abuse 4*(3/4), New York: The Haworth Press.

Kandel, D.B. & Faust, R. (1975). Sequence and stages in patterns of adolescent drug use. *Archives of General Psychiatry 32*, 923-932.

Kandel, D.B., Kessler, R., & Margulies, R. (1978). Antecedents of adolescent initiation into stages of drug use: A developmental analysis. *Longitudinal Research on Drug Use*, 73-99.

Lindesmith, A.R. (1947). *Opiate Addiction*. Bloomington, Indiana: Pricipia Press.

Lynn, D.E. (1986). The Process of Learning Parental and Sex-Role Identification. *Journal of Marriage and the Family 28*, 466-470.

McAuliffe, W.E. & Gordon, R.A. (1974). A test of Lindesmith's Theory of Addiction: The frequency of Euphoria among long-term addicts. *American Journal of Sociology 79*(4): 795-840.

McAuliffe, W.E. & Gordon, R.A. (1980). Reinforcement and the combination of effects: Summary of theory of opiate addiction. In *Theories on Drug Abuse: Selected Contemporary Perspectives* (pp. 137-141). Lettieri, Sayers and Pearson, (eds.). NIDA Research Monograph 30.

Nelson, D.D. (1978). *Frequently Seen Stages in Adolescent Chemical Use*. Minneapolis: Comp Care Publications.

Sadava, S.W. (1977). Stages of college student drug use: A methodological contribution to cross-sectional study. *Journal of Consulting and Clinical Psychiatry 38*(2), 298.

Schwartz, G. (1977). Telephone interview, *The Ventura County (CA) Star Free Press*, January 24.

Waldorf, Dan & D.W. Daily. (1975). Debunking Popular Myths about addicts and addiction. In Robert H. Coombs, Lincoln J. Fry & Patricia G. Lewis (eds.) *Socialization in Drug Abuse*. Cambridge, Massachusetts: Schenkman Publishing Co., Inc., Transaction Books.

Ethnic Family Differences in Adolescent Substance Use

Edward Kaufman, MD
Linda Borders, LCSW, MFCC

If we are to understand and reduce the problems of adolescent substance use, we must be knowledgeable of the ethnic influences which are transmitted through the family from one generation to the next. Ethnicity, as well as the integrally related issues of culture and religion, powerfully affects the family which in turn affects substance use and abuse. Adolescent use of drugs and alcohol are inextricably fused in most cases. Although alcohol is considered a drug, substance abuse is the term generally used to cover both drug and alcohol abuse. We will use "drug abuse" in those rare instances where we are referring specifically to drugs and substance abuse in all other circumstances.

Ethnicity exerts its effects on adolescent substance abuse in two major ways.

1. Ethnicity directly affects family attitudes toward substance use and abuse which in turn affects adolescent patterns of drug intake.
2. Ethnicity affects styles of family functioning which affect adolescent ego function, coping styles and vulnerability to substance abuse.

Edward Kaufman is Associate Professor and Director, Family Therapy Section, Department of Psychiatry and Human Behavior, University of California, Irvine Medical Center, 101 City Drive South, Route 81, Orange, CA 92668. Linda Borders is Associate Clinical Faculty, School of Social Work, University of Southern California and Associate Clinical Faculty, School of Social Work, University of California, Los Angeles.

In many families such as Italians, Episcopalians and Jews, youth are introduced to alcohol for its religious symbolism in highly controlled circumstances. Alcohol is also used in a controlled way as part of religious and secular celebrations. These cultural institutions often facilitate the control of substance use in these adolescents. Jews are protected by the concept that drug and alcohol abuse are only for non-Jews. Protestants are protected by their fear of loss of control and respectability (Ames, 1985). As adolescents move away from family values and particularly as they defy them, they become vulnerable to substance abuse. Still other ethnic cultures have practices which sanction substance abuse by youth. The Irish feel that the more you drink, the more Irish you become (Stivers, 1985). Mexican males drink together to bond their shared masculinity (Gilbert, 1985). Mexican youth are told that when they are old enough to earn a living, they are old enough to drink (Gilbert, 1985). Polish Americans believe that drinking is an expression of freedom and individualism (Freund, 1985). Thus, we see that ethnic cultural patterns can directly enhance or prohibit adolescent attitudes towards substance use and abuse. The effects of ethnicity on family function depend substantially on how many generations of the family have lived in the United States and the type of environment in which they live (Sluzki, 1979). If the family lives in a homogenous environment, in which the roles of the old country are continued, then intergenerational conflict can be minimized (Sluzki, 1979).

Many Jewish, Italian and Irish families lived in such "ghettos" in the early part of this century. This pattern has lessened over the past few decades only to be replaced by black ghettos and Hispanic barrios. However, when the family is pushed toward integration into contemporary society the adolescent more rapidly adopts the mores of that society, putting him/her into conflict with parents (Sluzki, 1979). Because of the disparity between their peer values and those of their parents, these adolescents are particularly vulnerable to substance abuse. They generally drop much of their ethnic identity, which they may rediscover after they bear their own children. These ethnic traits and related substance abuse modifying behaviors may reoccur in subsequent generations if there is a search for identity and roots (Sluzki, 1979).

When we examine the role of ethnicity directly and indirectly shaping substance abuse we must take great care not to overgeneralize about what these effects are. No ethnic group in the United States is homogeneous. Ethnic influences are a product of the country of origin of both parents as well as where in the U.S. the family and their kinship network settle. Although Hispanics have many similarities, there are also substantial differences among Hispanics depending on their country of origin, e.g., Mexico, Puerto Rico, Cuba, and Guatemala. Likewise Blacks may have origins not only from Africa but from Cuba, Jamaica, Haiti, Ethiopia, Nigeria or Puerto Rico. There are tremendous differences among Native Americans dependant on tribal origin and so on. However, there are many patterns in families from different ethnic groups which occur with great frequency and which must be taken into consideration if we are to understand and help change these families.

It is impossible to cite every ethnic group in the United States. This presentation will discuss family characteristics and needs for treatment in the following ethnic groups: Irish, Italian, Jewish, WASP, Black, Hispanic, Asian and Native American.

THE IRISH AMERICAN FAMILY

Parents in these families feel that adolescent substance abuse is a result of the family's sins (McGoldrick, 1982a). They are skillful with words but not in touch with their feelings. They do not praise their children for fear they will become overly confident. Hostility is not expressed directly but is dealt with indirectly through innuendos and sarcasm (McGoldrick, 1982a). The Irish often drink for reassurance and escape from their guilty burdens and their need to repress sexuality and aggression (McGoldrick, 1982a). Irish families are frequently ruled by domineering matriarchal mothers who continue their dominance of the family even when their children are middle aged (Ablon, 1980). Thus, we would expect Irish grandmothers to exert strong influences over their adolescent grandchildren and a general lack of separation on the part of all family members from their family of origin (Ablon, 1980). Cultural encouragement of procreation, and strictures against birth control, lead to the production of children before couples work out their dyadic relationship (Ablon, 1980). Many Irish fathers in inner cities work extra and evening hours in positions such as policemen which result in their absence from the family (Ablon, 1980). In addition, these fathers have a very strong, adult, role-oriented peer group, who influence their functions and values, and support their alcoholism (Ablon, 1980). This absentee father accentuates the need for the mother to be overinvolved and responsible for family function and tasks. This system, though culturally determined, encourages adolescent substance abuse and may account for the high incidence of such abuse in Irish adolescents (Ablon, 1980).

Irish youth are raised in the ambivalent dichotomy of mother, priest, antialcoholism versus father, political boss, pro-drinking. Those whose mothers most scold against the evils of alcohol are defiantly most likely to become alcoholic (Stivers, 1985).

THE ITALIAN AMERICAN FAMILY

The characteristics generally attributed by the family systems literature into Italian families are those of southern Italians who comprise 80% of Italian Americans (McGoldrick, 1982a). Northern Italians are much more like central Europeans in their family characteristics. In Italian American families the family of origin has the highest priority, often creating difficulties for the spouse, who must cope with the mate's intense and exclusive ties to the family of origin (McGoldrick, 1982a). In our experience, this is further complicated by the Italian male and his brothers so often working in the same business, and their expectations that their own sons will enter this business. The experience of the family business is intense and often characterized by conflict. However, the wife is often excluded from this aspect of Italian family experience.

The family support is so strong that leaving it is a severe problem and very stressful for individuals and family (McGoldrick, 1982a). Thus, these families have great difficulty with adolescent individuation, and their tight hold often leads to adolescent rebellion through substance abuse. Emotional security is related to dependency needs being met through the family, rather than through schooling and vocational achievements. Thus the adolescent is not encouraged to develop necessary coping skills, and drugs are used for alternate coping and immediate gratification for security and dependency needs (McGoldrick, 1982a). A critical problem is the low priority of the nuclear family in comparison to the extended family (McGoldrick, 1982a). The father is authoritarian and the head of the family. Any situation which threatens his total control, such as adolescent individuation, has a strong negative effect on the extended family (McGoldrick, 1982a). If the adolescent conforms to the need to uphold the family honor, he will not drink to the point of intoxication. The mother is the heart of the home, but her primary obligations are to the entire three generational system, not to her own family of procreation (McGoldrick, 1982a). Rigidity in the executive subsystem and few shared parental responsibilities contribute to adolescent drug abuse. The extended family business often serves as a vehicle for perpetuating adolescent substance abuse. Teenagers are provided with jobs which supply the money for drugs, regardless of their ability to perform (Kaufman, 1981). It is very difficult for these fathers to release their sons from the family business. These fathers are enmeshed with the substance abuser and not at all disengaged (Kaufman, 1981). The father frequently beats his male children as a form of discipline, but feels justified in doing so because it imitates the way in which his own father demonstrated love to him (Kaufman, 1981).

THE JEWISH AMERICAN FAMILY

There is a very strong family orientation in these families, with marriage and children central (Herz & Rosen, 1982). There is also a strong sense of family democracy, with consensual decision making and diffuse generational boundaries (McGoldrick, 1982a). They place a high value on verbal explanation and on reassuring in child rearing and do not use strong authoritarian directives or threats (McGoldrick, 1982a). They value education, credentials and success. Underachievement is viewed as a reflection on the mother, the entire family and the race (McGoldrick, 1982a). These values are transmitted with considerable guilt about noncompliance, encouraging parents to make great sacrifices towards the successes of their children (Herz & Rosen, 1982). Jews are taught that substance abuse problems occur only in Gentiles. They are taught to integrate moderate drinking into their social and religious activities. Most Jews take their first drink with their family yet also learn techniques as to how to avoid social pressures to use drugs and alcohol.

Feelings are expressed vigorously and verbally with a strong emphasis on arguing, which derives from the Talmud and Torah (McGoldrick, 1982a). Suffering is considered work, and a magical way to deal with adversity, which is to be shared and experienced, not overcome. Conflicts and hostility are direct and total. Lifetime emotional cutoffs can occur when loyalty standards are not met such as by marriage to a person who is not Jewish (McGoldrick, 1982a). Rituals such as the Bar Mitzvah, weddings, and mourning reinforce extended family closeness. There are strong pulls for the nuclear family to dine together on the sabbath and for the extended family to meet during the Jewish holidays (McGoldrick, 1982a). These strong ties in Jewish families make separation and individuation particularly difficult for adolescents, and may lead to substance abuse, though not as commonly as in other ethnic groups.

Jewish children experience the mixed message of demands to stay close to parents on the one hand and achieving and individuation in the outside world on the other (McGoldrick, 1982). Although this double bind could easily be dealt with by the pseudo-individuation provided by substance abuse, Jewish adolescents resort to drugs and alcohol less than most other ethnic groups. They are perhaps spared because of the warmth and other positive features in these families as well as negative sanctions against substance abuse.

There are commonalities in enmeshed family three generational systems such as Jews and Italians. Once substance abuse has occurred, the behavior of the identified patient (IP) is a systems maintaining and maintained mechanism, particularly in Italian and Jewish families. In these families, the family system frequently revolves around the drug abuser as a scapegoat, upon whom all intrafamilial problems are focused. Guilt is a frequent currency of manipulation. It is used by the drug abuser to coerce the family into continued financial and emotional support of drug use or by parents to curb individuation (Kaufman, 1981). In these families mothers often have severe depression, anxiety or psychosomatic symptoms which are blamed on the IP, thereby reinforcing the pattern of guilt and mutual manipulation (Kaufman, 1981). Mother's drug and alcohol abuse and suicide attempts are also blamed on the drug abuser. Fathers have been characteristically described as disengaged in samples of substance abusing families which do not consider ethnicity. However, Italian and Jewish fathers stay enmeshed with the substance abuser and the total family. Love and affection is often used in these families to deny and obliterate individuation or conflict.

ANGLO-SAXON PROTESTANT FAMILIES

The acronym WASP has been used to describe mainly White Protestants of British origin. However, it is also used to refer to many established American families of vague or mixed origins (McGill & Pearce, 1982). In our contact with these families, there is a strong emphasis on independence, which excludes children from the family at an early age, and does not put a premium on taking care of aging parents and relatives. This family type places great stress on autonomy, independence, self-actualization. Children are encouraged to stand on their own two feet early in life. There is little or no toleration for leaning on others or not taking care of oneself (McGill & Pearce, 1982). Adolescents are not taught to use alcohol moderately at family functions and excess substance use is well hidden. The basic family interactional pattern is often dull and lifeless and only becomes alive when mobilized to deal with the crises of drug abuse (Reilly, 1975). The children of WASP families are inculcated with the tenets and precepts of the Protestant-Calvinist Work Ethic and are consistently reinforced in the belief that worth is defined through work and occupational status (McGill & Pearce, 1982).

WASPs were the founding fathers of this nation and came to the continent as a dissenting group and as nonconformists. They were literally excluded from their homeland. They practiced these same exclusionary tactics when they came to this country, as they were the ruling majority and harbored superior sense of self-worth (McGill & Pearce, 1982). WASPs have a built-in code of justice, a sense of righteousness and fair play. They teach that one should not take unfair advantage of other persons. This helps prevent scapegoating, taking sides and playing favorites among the sibling subsystem. They have a great fear of failure because of their need to be superior. They isolate and punish failures. They may have difficulty in communication and are emotionally staid, with an inadequate sense of self-worth (McGill & Pearce, 1982).

The urban Anglo-Saxon American family clearly fostered and fosters the development of the nuclear family and its lack of involvement with the extended family (McGill & Pearce, 1982). This family can at times be demanding, distant, unemotional and cold (McGill & Pearce, 1982). Children are held personally responsible for everything they do. We find that this works well as long as there are no limitations or differences; like substance abuse or unmet dependency needs. They enter treatment with guilt for failing to resolve their own problems, and a low expectation of help from others. The family's response to substance abusing adolescents is more emotionally disengaged than other Anglo groups and justified by their intolerance of weakness and nonconformity.

BLACK AMERICANS

Racism and discrimination exert a constant impact on the Black family. While all groups of immigrants have acculturation problems they eventually become substantially acculturated. Black families have continued to battle social and economic hardships for centuries because of color discrimination (Hines & Boyd-Franklin, 1982). Although females head more Black families than white families, the two-parent family is still the norm among Blacks. Black fathers are much less peripheral than often depicted (McGoldrick, 1982a). They play a bigger role in child rearing and nurturing than white fathers. Disciplining of children is strict but social structures lead to a high incidence of substance abuse in youth. Black families must be understood in the context of their strengths which include strong kinship bonds, flexibility of family roles and high values for religion, education and work (Hill, 1972).

Strong Black kinship bonds evolved when the black family was devastated by slavery. Contemporary versions of these networks continue in Black ghettos as a major mode (Hill, 1972) for coping with the pressures of an oppressive society.

The cooperative domestic exchange of the Black urban family is an active lifelong network which includes uncles, aunts, cousins, boyfriends, older siblings, and preachers. Any one or all of these figures may be critical to the success of family intervention with ghetto Black families. Conflict between spouses is dealt with indirectly rather than through confrontation. There is a strong tradition to remain together for the children. In addition, Black women have even fewer opportunities to leave than White women of comparable social station.

This brief summary of the Black family illustrates how critical involvement with this family's ecosystem is, if meaningful change in family therapy is to occur.

HISPANIC AMERICAN FAMILIES

The Hispanic group includes many different cultures. We will focus on Mexican Americans. However, Puerto Rican, Cuban, and Central American Hispanics all show considerable variations of the same family roles and systems.

Mexican Americans

Over 8.9 million Mexican Americans live in the United States. They are the second largest minority group to live in this country. Most of these Mexican Americans are what is known as "mestizo" or of mixed Spanish and Indian descent. They trace their heritage back to the Indian groups who were responsible for the civilizations in Mexico long before the 1500s when the Spanish explorers arrived (McGoldrick, 1982).

In Mexican American families, the typical nuclear family is embedded in an extended family with flexible and open boundaries which at times appear enmeshed and overinvolved. Further observation of these families reveal clear and fluid boundaries which include all family members such as cousins, aunts, uncles, and grandparents. Besides blood relatives, the extended family includes friends, orphans and single family-less individuals (Madsen, 1964).

The following are five characteristics which distinguish Hispanic families from other ethnic varieties. They are:

1. Interdependence among members of the same and other generations;
2. High level of togetherness and cohesion;
3. Well-defined hierarchial organization of long standing;
4. Loyalty among members of the same and other generations;
5. Family-group identity and loyalty are more important than autonomy and independence (nuclear families attempt to preserve their identity and boundaries by living in separate households, but near to the extended family of origin) (Falicov, 1982).

The large size of the Mexican American family has a major structural influence on the unit. Mexican American families have a significantly higher birth rate than Anglo-Americans and this is most likely encouraged by the Catholic Church's stand against birth control (Falicov, 1982).

Like most families, there are three critical subsystems in the Mexican family. They are the marital, executive, and sibling subsystem. In the marital subsystem there is a complementarity between the spouses, whereby the husband is the provider and protector of the family and the wife is the homemaker and caretaker. This complementarity of roles is rooted in Spanish beginnings and expressed in the hierarchies of male dominance and female submission. The marital couple maintains a focus on parental and grandparental functions due to the large number of children (Falicov, 1982) and their intense connectedness with the parents during adulthood (Falicov, 1980, 1982).

In the executive subsystem, there is also a complementarity of parental functions. The father disciplines and controls while the mother provides nurturance and support. Hierarchies are clearly defined and most parents do not expect to be friends with their children. There is a very relaxed attitude towards developmental milestones with the major focus being on obedience and respect rather than competition or achievement. Extended family members perform parental duties and functions. They also provide adult attention which is hard to come by in a large family (Falicov, 1980, 1982).

In the sibling subsystem the ties are very strong and cousins, as well as siblings, are constant childhood companions. It is common to have few peer friendships outside the sibling subgroup. Quarrels and resentments among adult siblings are common and are often resolved through the reunion of life cycle rituals. Godparents are like an additional set of parents who act as guardians or sponsors of the godchildren and who have a very strong tie and relationship with the natural set of parents (Falicov, 1980, 1982).

In the assessment, evaluation and treatment of the Mexican American family it is important to take into account the sociocultural background and expectations of the Mexican American family when the adolescent has been identified as a substance abuser (McGoldrick, 1982) (Falicov, 1980).

According to the 1980 census, there were 5.7 million non-Mexican Hispanics in the U.S. including 2.2 million Puerto Ricans, 1.1 million Central and South Americans, and 880,000 Cubans. Puerto Ricans are heavy abusers of drugs and alcohol. Central Americans interestingly have a long tradition of positive involvement with Alcoholics Anonymous, particularly Guatemalans. Each Hispanic culture has several unique features and it is critical to not overgeneralize from one to the other.

ASIAN AMERICAN FAMILIES

The American Asian family comes from powerful historical background with roots in the longest continuing recorded civilization in the world (Shon & Ja, 1982). Confucianism and Buddhism are the philosophical and religious base which influence the entire ethnic-family system or structure. From this belief system, the individual is overshadowed and transcended by the family group. An individual's response to this way of thinking becomes a reflection not of him but of the family and kinship network to which he or she belongs. The clan is responsible for keeping up the family name, lineage and image. All relationships are prescribed by the system and little is left to spontaneity or natural affinity. Male offspring are valued much more highly than female, and the roles and expectations of each sex are quite different (Shon & Ja, 1982).

The structure of the family is greatly influenced by Confucianistic principles and the special concept of time surrounding the Asian family is critical in understanding the concept of ongoing continuity. Within the Asian family framework the family is not, like Anglo-American families, time limited. The concept of time and the family extends both backwards and forwards with an ever-flowing sense of movement and dynamic growth. Many families can trace their ancestors back over centuries of generations. Thus, the burden of responsibility is not on the individual, but more concerned with what went before and what is to become and go beyond (McGoldrick, 1982).

In the marital subsystem, the male is considered more important than the female since marriage does not mark the creation of a new family, but rather the continuation of the man's family line. Under this patriarchal system, the status of the wife is lower than that of her husband, his parents and his older siblings (Shon & Ja, 1982).

In the executive subsystem, there is complementarity of spouses in that the father is the leader of the family and mother the nurturant caretaker of both her husband and children. The father is the provider of food, clothing, and shelter and is the primary disciplinarian. The strongest emotional attachment in the Asian family is to the mother which is not only important in childhood, but in later life after the death of the father (Shon & Ja, 1982).

In the sibling subsystem, the sons are more valued than the daughter. The oldest child is a role model for his siblings and has status and authority over them. The oldest male sibling is groomed to take over when the father and leader of the household dies (Shon & Ja, 1982).

Dysfunctional Asian families usually emerge when there is rigid adherence to the old traditional ways of problem solving with too much reliance on male dominance, hierarchical authority and lack of emotional giving (Shon & Ja, 1982).

AMERICAN INDIAN FAMILIES

The U.S. Census indicates that in 1980 there were approximately 1.8 million American Indians living in the U.S. and this is a 60% increase since the last report. The Bureau of Indian Affairs and the Indian Health Service indicate that an increase in medical services has significantly lowered the infant mortality rates and this has contributed to the emphasis on young families in this ethnic group today (Attneave, 1982).

The structure of the traditional American Indian family focuses on all three or four living generations and members of the extended family. Since children are highly valued in this ethnic group the entire extended family makes sure that they are provided guidance, discipline, and control (Attneave, 1982). The primary tasks of the executive subsystem are shared responsibilities delegated among aunts, uncles, grandparents as well as parents. As these parental tasks are provided by nonparent adults of the extended family, the parents are freed to occupy themselves with matters of economic and material support. The high level of involvement of the nonparent adults frees up the natural parents to have a more relaxed and spontaneous relationship with their highly cherished offspring. Often the emotional bond which is created between grandparents and grandchildren is a deep and long lasting one which persists until the death of the older generation (Attneave, 1982).

Among all American Indian families there are numerous tribal differences with the phenomenon of the tri-generational extended families being the most fundamental and important constant. No matter how this complex family organization varies, there is usually an older man or woman who holds a key administrative role (McGoldrick, 1982). Historically, American Indian families had a high level of closeness between generations but not necessarily to a degree that the extended family unit was dysfunctional. To the contrary, this allowed for more freedom of movement for both the children and adults and allowed all family members many different levels and intensities of interpersonal interaction. The usual family therapy intervention of separating the generations would not necessarily be the most appropriate intervention for this ethnic family group (McGoldrick, 1982).

DIFFERENT TYPES OF SUBSTANCE ABUSE IN DIFFERENT ETHNIC GROUPS

In a study (Carlisi, 1979) conducted by the National Center for Urban Ethnic Affairs (NCUEA), Italian adolescents abused marijuana most frequently, followed by alcohol. In a large sample of

Italian adolescents in treatment, conducted by the National Youth Polydrug Study (NYPS) (Carlisi, 1979) the next most commonly abused drugs were opiates, barbiturates, sedatives and amphetamines. However, among Italian inner city adolescents not in treatment, barbiturates were abused most frequently after pot and alcohol, followed by illegal methadone, inhalants and tranquilizers all at the same level. The Irish group in these studies showed the highest incidence of alcohol and drug abuse, and a German group the lowest, with Italians falling in between (Carlisi, 1979). The NCUEA study found that Whites used mainly alcohol and marijuana and were less involved in the use of heroin and barbiturates that non-Whites (Carlisi, 1979). Other studies have found that Whites are more likely than Blacks to have tried alcohol, marijuana, barbiturates, amphetamines, psychedelics and inhalants, but less likely to have tried cocaine or heroin (Kandel, Kessler & Margulies, 1978). As drug trends have changed more recently, it is our observation that more and more White youths have at least tried cocaine. PCP has been widely abused by Mexican youths in Los Angeles and San Bernardino Counties for the past 5 to 10 years.

The NCUEA study found that Italian drug abusers had stronger negative reactions to their parents than Irish and Germans. Both male and female Italian alcohol users had less positive perceptions of their mothers than nonusers. Male, Italian, illicit drug users had less positive perceptions than nonusers of their mothers and fathers (Carlisi, 1979).

TREATMENT OF ADOLESCENT SUBSTANCE ABUSE IN THE CONTEXT OF ETHNIC FACTORS IN THE AMERICAN FAMILY

We have found that treatment of adolescent substance abuse is based on a knowledge of patterns in these different cultural groups and a fusion of two approaches: establishing a method for controlling or eliminating substance abuse and restructuring the maladaptive aspects of the family system.

A major issue which is focused on, and included at the therapeutic contract made in the beginning of treatment, is how the family will deal with substance abuse. If both parents can agree on clear limits and expectations and how to reinforce them, mild to moderate drug and alcohol abuse often can be controlled. Other aspects of the relationship between parents, such as decision-making, roles and sexuality, may also be worked through and resolved. If this method is not sufficient or if the adolescent's substance abuse is more severe, other methods to curtail drug use must be utilized. In the latter case, total abstinence from drug or alcohol use has a better chance for succeeding than controlled use. To achieve abstinence, the family is given a choice of hospitalization or intensive, comprehensive outpatient approach. If the adolescent is dependent on drugs or alcohol to a point of tolerance and withdrawal symptoms, then hospitalization is insisted on for detoxification. The first few sessions focus on the family's implementing hospitalization.

Although many adolescents may complain bitterly about hospitalization at first, they generally comply with and relax into the hospital routine after the first day or two. Even when dependence is not in evidence, hospitalization serves many functions including (1) observation of the extent of substance abuse (psychological and physical dependency), (2) establishment of a therapeutic alliance with the IP, (3) introduction to and total immersion in the concepts of a drug free existence, and (4) cooling down a chaotic family system so that communication and negotiations can occur.

If outpatient treatment is to be successful, we prefer a system of interlocking group therapies to supplement work with the individual family (Kaufman & Kaufman, 1981). These groups include multiple family groups (three or more families) with an adolescent substance abuser, parent groups, and groups for the adolescents themselves. Individual psychotherapy for the drug abusing adolescent is also used, although it is done at the risk of solidifying the family's view of the adolescent as the major problem in the family. Alcoholics Anonymous or Narcotic Anonymous groups which focus on adolescents are extremely helpful if not essential. Also recommended are Alanon groups which focus more on parental issues than on being the spouse of an alcoholic. Although we prefer AA and Alanon groups which meet these special needs, nonfocused groups can also be very helpful, particularly if the family is well motivated to attend such groups.

Basically, developing a system for controlling problematic adolescent substance abuse is a prerequisite for changing family structures to a point where there is no further need for the adolescent to use and abuse substances (Kaufman & Kaufman, 1979). At times families will then restructure rather easily, but in some cases intensive, long-term family therapy may be necessary.

In general, when dealing with differences in families of substance abusers, there are a series of fundamental approaches which should be undertaken which must consider ethnic differences in shaping behavior and responsiveness to change maneuvers.

The first task of the treatment is to support and fortify the executive subsystem and put it back into control. The second most important intervention is to decentralize the overinvolved executive subsystem leader (usually the mother) and restore to importance, the underinvolved executive subsystem member (usually the father). In the case of the single parent, it may be necessary to attend to the overworked, burnt-out depletion faced by most single parents and to fortify this subsystem by bringing in previously unrecognized support systems. Thirdly, free and open communication must be reestablished with parental hostility and criticism blocked or rechanneled by the family therapists. The fourth intervention involves diminishing the power of the peer group of the substance abusing adolescent by teaching the IP to say no and by building his/her self-esteem. The therapist's final emphasis is to refocus the parents away from the IP and into the quality of their own dyadic relationship. The healthier and more intimate the spousal relationship becomes, the more likely the entire family will be able to sustain higher functioning including maintenance of sobriety of each family member.

Basic family structures in each ethnic group must be recognized and techniques utilized which consider these inherent ethnic characteristics.

The Irish American family in therapy has been well described by McGoldrick (1982b). They tend to view therapy in the same way they view confession, i.e., to relate sins and gain forgiveness; yet if the therapist uncovers their sins, they will feel embarrassed. They are not assertive and do not let the therapist know if they are being inconvenienced. Because of the politeness and loyalty they may comply with the therapist without really changing. They view the therapist as a priest-authority and thus respond well to a structured, problem oriented approach, or to a specific, clearly spelled out plan, such as behavioral therapy. Bowen's systems therapy may work well because of its respect for individual and subsystem boundaries. These families also respond well to paradoxical techniques which encourage change without exposing inner feelings.

Irish families rarely seek out therapy on their own so that court mandated therapy for an acting out, substance abusing adolescent is a very common reason for referral (McGoldrick, 1982b) and embarrassing and humiliating for the family (McGoldrick, 1982b). Involving the distant father in these families is often essential to correcting the maternally dominated imbalance (Kaufman, 1981). Some Irish fathers have been so totally removed from the family that it has been impossible to get them to come into therapy. Adolescent males in these families identify strongly with their fathers, although this is a very difficult concept for them to accept. With the help of other family members, this identification can be pointed out and the IP helped to extrude the extreme emotional distancing attitude of their fathers (Kaufman, 1981).

Though the therapy may be very uncomfortable for these families, their deep sense of personal responsibility often leads them to continue therapeutic work on their own after termination of formal therapy (McGoldrick, 1982b).

Therapy with Italian American families must focus on the renegotiation of their rigid system boundaries, which keep the extended family out of contact with the outside world (Rotunno & McGoldrick, 1982). They talk openly and with exaggerated feeling, yet hide their family secrets, which are plentiful. Secrets must be dealt with delicately, as their being made known to the therapist may constitute family betrayal (McGoldrick, 1982b).

The therapist must overcome being distrusted as an outsider, so that the authority necessary to change the family can be established. This may involve patiently surviving the family's many tests of the therapist's loyalty and the therapist's skills (Rotunno & McGoldrick, 1982). Then the therapy can focus on helping the adolescent differentiate from the family in more adaptive ways than through substance abuse, yet permit them a face-saving way to remain within the family (Rotunno & McGoldrick, 1982).

We have found that multiple family groups (Kaufman and Kaufman, 1979) can be very helpful in providing Italian families the support that they need to let go of their adolescents. Given the insularity of the Italian extended family, their willingness to open up and change in a group of other families is surprising. This openness to change may occur because of the devastating effect of a heroin-addicted youth in the family. The use of an Italian cotherapist, their view of the doctor as respected expert and other Italian families in the group who supported the letting go process may also be responsible.

Jewish American families value credentials and education, and the therapist should not feel threatened by questions about these issues. When credentials are established, they readily consult with the therapist as a wise person, but still retain the right to make the final judgment about which interventions they will or will not use. They prefer complex, sophisticated interventions and consider behavioral types of techniques to be superficial (McGoldrick, 1982a). Talking and expressing their feelings are more important to Jewish American families than actively changing, and thus they prefer analytic techniques to strategic ones (Herz & Rosen, 1982). However, tasks are essential to shift from intellect to action, and they can be given in the families own complex terms, utilizing their language and rituals.

The therapist must respect the rules which support enmeshed togetherness in Jewish families at the same time as he/she facilitates some essential boundary making. This can be done by working with the more flexible parts of the system, such as the adolescent subsystem. They can be encouraged to accept less threatening parental gifts while they reject those which are infantilizing (Herz & Rosen, 1982). The therapist can readily join with the children in these families, without threatening the parents, because of their basic sense of democracy and egalitarianism (Herz & Rosen, 1982).

In WASP families, adolescent difficulties are perceived as the child's problem, not the family's (McGill & Pearce, 1982). Thus WASP families should be encouraged to stay involved, to provide support and to assume control of the problem. The substance abusing adolescent is encouraged to share his/her pain with the family so they are able to share the responsibility (McGill & Pearce, 1982).

Since asking for help is so difficult for WASP families the therapist should support, rather than confront, these families in the early stages of therapy, and should build trust in order that their feelings of vulnerability will not be intensified (McGill & Pearce, 1982). Once the problem is clearly defined and a treatment contract is made they will proceed with hard work in therapy, with the belief that this will be sufficient for success in therapy as it is in life. Thus they respond well to taking didactic courses and planned interventions such as Parent Effectiveness Training.

They are so understated that they may make significant progress in therapy or be deeply affected without telling the therapist. However, their lack of attachment makes termination of therapy an easy process (McGill & Pearce, 1982).

In working with Black and Hispanic families it is critical to separate ethnic issues from those of poverty. It is also essential in both types of families to involve the extended network. Mexican American adolescent males feel that if they are employed, they have the right to drink, particularly with their fellow workmen and relatives. The therapist must deal with this "right to drink" with the same cultural sensitivity necessary to deal with Hispanic paternalism.

Asian adolescents, particularly those who are acculturated do not seem to be offered substantial protection against alcoholism via flush related responses. In Chinatowns, adolescents may be quite involved with gang related activities which are also conducive to drug abuse. The strong positive family and network ties should be used to the fullest in work with these families, although by the time the adolescent is involved with gangs, it may be too late for family interventions. A Japanese version of AA, the All Nippon Sobriety Association (ANSA) could be developed in this country to aid that ethnic group. A Hong Kong version of NA is another effective model which could be utilized. With the recent growth of the Hmong Tribe from Asia's golden poppy growing triangle, we should watch for a shift upon migration from opium to alcohol.

We are in agreement with Fishman et al. (1982), who state that the therapy of these adolescents should be much more structural than strategic since the goals are an intact family with a restructured parental hierarchy. Thus techniques used with adolescents include reframing their behavior as competent so they can be trusted or voluntary and delinquent so it can be controlled. It may also be necessary to diminish parental overcontrol in order to lessen the adolescent's need to rebel (Fishman et al., 1982).

Marking boundaries is very important with those families which are enmeshed. After we have observed the adolescent's interfering role in parental decision making during an actualization, we will work with the parents to restrict the adolescent from such interference while respecting the adolescent's right to his/her privacy. We often ask the adolescent subsystem to leave the room while parents are agreeing on limits to underline the importance of making such decisions without the adolescent being present or influencing their parents. Once decisions have been made, then the adolescent can participate in negotiations as long as an intergenerational coalition or triangle can be avoided. After several decisions have been made with everyone present throughout the process we are able to evaluate the extent to which the systems can maintain its boundaries outside therapy.

One situation which occurs frequently in our experience with these families is parental substance abuse which may be more extensive than that of the adolescent. However, if the adolescent is clearly labeled the problem by the family, then it is very important that the family be given some relief from the adolescent's behavior and/or substance abuse before the drug/alcohol or behavior problems of the parent(s) are addressed (Minuchin, 1974). On the other hand, if the adolescent's problems are only a means to get the more seriously disturbed parent into the session and the family clearly labels the parents' problems as a major problem, it is our experience that primary parental difficulties can be addressed and even made a part of the initial treatment contract. In the former case, once there is some relief for the family from the adolescent's problems, then parental substance abuse and other problems can be dealt with. When the parents themselves are dependent on drugs or alcohol it is very difficult for them to acquire appropriate parenting skills, thus their finding a system for abstaining becomes a very high priority in the treatment.

We feel that once the therapist has developed a method of working with families to achieve a drug and alcohol free state and has gained an understanding of the specific culturally determined patterns in these families, a firm base for their psychotherapy is established. Upon this cornerstone, a therapist can impose any workable system of family change, given the constraints developed for each ethnic group in this article. Our preference for a therapeutic family method is an integrated approach which draws from such contemporary family therapy modalities as strategic, structural, behavioral, and psychodynamic. These techniques are then adapted to meet the needs of each individual family with great attention paid to ethnic differences.

REFERENCES

Ablon, J. The significance of cultural patterning for the alcoholic family. *Family Process*, 19(2): 127-144, 1980.

Alexander, B.K. and Dibb, G.S. Opiate addicts and their parents. *Family Process*, 14:499-514, 1975.

Ames, G.M. Middle class Protestants: Alcohol and the family. In L.A. Bennett and G.M. Ames (Eds.), *The American Experience with Alcohol*. Plenum Press, New York, pp. 435-460, 1985.

Attneave, C. Therapy in tribal settings and urban network interventions. *Family Process*, 8:192-210, 1969.

Attneave, C. American Indians and Alaska native families: Emigrants in their own homeland. In M. McGoldrick (Ed.), *Ethnicity and Family Therapy*. Guilford Press, New York, 1982.

Benedict, R. *Patterns of Culture*. Houghton Mifflin, Boston, 1959.

Biggs, J.T. Psychosocial factors related to substance abuse among delinquent females. *American Journal of Orthopsychiatry*, 52(2):261-271, 1982.

Blum, R.H. *Horatio Alger's Children*. San Francisco, Josey-Bass, 1972.

Brook, J., Lykoff, I. and Whiteman, M. Family socialization and adolescent personality and their association with adolescent use of marijuana. *Journal of Genetic Psychology*, 133:261-271, 1978.

Carlisi, J.A. Unique aspects of white ethnic drug use. In G.M. Breschner and A.S. Friedman (Eds), *Youth Drug Abuse: Problems, Issues and Treatment*. Lexington Books, Lexington, MA, 1979.

Falicov, C. Mexican families. In McGoldrick M. (Ed.), *Ethnicity and Family Therapy*. Guilford Press, New York, 1982.

Falicov, C. and Darrer, B. Cultural variations in the family life cycle: The Mexican-American family. In E. Carter and M. McGoldrick (Eds.), *The Family Life Cycle and Family Therapy*. Gardner Press, New York, 1980.

Fishman, H.C., Stanton, M.D. and Rossman, B.L. Treating families of adolescent drug abusers. In M.D. Stanton and T.C. Todd (Eds.), *The Family Therapy of Drug Abuse and Addiction*. Guilford Press, New York, 1982.

Freund, P.J. Polish American drinking: Continuity and change. In L.A. Bennett and G.M. Ames (Eds.), *The American Experience with Alcohol*. Plenum Press, New York, pp. 77-92, 1985.

Gilbert, M.J. Mexican Americans in California: Intracultural variation in attitudes and behavior related to alcohol. In L.A. Bennett and G.M. Ames (Eds.), *The American Experience with Alcohol*. Plenum Press, New York, pp. 255-278, 1985.

Gonzales, E. The role of Chicano folk beliefs and practices in mental health. In C.A. Hernandez, M.J. Hauf, and N.N. Wagner (Eds.), *Chicanos: Social and Psychological Perspective*. C.V. Mosby, St. Louis, 1976.

Haley, J. *Problem Solving Therapy*. San Francisco: Josey-Bass, 1977.

Herz, F.M. and Rosen, E.J. Jewish families. In McGoldrick, J. Pearce, and J. Giordano (Eds.), *Ethnicity and Family Therapy*. Guilford Press, New York, 1982.

Hill, R. *The Strengths of Black Families*. Emerson Hall, New York, 1972.

Hines, Paulette Moore and Boyd-Franklin, Nancy. Black Families. In Monica McGoldrick, John Pierce and Joseph Giordano, *Ethnicity & Family Therapy*. Guilford Press, New York, pp. 84-107, 1982.

Kandel, D.B., Kessler, R.C. and Margulies, R.Z. Antecedents of adolescent initiation into stages of drugs use: A developmental analysis. *Journal of Youth and Adolescence*, 7(1):3-14, 1978.

Kaufman, E. and Kaufman, P. *Family Therapy of Drug and Alcohol Abuse*. Gardner Press, New York, 1981.

Kaufman, E. Family Structures of Narcotic Addicts. *Int. J. Addictions*, 16(2):273-282, 1981.

Madsen, W. *The Mexican American of South Texas*. Holt, Rinehart, and Winston, New York, 1964.

McGill, D. and Pearce, J.K. British Families. In M. McGoldrick, J. Giordano and J.K. Pearce (Eds.), *Ethnicity and Family Therapy*. Guilford Press, New York, 1982.

McGoldrick, M. *Ethnicity and Family Therapy*. Guilford Press, New York, 1982.

McGoldrick, M. Normal families: An ethnic perspective. In F. Walsh (Ed.), *Normal Family Processes*, Guilford Press, New York, 1982a.

McGoldrick, M. Irish Families. In M. McGoldrick, J.K. Pearce, and J. Giordano (Eds.), *Ethnicity and Family Therapy*. Guilford Press, New York, 1982b.

Minuchin, S. and Fishman, H.C. *Family Therapy Techniques*. Harvard University Press, Cambridge, Massachusetts, 1981.

Minuchin, S. *Families and Family Therapy*. Harvard University Press, New York, 1974.

Olson, D.H., Spreennkle, D.H. and Russell, C.S. Circumplex model of marital and family systems: Cohesion and adaptability dimensions, family types, and clinical applications. *Family Process*, 18:3-28, 1979.

Reilly, D.M. Family factors in the etiology and treatment of youthful drug abuse. *Family Therapy*, 2:149-171, 1975.

Rotunno, M. and McGoldrick, M. Italian families. In M. McGoldrick, J.K.

Pearce, and J. Giordano (Eds.), *Ethnicity and Family Therapy*. Guilford Press, New York, 1982.

Shon, S.P. and Ja, Davis, Y. Asian families. In M. McGoldrick (Ed.), *Ethnicity and Family Therapy*. Guilford Press, New York, pp. 208-228, 1982.

Sluzki, C.E. Migration and Family Conflict. *Family Process*, 18(4):379-390, 1979.

Stivers, R. Historical meaning of Irish-American drinking. In L.A. Bennett and G.M. Ames (Eds.), *The American Experience with Alcohol*. Plenum Press, New York, pp. 255-278, 1985.

Sue, S. and McKinney, H. Asian Americans in community mental health care system. *American Journal of Orthopsychiatry*, 45(1):111-118, 1975.

Personality, Family, and Ecological Influences on Adolescent Drug Use: A Developmental Analysis

Judith S. Brook, EdD
Martin Whiteman, PhD
Carolyn Nomura, MA
Ann Scovell Gordon, MA
Patricia Cohen, PhD

DEVELOPMENTAL PERSPECTIVES ON ADOLESCENT DRUG USE

Investigators into the causes and consequences of adolescent drug use increasingly have taken a developmental approach. This

---

Judith S. Brook is Associate Professor of Psychiatry and Carolyn Nomura and Ann Scovell Gordon are Research Analysts, Department of Psychiatry, Division of Child and Adolescent Psychiatry, Mount Sinai School of Medicine. Martin Whiteman is Professor of Psychology, Columbia University School of Social Work. Patricia Cohen is Associate Professor of Epidemiology, Columbia University School of Public Health and Principal Research Scientist, New York State Psychiatric Institute.

Preparation of this article was facilitated by a Research Scientist Development Award (Grant DA00094) to Judith Brook and Grant DA03188, both from the National Institute on Drug Abuse. The authors are particularly grateful to Dr. Coryl Jones for her valuable input, to Sandy Stillman for program analysis, and to Susan Karaban for typing several versions of the manuscript. Finally, the authors would like to thank Dr. Jesse Smith and Claudia Hartmark for supervising the collection of data.

Requests for reprints should be addressed to Dr. Judith Brook, Mount Sinai School of Medicine, One Gustave Levy Place, Annenberg 22-74, New York, NY 10029.

concern with the developmental processes involved in drug use has led to efforts at integrating the various extant theories of delinquency, deviance, and drug use that offer narrower explanatory frameworks for the why and how of substance use by adolescents. These frameworks, some of which were reviewed in 1980 by Kandel, are based on cross-sectional or longitudinal data from only one developmental period, i.e., adolescence. One consequence of this concentration on adolescence has been a particular emphasis on peer influences, with friends' use or nonuse of drugs as an explanatory variable, although in more recent research there also has been a focus on the crucial features of family dynamics that have to be borne in mind when considering possible causal effects.

The work of several research groups, especially Jessor, Kandel, and Brook/Whiteman and colleagues, has contributed to the consideration of adolescent drug use from a developmental perspective. Their theories, which present different but complementary approaches to a developmental understanding of adolescent drug use, will be described below.

The psychosocial theory of problem behavior put forth by Jessor and Jessor (1977) views certain adolescent behaviors as indicative of transition-proneness, because their adoption is characteristic of a movement from one developmental stage to another. According to this theory, the developmental process marked by drug behavior (alcohol and marijuana use) includes such other behaviors as sexual promiscuity and delinquency. Thus, drug use is part of a larger constellation of factors collectively called "problem behavior" which occurs in a transitional developmental stage also distinguished by the growing autonomy of late adolescence and pre-adulthood. Problem behavior is so labeled because it presents a problem both to the caretakers of adolescents and to the larger society. The Jessors' studies bore out their hypothesis that the attributes associated with onset of problem behavior include lower value on achievement, greater value on independence, greater social criticism, greater tolerance of deviance, and less religiosity; less parental control and support, greater influence of friends, and more modeling of and approval for drug use by friends as perceived by the adolescent; and adolescent behavior characterized by less church attendance and lower school achievement.

Kandel has taken another approach to the developmental process involved in adolescent drug use. She has identified four distinct developmental stages in adolescent drug involvement which form a sequence from the use of legal drugs to illegal drug use: (1) beer or wine, (2) cigarettes or hard liquor, (3) marijuana, and (4) illicit drugs other than marijuana (Kandel, 1975). Evidence for stages in drug use is based on Guttman scales analysis and findings that different variables identify adolescents who are likely to progress from one stage to the next (Kandel, 1975; Kandel, Kessler & Margulies, 1978). Specifically, involvement in delinquent activities, parental modeling, and peer sociability predict initiation into the use of hard liquor, while association with drug-using peers and the adolescent's own beliefs and values are the dominant factors in onset of marijuana use. A poor parent-child relationship, psychological distress, and modeling by one's friend precede the use of illicit drugs other than marijuana.

Frequency of use at each of the stages of drug use has also been studied in recent years (Baumrind, 1985; Brook, Whiteman & Gordon, 1982). Brook et al. (1982) found that while the same personality and peer factors differentiated stages and levels (nonuse, experimental use, regular use) of adolescent drug use, family factors were more powerfully related to stage than to frequency. Moreover, each of the sets of personality, family, and peer variables had a direct impact on stage of drug use, whereas the family and personality variables had an indirect influence on frequency of drug use by operating through characteristics of the peer group. The implication is that family and personality factors determined whether the adolescent would use a particular drug, while friends were especially potent in determining the occasions for drug usage by the adolescent.

A developmental approach taken by Brook, Whiteman, and their associates focuses on the interrelation of family relationships, adolescent personality attributes, peer associations, and the adolescent's use of marijuana (e.g., Brook, Whiteman & Gordon, 1983b). According to this conception, parental introjection of traditional societal values is related to a warm and conflict-free parent-adolescent attachment relationship, which in turn is linked with the adolescent's greater identification with the parent. As a consequence of this attachment and identification, the adolescent introjects the parent's conventional values and behavior, which are then manifested in the adolescent's own conventional behavior and attitudes and psychological adjustment. This greater adolescent conventionality and psychological well-being insulate the adolescent from association with peers who use drugs, and also make him or her less peer-oriented relative to parents.

Several other investigators, such as Kaplan, Akers, Robins, Clayton, and Bentler, have made important contributions to an understanding of drug use by adolescents. Excellent summaries of their work have appeared in recent years (see Braucht, Brakarsh, Follingstad & Berry, 1973; Jessor, 1979; Kandel, 1980; Lettieri, 1985).

A few investigators employing longitudinal data also have explored the childhood antecedents of adolescent drug use (Baumrind, 1985; Block, Keyes & Block, 1986; Kellam, Ensminger & Simon, 1980; Pulkkinen, 1983). These studies focus on the possible psychosocial and environmental antecedents in childhood of adolescent drug use. Block et al. (1986) report that a configuration of childhood attributes, including lack of compliance, rebelliousness, and a lack of social skills, is associated with substance use among adolescents living in an urban, middle-class environment.

Of all the childhood personality factors associated with adolescent drug use, aggression appears to be the most potent. This is demonstrated in the Woodlawn study of a population of poor inner-city blacks (Kellam et al., 1980), as well as in the research of Pulkkinen (1983), who found that childhood aggression related at age 20 to smoking for both males and females, and to heavy drinking for males. With regard to childhood family and environmental factors linked to adolescent illicit drug use, the following have appeared in the literature: a poorly structured environment characterized by conflict (Block et al., 1986); lack of traditionality, nonintact family structure, and lack of monitoring and firmness (Baumrind, 1985); and parental modeling of legal drug use (Pulkkinen, 1983).

Although the adolescent exists in an environment which must differ significantly from that of the child, there is evidence that fundamental aspects of the family environment tend to persist over time. Parental child-rearing techniques are somewhat stable throughout the childhood years into adolescence (Roberts, Block & Block, 1984; Schaefer & Bayley, 1963). The quality of the parent-child relationship, first established during infancy, naturally changes as the child undergoes developmental reorganization; but the relationship is a continuing one in which previous dynamics affect later interactions (Youniss & Smollar, 1985).

Childhood personality traits associated with adolescent drug use usually have been viewed as consequences of parental and other external influences rather than as intrinsic personal characteristics. Although there is some suggestion that temperamental characteristics, such as slow adaptability and negative mood, are associated with eventual substance use (Lerner & Vicary, 1984), the empirical data suggest that environmental factors have the strongest impact on the personality precursors in childhood of later problem behavior (Elder, Caspi & Downey, 1986; McCord, 1979; Robins, 1974).

Besides childhood, another important part of the "life cycle" of drug use involves the post-adolescent period. A decline in illicit drug use appears to take place in young adulthood as young people begin to take on adult roles (Kandel & Logan, 1984). In particular, marriage and parenthood are associated with steep declines in drug use (Yamaguchi & Kandel, 1985). By the same token, adolescents who are unable to negotiate the difficult transition to adulthood may choose to escape from developmental disequilibrium through either compulsive drug use or the total avoidance of drugs (Baumrind & Moselle, 1985). As is true of adolescent drug users, young adults who use illicit drugs on a regular basis maintain drug-using peer networks and show greater dissatisfaction with social institutions (Kandel, 1984).

INTERPLAY AMONG ECOLOGICAL AND SOCIALIZATION FACTORS, ADOLESCENT PERSONALITY/ATTITUDES/BEHAVIOR, AND ADOLESCENT DRUG USE

In the first part of this section, we will discuss the association of ecological factors with socialization factors, with adolescent personality/attitudes/behavior, and with adolescent drug use. The second part of this section will address the links between socialization factors and adolescent substance use. Finally, a third part will focus on the adolescent personality, attitudinal, and behavioral factors involved in drug use by adolescents.

Ecological Factors Related to Socialization Factors, Adolescent Personality/Attitudes/Behavior, and Adolescent Drug Use

Ecological factors are structural elements of the environment that constitute the objective context of behavior, that is, the real-life settings within which people behave and over which they have little control (Barker, 1968).

There is clear evidence that one type of ecological variable, socioeconomic status (SES), is related to the socialization factor of parental child-rearing practices (Elder, Liker & Cross, 1984; Gecas, 1979; Kohn, 1977; Lytton, 1980), and is also associated with the child's own attitudes and behavior (Brook, Whiteman, Peisach & Deutsch, 1974; Cohen & Hodges, 1963; Gough, 1946; Liddle, 1958; Rosenberg, 1965). Socioeconomic status has not been found to have a large impact on adolescent drug use, especially alcohol and marijuana use (Coombs, Fawzy & Gerber, 1986; Kandel, 1980). As noted in Kandel's review (1980), when a relationship does emerge, it is for more extreme forms of the behavior, and usually occurs as an SES difference between individuals in the lowest social class and all others (e.g., for heavy drinkers). Cocaine once was an exception to the foregoing, primarily because of its high cost and pattern of distribution which made it most prevalent and heavily used among higher-SES groups (Grabowski, 1984). However, with the advent in the mid-1980s of "crack," a cheap (per unit of dosage) form of smoked cocaine, the drug became distributed among all the socioeconomic strata (Morganthau, 1986).

The general finding that social class is relatively unimportant as a direct influence on drug use may be because SES has been examined singly in its effects. It is possible that if SES was looked at in conjunction with other aspects of the child's ecological and social environment, such as family structure or material resources, social class would have a greater impact on drug use behavior.

The home's material environment is another ecological factor that influences the child's development (Wohlwill, 1983). It may also affect the interactions between parent and child, since conditions such as the availability of books and toys, quality of furnishings, and physical space together create a setting for a family's day-to-day social and emotional life. Block, Keyes, and Block (1986) found that a poorly maintained and relatively disordered home environment in childhood was associated with "hard" substance use in adolescence.

With regard to family structure, studies show that parent-child interaction is strongly affected by such patterns of organization as single parenting (e.g., Rutter, 1981). One frequent, though inconclusive, finding in the literature is the positive linkage between nonintact family structure and adolescent marijuana use (Brook, Whiteman & Gordon, 1985; Penning & Barnes, 1982).

Although the school's effect on the child's development is well-established (Busch-Rossnagel & Vance, 1982; Minuchin & Shapiro, 1983), the direct effect of the school on adolescent drug use appears to be limited (Minuchin & Shapiro, 1983). Drug education programs by and large have not succeeded in discouraging students from using drugs, and in some cases have been found to increase drug usage (Minuchin & Shapiro, 1983). Nonetheless, there is considerable evidence that disaffection from the school, as indicated by low academic achievement or underachievement and dislike of school authorities, is a correlate of alcohol and other drug use by early and middle adolescents (see, for example, Hawkins, Lishner & Catalano, 1985; Schwartz, Hayden, Getson & DiPaola, 1986).

The church also is an ecological construct known to have effects related to adolescent substance use. Religiosity, as demonstrated for example by church attendance, bears a strong negative relationship to drug use (Gersick, Grady, Sexton & Lyons, 1981; Khavari & Harmon, 1982). The findings are equivocal with respect to denominational affiliation (Gersick et al., 1981; Penning & Barnes, 1982).

In addition to those discussed above, a variety of other ecological factors can foster drug use by adolescents. Neighborhoods characterized by cultural diversity, high population turnover, and physical deterioration produce cultural and social disorganization which, with accompanying availability of drugs, increases youthful vulnerability to drug use (Elliott, Huizinga & Dunford, 1983). Ethnicity, cohort effects, secular trends, and historical circumstance and change also appear to affect patterns of illicit drug use behavior among adolescents, although the research findings by no means are consistent (Gersick et al., 1981; Johnston, 1985; Penning & Barnes, 1982; Robins, 1980).

Socialization Factors Related to Drug Use

The process of socialization is one in which the individual develops socially-relevant patterns of behavior, values, and attitudes through interchange with other people (Zigler & Child, 1969). Although there are many arenas in which socialization takes place, the family generally is considered the most influential (Maccoby & Martin, 1983).

Before examining the effect of family factors on adolescent drug use, several issues need to be addressed with regard to family influences on child development. To begin with, it is important to recognize that while the mother may serve as the main attachment figure for the child, other members of the family also play important roles. Within the last decade, for instance, a number of investigations have focused on the father-child relationship (e.g., Lamb, 1981). Attention also has been given to the alterations in children's development as a result of their interactions with siblings (e.g., Dunn, 1983). Second, there is now clear evidence that family influences are not unidirectional, that is, from a particular family member to the child. The relationship between parent and child can best be described as bidirectional: the parent affects the child at the same time as the child affects the parent (Bell, 1979; Lerner & Spanier, 1978; Olweus, 1980). Even within the same family, parents may respond to each of their children differently, depending on their individual characteristics (Daniels & Plomin, 1985). Third the relationship between parent and child does not exist in a vacuum; rather, the child's relationship with the parent is affected by the child's relationships with other members of the family unit. For instance, in recent studies it has been demonstrated that the father's relationship with the child is affected by the mother's relationship with the child (Brook, Whiteman, Gordon & Brook, 1983; Brook,

Whiteman, Gordon & Brook, 1985). Fourth, while there is considerable stability in the dynamics of the family, a certain amount of change occurs over time (Jersild, Brook & Brook, 1978). To our knowledge no framework exists for identifying those factors that have an impact on the stability of the family.

Socialization within the family as it specifically concerns adolescent drug users and their parents centers on two aspects of interpersonal influence: (a) modeling, and (b) child-rearing practices.

The modeling effects of parental drug use behavior on adolescent drug use are well-documented, although the associations vary depending on the drug in question. The overall evidence indicates that perceived parental use of alcohol, tobacco, and tranquilizers is associated with adolescent marijuana use (for review, see Penning & Barnes, 1982), although Kandel and her colleagues (1978) did not find an association between parental use of liquor and psychoactive drugs and adolescent use of marijuana. Brook et al. (1983b) found a significant but weak correlation between both maternal and paternal use of alcohol, marijuana, and psychoactive drugs and stage of adolescent drug use. They also found that maternal drug use interacted significantly with peer modeling and socialization, such that adolescents at higher stages of drug use had both maternal models of drug use and friends who either used drugs or were negative and rejecting. Maternal marijuana use also interacted significantly with the adolescent's rebelliousness to produce a higher stage of drug use.

Child-rearing practices constitute the principal means by which parents affect the drug use of their offspring, with each of the three major parenting dimensions of warmth, control, and involvement (Maccoby & Martin, 1983) exerting a distinctive influence on the overall quality of the parent-child relationship.

Numerous investigators have reported negative correlations between measures of parental warmth and illicit drug use (see Hawkins et al., 1985, for review). The nature of the affective bond between parent and child has been explored through such variables as parental support, communication, responsiveness, and affection, the child's identification with the parent, and the harmony of the parent and child relationship. Many of these variables are particularly potent in their association with drug use when adolescents have formed an attachment to conventional or traditional parents

(Brook, Whiteman, Gordon & Brook, 1984). In addition, Brook et al. (1984) have demonstrated that a close parent-adolescent relationship can offset risks in the adolescent's personality as well as risks stemming from his or her peer environment. The importance of the affective bond between parent and child in insulating the youngster from drug use has been shown in both cross-sectional and longitudinal research.

The control dimension of parenting also has been found to be of importance in the etiology of drug use by adolescents (Hawkins et al., 1985). This dimension encompasses all forms of discipline including punitive vs. nonpunitive, restrictive vs. permissive, and psychological control techniques such as control through guilt and love withdrawal. As regards the punitive component of discipline, children who experience deprivation of privileges and threats of physical punishment tend to develop into less conventional adolescents who are more likely to initiate illicit drug use (Baer & Corrado, 1974; Brook, Whiteman & Gordon, 1985).

Overpermissiveness, as assessed by a lack of rules and regulations regarding the adolescent's behavior, and psychological control through guilt are associated with higher drug stages (Block et al., 1986; Brook, Whiteman, Gordon & Cohen, 1986b).

The third major parenting dimension, parental involvement, has qualitative and quantitative aspects that have been found to relate to adolescent drug use behavior. Parents who are committed to their parenting roles and spend time with their children in caregiving, teaching, and recreational activities develop strong parent-child relationships (Maccoby & Martin, 1983). The importance of parental involvement in the etiology of marijuana use has been emphasized in the various studies of Brook et al. (1981, 1984, 1986b).

The nature of parental influence on adolescent drug use is similar for both mothers and fathers, but there are some interesting and important gender differences between them. For instance, it appears that maternal control (as assessed by permissiveness, control through guilt, punitiveness) more strongly influences adolescent drug use than does paternal control (Brook et al., 1986b; Miller, 1976). Moreover, girls' drug use appears to be more affected by the parental control dimension (e.g., restrictiveness) than is boys'

(Baumrind, 1985; Pandina & Schuele, 1983), with maternal control especially salient for the daughter (Miller, 1976).

To date, the exploration of familial influences other than parental on adolescent drug use has been limited, but sibling influence appears to be a very important factor. Older brothers have been found to influence their younger siblings' drug use, independent of peer influences (Brook, Whiteman & Gordon, 1983a; Needle, McCubbin, Wilson, Reineck, Lazar & Mederer, 1986). The indication is that older siblings are more potent than parents in modeling drug use behavior.

Aside from the family, the peer group commonly serves as a primary socialization influence on the adolescent's behavior and attitudes. The strong positive relationship between friends' drug use (modeling) and self-drug use is well-documented; and investigators generally agree that peer influences are the most powerful immediate determinants of adolescent substance use (for reviews, see Kandel, 1980, and Hawkins et al., 1985). A dual process of selective association and socialization by peers appears to best explain how peers influence adolescent drug use (Kandel, 1985).

Personality/Behavioral/Attitudinal Factors in Adolescent Drug Use

In recent years advances have been made in identifying the personality traits involved in the etiology of adolescent drug use and the manner in which they operate. Attitudinal and intrapsychic components of personality have been found to have a greater impact on illicit drug use than have temperamental traits. It is the adolescents who reject dominant social norms who are most likely to initiate and sustain drug use. These adolescents tend to be deviant, sensation seeking, tolerant of deviance, impulsive, rebellious, to value independence over achievement, and to be less responsible and less interested in the goals of conventional institutions (Block et al., 1986; Brook, Whiteman, Gordon & Cohen, 1986a; Jessor, Chase & Donovan, 1980; Kay, Lyons, Newman, Mankin & Loeb, 1978; Mellinger, Somers & Manheimer, 1975; Smith & Fogg, 1978). A study by Wingard, Huba, and Bentler (1979, 1980) explores how nonconventionality predisposes adolescents toward general substance use and predicts later drug use. They found that general substance use was correlated with a personality cluster marked by nonabidance with the law, liberalism, leadership, extroversion, and lack of both diligence and deliberateness. Nonconventionality measures were related to drug use patterns regardless of whether the pattern primarily reflected alcohol use or use of marijuana and other illicit drugs. Although a number of intrapsychic factors have been studied, further investigation of the degree to which depression, anxiety, self-esteem, and other measures of intrapsychic functioning can predict illicit substance use are needed. Within the interpersonal sphere, less inhibition and greater aggression appear to be attributes of the drug user (Baumrind, 1985; Block et al., 1986; Brook et al., 1986a; Kay et al., 1978; Kellam et al., 1980).

A LONGITUDINAL STUDY OF CHILDHOOD DETERMINANTS OF ADOLESCENT MARIJUANA USE

The present study was designed to explore empirically some of the developmental issues discussed in the foregoing review with regard to adolescent drug use. Its longitudinal design afforded a rare opportunity to examine childhood personality, family, and ecological determinants of marijuana use in adolescence, and to identify some of the processes residing in the parent-adolescent relationship and the adolescent's personality that may link childhood factors with adolescent marijuana use. (Our drug use variable in this study was frequency of marijuana use. However, when the major analyses were run with stage of drug use or age at onset of marijuana use as the dependent variables, the findings were not substantially different.)

Several alternative models could have been proposed as possibilities for depicting the developmental interrelationship of the domains of childhood factors, adolescent personality traits, and parent-adolescent relations vis-à-vis frequency of adolescent marijuana use (see Brook et al., 1986a, for a description of various models). We hypothesized that a *mediational model* would best explain this interrelationship (see Figure 1). According to this model, the impact of childhood influences on adolescent marijuana use would be completely mediated by the adolescent's personality and the nature

Figure 1

The Mediational Model

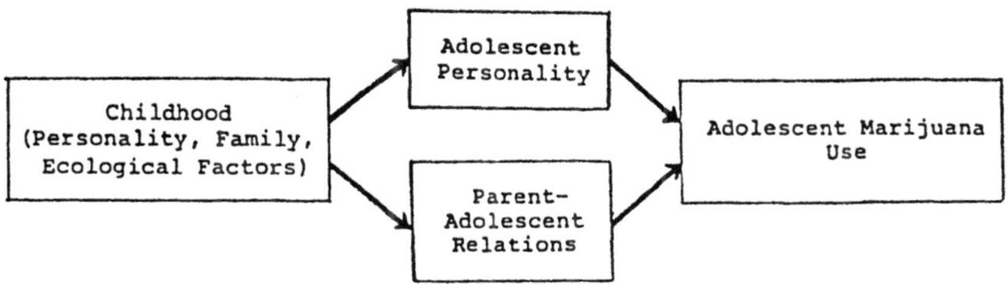

of the parent-adolescent relationship. In other words, the childhood domain would be related to both of the adolescent domains, which in turn would relate to the adolescent's use of marijuana.

The primary basis for selecting the two adolescent domains (adolescent personality and parent-adolescent relations) as mediating links between childhood factors and adolescent marijuana use was their ties in our previous research and theory to earlier childhood factors on the one hand, and to adolescent drug use on the other (Brook et al., 1986a). Moreover, as indicated in the first part of this chapter, there is considerable evidence that childhood personality, family, and ecological factors are associated with the adolescent's personality traits and his/her relations with parents (Brim & Kagan, 1980; Elder et al., 1986; Langner, Gersten, Wills & Simcha-Fagan, 1983; McCord, 1979).

We also wanted to provide a more complete picture of the developmental precursors of adolescent drug use than exists in the literature, and therefore included major ecological variables in the childhood domain, along with family and personality factors. Specifically, the ecological variables were family stability (the structural stability of the parental dyad), residential stability, household amenities (the home's material environment), and SES.

In our view, mutual attachment is a useful concept for examining the association of parent-adolescent relations and adolescent marijuana use. Based on previous research, we have attempted to delineate four separate dimensions of parent-adolescent mutual attachment: (1) identification; (2) parent-child conflict; (3) warmth; and

(4) parental involvement. Although most investigators have not systematically looked at parent-adolescent mutual attachment as it relates to adolescent drug use, several have incorporated some components of the attachment relationship in their studies of drug use (Hendin, Pollinger, Ulman & Carr, 1981; Jessor & Jessor, 1977; Kandel et al., 1978; Mercer, Hundleby & Carpenter, 1978; O'Donnell & Clayton, 1979).

Another important aspect of the parent-adolescent relationship, parental techniques of control, will be explored in this study in connection with adolescent marijuana use. As discussed earlier, such control variables as overpermissiveness and the use of harsh discipline are known to be associated with greater adolescent drug use.

Numerous researchers have identified several prominent personality dimensions associated with adolescent drug use (Brook et al., 1983; Gersick et al., 1981; Jessor & Jessor, 1977; Johnston, O'Malley & Eveland, 1978; Kaplan, Martin & Robbins, 1982). This study therefore includes the following four major personality dimensions: (1) conventionality (e.g., tolerance of deviance); (2) control of emotions (e.g., impulsivity); (3) intrapsychic functioning (e.g., depression); and (4) interpersonal relatedness (e.g., aggression against siblings).

To summarize, this research was designed to identify some of the processes residing in the parent-adolescent relationship and the adolescent's personality that may serve to mediate the influence of childhood personality, family, and ecological factors on the adolescent's use of marijuana.

METHOD

Subjects and Procedure

The sample consisted of 435 mothers and their offspring, predominantly white, with approximately equal numbers of male and female children. The mothers were seen at two points in time, Time 1 (T1) when the children were ages 5 to 10 and eight years later (T2) when the children were 13-18, at which time they were also interviewed. The original T1 sample consisted of 583 mothers. As described in a previous paper (Brook et al., 1986a), the sample was essentially the same at both points in time in terms of demographics.

At T1, trained interviewers questioned the mothers in their own homes regarding their child's personality, behavior, and development as well as about child-rearing techniques, family structure, family health, and demographics. At T2, both mothers and children were seen by trained interviewers, again at home. Protocols given to mothers included a parallel version of the T1 interview and a self-administered questionnaire assessing her relations with the child. The adolescent protocols included a self-administered questionnaire assessing personality/attitudes/behavior (including drug use) and interpersonal relationships.

Instruments

Scales were developed from the separate questionnaires based on item intercorrelations. Table 1 presents each measure, when it was obtained (T1, T2, or both), and whose report was used (mother or adolescent). The scales were grouped into

I. Child Personality/Attitudes/Behavior Measures,
II. Family Measures, and
III. Ecological Factors Measures.

The source and Cronbach alpha for each scale appear in previous work (Brook et al., 1986a).

The dependent variable was the adolescent's report of his/her frequency of marijuana use ("On the average, how often have you ever used marijuana or hashish?"). The distribution was as follows: never = 240; a few times a year or less = 113; about once a month = 34; several times a month = 13; once a week = 11; several times a week = 14; or every day = 10.

RESULTS

Regression analyses were run to test the interactions of demographic characteristics (age, sex) with the independent variables (childhood personality, family, and ecological measures; adolescent personality and parent-adolescent relationship measures) in terms of adolescent frequency of marijuana use. Fewer than 5% of

TABLE 1. T1 and T2 Measures of Child Personality/Attitudes/Behavior, Family, and Ecological Factors

Measure	When Measured
I. Child Personality/Attitudes/Behavior Measures	
A. Conventionality	
Achievement (general)[a]	Both times
Church attendance[b]	T2
Compliance[a]	Both times
Delinquency[a]	Both times
Deviancy[b]	T2
Educational aspirations[b]	T2
Educational expectations[b]	T2
Rebelliousness[b]	T2
Responsibility[b]	T2
School achievement[b]	T2
School behavior[a]	Both times
Sensation seeking[b]	T2
Task persistence[a]	Both times
Tolerance of deviance[b]	T2
B. Control of Emotions	
Anger[a]	Both times
Crying/demanding[a]	Both times
Impulsivity[b]	T2
Temper[a]	Both times
C. Intrapsychic Functioning	
Anxiety[b]	T2
Coping[b]	T2
Depression[b]	T2
Depressive mood[a]	Both times
Ego integration[b]	T2
Guilt[b]	T2
Obsessiveness[b]	T2
Self-esteem[b]	T2
D. Interpersonal Relatedness	
Aggression against peers[a]	Both times
Aggression against siblings[a]	Both times
Interpersonal aggression[b]	T2
Interpersonal difficulty[b]	T2
Peer isolation[a]	Both times
Social inhibition[a]	Both times

[a]Mother's report.

[b]Adolescent's report.

TABLE 1 (continued)

E. Other	
Eating problems[a]	Both times
Hyperactivity[a]	Both times
II. Family Measures	
A. Parent-Child Mutual Attachment	
Affection - maternal[a] and paternal[b]	T2
Availability (emotional) - maternal[a]	T2
Availability (physical) - maternal[a]	Both times
Child centeredness - maternal[a] and paternal[b]	T2
Communication - maternal[a] and paternal[b]	T2
Conflict - maternal-child[a] and paternal-child[a]	T2
Encourages child's ideas - maternal[a]	T2
Identification - child with father[b] and child with mother[b]	T2
Involvement - maternal[a]	T1
Involvement - paternal[a]	Both times
Possessiveness - maternal[a]	T1
Satisfaction with child - maternal[a]	T2
Support - maternal[a]	T2
Time spent with child - maternal[a] and paternal[a]	T2
B. Parent Control	
Cognitive discipline - maternal[a]	Both times
Consistency in discipline - maternal[a]	T2
Control through guilt - maternal[a]	T2
Orientation to parental authority - maternal[a]	T2
Permissiveness vs control - maternal[a] and paternal[b]	T2
Power-assertive discipline - maternal[a] and paternal[b]	T2
Punitive discipline - parents combined[a]	Both times
Strictness - parents combined[a]	Both times
Tolerance of child's cigarette use - maternal[a]	T2
Tolerance of child's marijuana use - maternal[a]	T2
C. Other	
Educational goals for child - maternal[a]	Both times
Religious involvement - family[a]	Both times
Sociopathy - parents combined[a]	Both times

[a]Mother's report.

[b]Adolescent's report.

TABLE 1 (continued)

III. Ecological Factors Measures	
Family stability[a]	Both times
Household amenities[a]	Both times
Residential stability[a]	Both times
Socioeconomic status[a]	Both times

[a]Mother's report.
[b]Adolescent's report.

the interactions were significant (data not presented). Therefore, the subgroups were combined in all subsequent analyses.

T1 Childhood Correlates of Adolescent Marijuana Use

Pearson correlations were computed between the T1 personality, family, and ecological measures and T2 adolescent frequency of marijuana use.[1] Only the following measures were significantly related to more adolescent marijuana use: maternal noninvolvement ($r = .32$) and physical unavailability (.17); the child's low social inhibition (.13), low peer isolation (.12), and greater task persistence (.10). However, when the entire set of T1 measures was examined, it was significantly related to adolescent marijuana use, as will be discussed subsequently.

T2 Adolescent Personality and Parent-Adolescent Relationship Correlates of Adolescent Marijuana Use

Table 2 contains the significant correlations between the hypothesized mediating variables at T2 (adolescent personality and parent-adolescent relationship characteristics) and the adolescent's frequency of marijuana use. As shown in Table 2, measures of unconventional attitudes and behavioral/psychological maladjustment were associated with more frequent marijuana use. As regards the parent-adolescent relationship variables, less than optimal maternal-child attachment (e.g., less maternal time spent with child, less identification of child with mother) and maternal control tech-

TABLE 2. Correlation of Significant T2 Variables with T2 Adolescent Frequency of Marijuana Use

Variable	Adolescent Marijuana Use r
I. Adolescent Personality/Attitudes/Behavior	
A. Conventionality	
Achievement (general)[a] (less)	.13**
Compliance[a] (less)	.26***
Delinquency[a] (more)	.28***
Deviance[b] (more)	.49***
Educational aspirations[b] (less)	.19***
Educational expectations[b] (less)	.20***
Rebelliousness[b] (more)	.43***
Responsibility[b] (less)	.31***
School achievement[b] (less)	.24***
School behavior[a] (poor)	.33***
Sensation seeking[b] (more)	.40***
Task persistence[a] (less)	.11*
Tolerance of deviance[b] (more)	.51***
B. Control of Emotions	
Anger[a] (more)	.10*
Impulsivity[b] (more)	.18***
Temper[a] (more)	.12**
C. Intrapsychic Functioning	
Depression[b] (more)	.13**
Depressive mood[a] (more)	.14**
Ego integration[b] (less)	.21***
Obsessiveness[b] (more)	.10*
D. Interpersonal Relatedness	
Aggression against peers[a] (more)	.10*
Interpersonal aggression[b] (more)	.11*
Social inhibition[a] (less)	.10*
II. Parent-Adolescent Relations	
A. Mutual Attachment	
Affection - paternal[b] (less)	.30***
Availability (physical) - maternal[a] (less)	.20***
Child centeredness - paternal[b] (less)	.24***

Note. The significant correlations of the T1 measures with marijuana use are reported in the text.

[a]Scale based on maternal report.

[b]Scaled based on adolescent report.

*$p < .05$. **$p < .01$. ***$p < .001$.

TABLE 2 (continued)

Communication - paternal[b] (less)	.18***
Conflict - maternal-child[a] (more)	.32***
Conflict - paternal-child[a] (more)	.33***
Identification - child with father[b] (less)	.19***
Identification - child with mother[b] (less)	.20***
Involvement - paternal[a] (less)	.16***
Satisfaction with child - maternal[a] (less)	.22***
Time spent with child - maternal[a] (less)	.23***
Time spent with child - paternal[b] (less)	.20***
B. Parent Control	
Consistency in discipline - maternal[a] (less)	.19***
Control through guilt - maternal[a] (more)	.19***
Permissiveness - maternal[a] (more)	.19***
Permissiveness - paternal[b] (more)	.14**
Power-assertive discipline - paternal[b] (more)	.19***
Strictness - parents combined[a] (less)	.14**
Tolerance of child's cigarette use - maternal[a] (more)	.27***
Tolerance of child's marijuana use - maternal[a] (more)	.20***
C. Other	
Educational goals for child - maternal[a] (less)	.12**
Religious involvement - family[a] (less)	.14**

Note. The significant correlations of the T1 measures with marijuana use are reported in the text.

[a]Scale based on maternal report.

[b]Scaled based on adolescent report.

*p < .05. **p < .01. ***p < .001.

niques (e.g., more permissiveness, more control through guilt) were positively related to marijuana use by the adolescent. Most of the paternal-child attachment and paternal control variables showed similar relationships to adolescent marijuana use.

Interrelationship of T1 Childhood and T2 Adolescent Domains and T2 Frequency of Marijuana Use

In order to examine whether the mediational model was consistent with the data, a series of hierarchical multiple regression analyses was run. The demographic variables (age and sex) were entered as a control set. Each of the three domains (T1 childhood ecological, family, and personality variables; T2 adolescent personality; and T2 parent-adolescent relations) was then examined, partialing out the effects of the other domains. All the childhood variables were included in the T1 childhood factor set; however, only the T2 personality and parent-adolescent relationship attributes significantly related to marijuana use were included in the T2 sets. (The reason for including only the significant T2 variables is that we wanted to reduce the large number of variables in the T2 set.)[2] The dependent variable in the regressions was T2 frequency of marijuana use.

The regression results are summarized in Table 3. As shown in the table, all three sets were significantly related to T2 frequency of marijuana use *without* partialing. However, *with* partialing the T2 domains and control on the demographic set, the T1 set lost its significant relationship to marijuana use, whereas each of the T2 sets remained significant when the other sets were partialed. The findings therefore supported the mediational model: the domain of T1 childhood factors was associated with the domains of T2 parent-adolescent relations and T2 personality factors, which in turn were associated with T2 frequency of marijuana use. Altogether, the

TABLE 3. Multiple *Rs* for T1 and T2 Domains and Frequency of Marijuana Use

	Without Partialing			With Partialing Other Domains and Control on Demographic Set		
Domain	R^2	*F*	*df*	R^2	*F*	*df*
A. T1 childhood factors	.18	2.91**	(28,374)	.02	.50	(28,327)
B. T2 parent-adolescent relations	.28	6.79**	(22,380)	.05	1.64*	(22,327)
C. T2 adolescent personality	.41	11.64**	(23,379)	.16	5.07**	(23,327)

Note. All T1 variables are included in Domain A. Only those variables significantly related to frequency of marijuana use are in Domains B and C.

*$p<.01$. **$p<.001$.

three domains and the demographic set explained 54% of the variance in frequency of marijuana use.

It was also of theoretical interest to determine whether each of the T2 domains served as a separate mediator for the T1 childhood domain. The results of separate regressions indicated that the impact of the T1 childhood domain was indeed mediated by each of the T2 domains (data not presented).

Because the results supported a mediational model (that is, T1 childhood personality, family, and ecological characteristics were associated with T2 adolescent personality traits and T2 parent-adolescent relations, which in turn were related to adolescent marijuana use, it was of interest to examine the relationship between the set of T1 variables and each of the two T2 sets of mediating variables using canonical analysis.

Childhood Factors by Mediating Adolescent Personality Traits

To determine the magnitude and patterning of the relationship between T1 childhood variables and the T2 personality variables, a canonical correlation analysis between the two sets was performed. Two features of the canonical results were noteworthy. What emerged from the first canonical correlation (to be presented below) is the importance of a childhood cluster consisting of SES and SES-related variables, such as low achievement and poor household amenities, in relation to adolescent personality measures of unconventionality, such as poor achievement motivation and lack of responsibility. The second noteworthy feature of the remaining canonicals (data not presented) is the importance of personality stability from childhood to adolescence. Thus, measures of social inhibition, achievement, anger, and aspirations showed continuity over an eight-year span.

Overall, five canonical correlations were significant. The first will be presented in detail; the remaining four were briefly summarized above.[3] The first significant canonical correlation indicated that 49% of the variation in the adolescent personality vector was accounted for by the childhood vector. The correlations of the individual variables with the canonical variates appear in Table 4. The

TABLE 4. Canonical Correlation Analysis of T1 Childhood Variables by T2 Adolescent Personality Variables

First T1 Childhood (Personality, Family, Ecological Factors) Canonical Variate	Structure Coefficient	First T2 Adolescent Personality Canonical Variate	Structure Coefficient
Less achievement (general)	.79	Less achievement (general)	.86
Low SES	.60	Less school achievement	.67
Less task persistence	.44	Less educational expectations	.59
Less maternal educational goals for child	.40	Less educational aspirations	.56
Less household amenities	.35	Less task persistence	.45
More temper tantrums	.34	Poor school behavior	.41
Less family stability	.33	Less compliance	.35
Less parental sociopathy	.26	More temper tantrums	.31
Less maternal availability (physical)	.26	Less responsibility	.28
More aggression against siblings	.25		
Less compliance	.22		
More delinquency	.21		

findings based on this first canonical correlation indicated that low economic and social support in conjunction with the child's low achievement and difficulty in controlling emotions were associated with poor achievement motivation and lack of responsibility in the adolescent.

Childhood Factors by Mediating Parent-Adolescent Relationship Variables

Next, the magnitude and nature of the relationship between the set of T1 childhood variables and the set of T2 parent-adolescent relationship variables were examined in canonical analysis. In this section, only the first and fourth of the five significant canonicals will be presented in detail because of their theoretical interest.

The first significant canonical correlation accounted for 54% of the variation in the T2 parent-adolescent relationship variate or vector. Correlations between each of the individual variables and the canonical variates appear in Table 5 (Panel A). The findings demonstrated that high economic and social support, in conjunction with an achieving and controlled child, led to high educational goals for the adolescent and a close and nonconflictual mutual parent-adolescent attachment.

The findings for the second canonical correlation indicated that an involved, punitive mother with weak ties to the community, and whose child had poor emotional control, resulted in an involved but

TABLE 5. Canonical Correlation Analysis of T1 Childhood Variables by T2 Parent-Adolescent Relationship Variables

A. First T1 Childhood (Personality, Family, Ecological factors) Canonical Variate	Structure Coefficient	First T2 Parent-Adolescent Relations Canonical Variate	Structure Coefficient
High SES	.72	More maternal educational goals for child	.89
More achievement (general)	.61	More family religious involvement	.49
More maternal educational goals for child	.60	Less maternal control through guilt	.38
More household amenities	.34	More strictness	.36
More task persistence	.34	More maternal satisfaction with child	.33
More maternal availability (physical)	.33	More paternal-child conflict	.30
More strictness	.32	More maternal-child conflict	.25
Less aggression against siblings	.31	More maternal time spent with child	.22
More family religious involvement	.29	More paternal control	.22
Less crying/demanding	.28	More maternal consistency in discipline	.20
More family stability	.27	More paternal affection	.20
More compliance	.26		
Less temper tantrums	.24		
More maternal involvement	.22		
Less hyperactivity	.21		

TABLE 5 (continued)

B. Fourth T1 Childhood (Personality, Family, Ecological Factors) Canonical Variate	Structure Coefficient	Fourth T2 Parent-Adolescent Relations Canonical Variate	Structure Coefficient
More punitive discipline	.49	Less paternal-child conflict	.71
More temper tantrums	.45	Less maternal satisfaction with child	.65
More anger	.44	Less maternal-child conflict	.62
More delinquency	.41	Less maternal consistency in discipline	.46
Less compliance	.40	Less maternal availability (physical)	.40
More aggression against peers	.40	More paternal power-assertive discipline	.33
More aggression against siblings	.35	More maternal control through guilt	.27
More depression	.29	Less paternal affection	.27
More crying/demanding	.26	Less paternal communication	.24
More eating disorders	.26	Less paternal child centeredness	.24
More cognitive discipline	.25	Less paternal involvement	.24
Less task persistence	.23		
More hyperactivity	.20		

punitive maternal profile during the child's adolescence. The third canonical correlation revealed that families which were religious and involved, but punitive, during the early years of the youngster's development were likely to have similar qualities during the youngster's adolescence. (Tabular data not presented for the second and third canonicals.)

As previously noted, the fourth canonical correlation was of considerable interest and predicted 37% of the variance in the T2 parent-adolescent vector. The correlations of individual variables with their canonical variates at T1 and T2 are presented in Table 5 (Panel B). Findings in the main indicated that the personality of the child at T1 was related to T2 parental child-rearing practices and the attachment relationship. More specifically, a child with poor emotional control and externally-directed anger and aggression seemed to bring forth child-rearing practices during adolescence marked by inconsistency and parental control through guilt, as well as a conflictual mutual detachment. It should be noted that this relationship is independent of the continuity of child-rearing practices demonstrated in the second and third canonical pairs presented above.

DISCUSSION

The findings of the present study were supportive of a mediational model in which a set of childhood personality, family, and ecological factors affected in good part two adolescent domains reflecting (a) the nature of the parent-adolescent relationship, and (b) the adolescent's personality traits. These adolescent domains, in turn, were related to the adolescent's frequency of marijuana use. Although the adolescent domains entirely mediated the domain of childhood factors, this does not signify that the childhood factors were of little importance in the etiology of adolescent marijuana use. It merely indicates that the influence of childhood factors was indirect, occurring through their contribution to the evolution of the adolescent's personality and to the development of the parent-adolescent relationship. Although our results supported a mediational model, other causal orderings of the childhood and adolescent factors and adolescent marijuana use are possible. For example, it could be that parent-adolescent relationship factors and adolescent personality traits are the result of drug use rather than its cause. If this were the case, the T1 set of variables would have to be considered as having a direct causal linkage with adolescent drug use, and the "disappearance" of the independent relationship between the childhood factors and drug use would be attributable to sheer redundancy. Given the relatively large sample size, and thus the power, this is not very likely. More theoretically likely would be a causal model showing feedback between the adolescent sets and drug use. A third data collection now under way will be helpful in further illuminating this issue.

Returning to the mediational hypothesis, the canonical findings give greater specification to the mediational pathways connecting the T1 childhood and T2 adolescent characteristics. Two types of linkages or linkage themes appear to be involved. The first features the importance of a set of T1 SES and SES-related variables (including personality) in its effect on the T2 parent-adolescent relationship and on the adolescent's personality. More specifically, a set of T1 variables involving strong economic and social support and an achieving child led at T2 to: (a) a close and nonconflictual parent-adolescent mutual attachment, characterized by appropriate control, and (b) adolescent personality traits of achievement, educational motivation, and responsibility.

A second linkage theme focuses more closely on the importance of T1 childhood personality (aside from its SES-related role) as it affected the two adolescent domains. As to the T1 and T2 personality linkages, social inhibition, nonachievement, and anger in the child were related to similar attributes in the adolescent, suggesting a greater stress in this second theme on the continuity of personality. Regarding the linkage between T1 personality and the T2 parent-adolescent relationship, childhood personality attributes involving poor emotional control and outwardly-directed anger and aggression apparently led to a parent-adolescent relationship marked by excessive and inconsistent parental control, conflict, and mutual detachment.

No studies to our knowledge have examined the child's personality in the context of the family and broader social situation and related these factors to subsequent parent-adolescent relations and personality attributes. However, some investigators have examined the specific influences of family, demographic background, or personality on parent-child relations and the child's personality development, and our findings are consistent with theirs. For example, our canonical finding that the broader social and material environment is important in its effect on parent-adolescent relations is in line with the research of others who have found that stressful external factors, including low SES, have a negative impact on parent-child interaction (Dill & Greywolf, 1982; Maccoby & Martin, 1983; Vaughn, Egeland, Waters & Sroufe, 1979). Moreover, SES and SES-related variables have been implicated in the development of child attributes, especially intellectual achievement (Laosa, 1982; Masten, Garmezy, Larkin & Tellegen, 1985).

As to the second linkage theme, although this study's examination of the relationship between a constellation of T1 personality, family, and ecological factors and adolescent personality traits associated with drug use has little precedence, there are some investigators who have examined personality and continuity alone. Their findings of stability in personality between childhood and adolescence are consistent with our own (Block, 1971; for review, see Moss & Sussman, 1980). Our study, however, has extended their results by linking personality stability with drug use behavior. Finally, of considerable interest is our finding that childhood personality factors also affected later parent-adolescent relations. This is in keeping with Bell's (1979) contention that the youngster plays a crucial role in shaping parent-child relations.

Because our data set has allowed us to examine SES factors and adolescent marijuana use in a unique context (that is, along with personality and family factors over time), we feel able to shed some light on a recurring theme in the literature which appears rather anomalous—the low correlation between socioeconomic status and marijuana use. Our own results showed that although SES by itself was not strongly related to adolescent marijuana use, nonetheless, there seemed to be an intricate relationship between these two factors. To begin with, examination of our findings suggested that the direct relationship between SES and marijuana use was weakened in three ways. First, SES was not related to some important predictors of marijuana use (such as the adolescent's sensation seeking in the personality area or parental identification in the family area), and so lost some of its power to act on the important mediators of marijuana use. Second, childhood SES was related to some adolescent factors (mainly family) *not* implicated in marijuana use, such as the mother's orientation to parental authority and her encouragement of the youngster's own ideas, and therefore had variance that was irrelevant to marijuana use. Third, high SES was negatively related to one of the most important insulators of adolescent marijuana use—intolerance of deviance. Despite this lack of a strong, direct SES-marijuana relationship, the canonical analyses revealed that SES, when viewed together with associated childhood background factors and early personality traits, was highly linked with parent-adolescent relationship and adolescent personality predictors of marijuana use.

So far the discussion has centered on the connections between T1 childhood factors and the T2 domains of parent-adolescent relations and adolescent personality traits. The focus now will be on which variables in the two adolescent domains were the most important mediating links between the T1 domain and adolescent marijuana use. In the parent-adolescent relations domain, two dimensions appeared to be of particular consequence with respect to adolescent marijuana use—parent-adolescent mutual attachment and parental control techniques. As to the first dimension of mutual attachment, a warm and conflict-free relationship wherein the adolescent identified with the parent was associated with less adolescent marijuana use. As regards the control dimension, a more structured and less punitive mode of control was related to less adolescent marijuana use. Although some of these findings have received support in the literature (e.g., Mercer, Hundleby & Carpenter, 1978; Pandina & Schuele, 1983; Prendergast, 1974), the results of the present study not only have demonstrated the relationship of parental attachment and control factors to adolescent marijuana use, but they also have linked these same parental factors with earlier childhood conditions and dispositions.

The adolescent personality traits implicated in marijuana use can be grouped into four dimensions—conventionality, control of emotions, intrapsychic functioning, and interpersonal relatedness. Of these dimensions, conventionality clearly was the most important in terms of marijuana use. Adolescents with nontraditional attitudes and behaviors were more likely to use marijuana. This finding is in accord with results from previous investigations (e.g., Jessor & Jessor, 1977; Smith & Fogg, 1978). Three personality characteristics, in particular, were very powerful correlates of marijuana use: sensation seeking, rebelliousness, and tolerance of deviance. Adolescents with an orientation to sensation seeking require greater stimulation from outside sources, and so may use marijuana as a means of providing themselves with external or new stimulation. Adolescents who are rebellious have fewer internalized personal controls and rules, and therefore are more likely to seek out that which is forbidden. Finally, within the conventionality dimension, not only were characteristics reflecting the adolescent's own personal behavior of importance, but his or her broader ethics involving traditional values were also relevant, as manifested in the high correlation between tolerance of deviance and marijuana use.

Of much less importance than the conventionality dimension, but still of significance, were the remaining three – emotional control, intrapsychic functioning, and interpersonal relatedness. As regards emotional control, we found that greater impulsivity, temper, and anger were related to more marijuana use, the latter two somewhat weakly. Support for this finding comes from studies by Mellinger et al. (1975), Segal (1977), and Hendin et al. (1981). It may be that adolescents who have difficulty in containing their emotions or impulses are unable to deny themselves immediate gratification when presented with something pleasurable even if potentially harmful. The significant variables in the intrapsychic functioning dimension indicated that adolescents who experience a great deal of intrapsychic distress (e.g., depressive mood, low ego integration) may try to cope with it by using marijuana (see Hendin et al., 1981; Paton, Kessler & Kandel, 1977). Last, in line with previous results (Brook et al., 1986a), those adolescents who had problems in the interpersonal sphere (e.g., more interpersonal aggression) were more likely to use marijuana. However, our finding that adolescents with more social inhibition were less likely to use marijuana is puzzling, although it has been corroborated by other researchers (Baumrind, 1985; Block et al., 1986). Perhaps such adolescents are less likely to use marijuana because they have fewer contacts with peers. It is possible, too, that their inhibitions in the social sphere may reflect a more general fear of "letting themselves go" by using drugs.

In sum, our findings on the etiology of adolescent marijuana use highlight the influential roles of parent-adolescent mutual attachment and adolescent personality as extensions of personality, family, and ecological factors salient during childhood. In its role as mediator, parent-adolescent attachment served as a mechanism by which the influence of childhood factors resulted in variation in adolescent marijuana use. Similarly, adolescent personality mediated the effect of childhood factors on adolescent marijuana use.

Thus, parent-adolescent relations and adolescent personality traits were seen to evolve from characteristics present during childhood, through a process of personal and interpersonal development occurring within a given sociocultural and material environment.

SUMMARY AND CONCLUDING REMARKS

As the literature demonstrates, and our research shows, issues concerning the etiology of drug use require that we study in depth the domains of personality, family relations, and ecological factors, as well as examine their interrelationship. Considerable work has already been done in these areas; but there is still much to be accomplished, particularly in looking at the interrelation of domains over time, starting with early childhood.

In line with this, there has been much interest in specifying possible childhood personality risk factors for adolescent drug use. Our own formulations, based on the present study, indicate that personality during childhood can operate in three ways to affect the adolescent's drug use. First, the interplay of childhood personality with family and ecological factors has an impact on adolescent drug use via the adolescent's personality and the parent-adolescent relationship. Second, continuity in personality traits between childhood and adolescence affects drug use, in that personality risk traits during childhood appear to set the foundation for the development of adolescent personality risk traits. Third, family factors impinge on the child's personality attributes, attitudes, and behavior. It is also clear that the child's characteristics are likely to determine to some extent the nature of the parent-adolescent relationship. For instance, our findings showed that childhood personality risk traits resulted in a parent-adolescent relationship characterized by detachment, which placed the adolescent more at risk for marijuana use.

There are strong reasons for believing that family factors also have a powerful effect on drug use. Our own research focused on the importance of the attachment and control dimensions as crucial mediating variables. On the one hand, these child-rearing variables seem sensitive to a configuration of ecological, family, and personal factors in childhood, while on the other, they appear to have an impact on drug use. Future investigations might examine separately the power of attachment and control factors, in order to determine whether these two child-rearing dimensions act independently, additively, or synergistically in affecting substance use.

In recent years research orientations with regard to parental child-rearing factors involved in adolescent drug use have come to recognize the need for dealing with the complex of techniques and conditions rather than with single variables. For instance, greater attention has been paid to examining configurations of child-rearing factors affecting adolescent drug use behavior. Nevertheless, this remains an area in which future theoretical development is necessary.

Several research directions appear to be especially deserving of attention to build on the accumulated research evidence and to contribute information that is critical for comprehending the youngster's development and behavior, such as drug use.

1. There is a need for more descriptive data on childhood factors that may be associated with adolescent drug use. Although a number have been identified, a more comprehensive mapping of biological, personal, and environmental areas is greatly needed. A call for data that are descriptive does not, of course, minimize the importance of theory. While we were able in our study to investigate several childhood predictors, we did not have access to data in some significant domains and had limited data in others. For example, there was a paucity of parent-child relationship variables during childhood, so we were unable to study the stability of these factors in great depth.

2. In our view the family is an open system which is likely to change with time. Therefore, it is important to identify the events or interventions that are capable of changing the quality of interactions among family members. Obviously, a great deal of information is needed before the conditions that determine both continuity and change in parent-child interactions can be specified.

3. It seems clear that separate intensive studies of the impact on drug use of personality, family, peer, and ecological factors must be done before an integrative theory or approach is possible. However, it appears that we are now at the point where some attempts

can be made to relate several domains to one another at different developmental periods. It appears critical to include in this research an examination of the interdependencies between the individual and the larger societal units and systems in which he or she functions. In part, this conclusion is based on the finding that a combination of ecological factors (such as SES) and personal/attitudinal/behavioral factors emerged as significant predictors in our longitudinal analysis.

4. On a methodological note, the need exists for the development of more reliable and valid measures of both behavior and context; for research that incorporates both actual behavior and self-report data; and for studies that utilize a multivariate approach. From a systems perspective, there is a need for more observational research in continuing systems, with the goal of clarifying the forces that alter or maintain the system. Such an approach is necessary for the study of the individual in complex natural systems.

At the present time there is intense and widespread interest in adolescent drug use. Such attention should broaden future investigations while at the same time providing a more solid base of evidence, all of which augers well not only for research in the etiology of adolescent drug use but also for effective interventions to prevent and counter drug use generally.

NOTES

1. Because of the large age span, correlations between the T1 and T2 measures and T2 adolescent marijuana use were also computed controlling for age. For the most part, the correlations were similar with and without control. However, for one measure, T1 *maternal noninvolvement*, there was a considerable reduction in the correlation (from .32 to .08), although both were significant.

2. In our previous work using similar data (Brook et al., 1986a), we demonstrated in the following manner that the use of only significant variables at T2 did not "force" a mediational model: first, we ran a series of regressions to test the models using only the significant T2 variables (as was done in the present study); then, we ran the regressions using parallel T1 and T2 measures regardless of their significance. In both cases, a mediational model was obtained. (For further detail, see Brook et al., 1986a.)

3. A more detailed presentation of these four canonicals appears in Brook et al. (1986a).

REFERENCES

Baer, D. J., & Corrado, J. J. (1974). Heroin addict relationships with parents during childhood and early adolescent years. *Journal of Genetic Psychology, 124*, 99-103.

Barker, R. G. (1968). *Ecological psychology: Concepts and methods for studying the environment of human behavior*. Stanford, CA: Stanford University Press.

Baumrind, D. (1985). Familial antecedents of adolescent drug use: A developmental perspective. In C. L. Jones & R. J. Battjes (Eds.), *Etiology of drug abuse: Implications for prevention* (Research Monograph No. 56, pp. 13-44). Rockville, MD: National Institute on Drug Abuse.

Baumrind, D., & Moselle, K. A. (1985). A developmental perspective on adolescent drug abuse among adolescents. *Advances in Alcohol & Substance Abuse, 4*(3/4), 41-67.

Bell, R. Q. (1979). Parent, child and reciprocal influences. *American Psychologist, 34*, 821-826.

Block, J. (1971). *Lives through time*. Berkeley, CA: Bancroft Books.

Block, J., Keyes, S., & Block, J. H. (1986, March). *Childhood personality and environmental antecedents of drug use: A prospective longitudinal study*. Paper presented at the meeting of the Society for Life History Research in Psychopathology, Palm Springs, CA.

Braucht, G. N., Brakarsh, D., Follingstad, D., & Berry, K. L. (1973). Deviant drug use in adolescence: A review of psychosocial correlates. *Psychological Bulletin, 79*, 92-106.

Brim, Jr., O. G., & Kagan, J. (Eds.). (1980). *Constancy and change in human development*. Cambridge, MA: Harvard University Press.

Brook, J. S., Whiteman, M., Brook, D. W., & Gordon, A. S. (1981). Paternal determinants of male adolescent marijuana use. *Developmental Psychology, 17*, 841-847.

Brook, J. S., Whiteman, M., & Gordon, A. S. (1982). Qualitative and quantitative aspects of adolescent drug use: Interplay of personality, family and peer correlates. *Psychological Reports, 51*, 1151-1163.

Brook, J. S., Whiteman, M., & Gordon, A. S. (1983a). Older brother's influence on younger sibling's drug use. *Journal of Psychology, 114*, 83-90.

Brook, J. S., Whiteman, M., & Gordon, A. S. (1983b). Stages of drug use in adolescence: Personality, peer, and family correlates. *Developmental Psychology, 19*, 269-277.

Brook, J. S., Whiteman, M., & Gordon, A. S. (1985). Father absence, perceived family characteristics and stage of drug use in adolescence. *British Journal of Developmental Psychology, 2*, 87-94.

Brook, J. S., Whiteman, M., Gordon, A. S., & Brook, D. W. (1983). Paternal correlates of adolescent marijuana use in the context of the mother-son and parental dyads. *Genetic Psychology Monographs, 108*, 197-213.

Brook, J. S., Whiteman, M., Gordon, A. S., & Brook, D. W. (1984). Paternal determinants of female adolescent's marijuana use. *Developmental Psychology, 20*, 1032-1043.

Brook, J. S., Whiteman, M., Gordon, A. S., & Brook, D. W. (1985). Father's influence on his daughter's marijuana use viewed in a mother and peer context. *Advances in Alcohol & Substance Abuse, 4*(3/4), 165-190.

Brook, J. S., Whiteman, M., Gordon, A. S., & Cohen, P. (1986a). Dynamics of childhood and adolescent personality traits and adolescent drug use. *Developmental Psychology, 22*, 403-414.

Brook, J. S., Whiteman, M., Gordon, A. S., & Cohen, P. (1986b). Some models and mechanisms for explaining the impact of maternal and adolescent characteristics on adolescent stage of drug use. *Developmental Psychology, 22*, 460-467.

Brook, J., Whiteman, M., Peisach, E., & Deutsch, M. (1974). Aspiration levels of and for children: Age, sex, race and socioeconomic correlates. *Journal of Genetic Psychology, 124*, 3-16.

Busch-Rossnagel, N. A., & Vance, A. K. (1982). The impact of the schools on social and emotional development. In B. B. Wolman (Ed.), *Handbook of developmental psychology*, (pp. 452-467). Englewood Cliffs, NJ: Prentice-Hall.

Cohen, A., & Hodges, H. (1963). Characteristics of the lower-blue-collar class. *Social Problems, 10*.

Coombs, R. H., Fawzy, F. I., & Gerber, B. E. (1986). Patterns of cigarette, alcohol and other drug use among children and adolescents: A longitudinal study. *International Journal of the Addictions, 21*, 897-913.

Daniels, D., & Plomin, R. (1985). Differential experience of siblings in the same family. *Developmental Psychology, 21*, 747-760.

Dill, D., & Greywolf, E. (1982). Daily lives, In D. Belle (Ed.), *Lives in stress: Women and depression* (pp. 54-64). Beverly Hills, CA: Sage Publications.

Dunn, J. (1983). Sibling relationships in early childhood. *Child Development, 54*, 787-811.

Elder, Jr., G. H., Caspi, A., & Downey, G. (1986). Problem behavior and family relationships: Life course and intergenerational themes. In A. Sorensen, F. Weinert, & L. Sherrod (Eds.), *Human development and the life course: Multidisciplinary perspectives* (pp. 293-340). Hillsdale, NJ: Erlbaum.

Elder, Jr., G. H., Liker, J. K., & Cross, C. E. (1984). Parent-child behavior in the Great Depression: Life course and intergenerational influences. In P. B. Baltes & O. G. Brim, Jr. (Eds.), *Life-span development and behavior, Vol. 6* (pp. 109-158). New York: Academic Press.

Elliott, D. S., Huizinga, D., & Dunford, F. W. (1983). Understanding delinquency and crime: A longitudinal multidisciplinary study of developmental patterns and conditions leading to criminal behavior. Unpublished proposal, Behavior Research Institute, Boulder, CO.

Gecas, V. (1979). The influence of social class on socialization. In W. R. Burr, R. Hill, F. I. Nye, & I. L. Reiss (Eds.), *Contemporary theories about the family: Vol. 1. Research-based theories* (pp. 365-404). New York: The Free Press.

Gersick, K. E., Grady, K., Sexton, E., & Lyons, M. (1981). Personality and sociodemographic factors in adolescent drug use. In D. J. Lettieri & J. P. Ludford (Eds.), *Drug abuse and the American adolescent* (Research Monograph No. 38, pp. 39-56). Rockville, MD: National Institute on Drug Abuse.

Gough, H. G. (1946). The relationship of socio-economic status to personality inventory and achievement test scores. *Journal of Educational Psychology, 37*, 527-540.

Grabowski, J. (1984). Cocaine 1984: Introduction and overview. In J. Grabowski (Ed.), *Cocaine: Pharmacology, effects, and treatment of abuse* (Research Monograph No. 50, pp. 1-14). Rockville, MD: National Institute on Drug Abuse.

Hawkins, J. D., Lishner, D. M., & Catalano, Jr., R. F. (1985). Childhood predictors and the prevention of adolescent substance abuse. In C. L. Jones & R. J. Battjes (Eds.), *Etiology of drug abuse: Implications for prevention* (Research Monograph No. 56, pp. 13-44). Rockville, MD: National Institute on Drug Abuse.

Hendin, H., Pollinger, A., Ulman, R. B., & Carr, A. C. (1981-82). The functions of marijuana abuse for adolescents. *American Journal of Drug and Alcohol Abuse, 8*, 441-456.

Jersild, A. T., Brook, J. S., & Brook, D. W. (1978). *The psychology of adolescence* (3rd ed.). New York: Macmillan.

Jessor, R. (1979). Marihuana: A review of recent psychosocial research. In R. L. Dupont, A. Goldstein, & J. A. O'Donnell (Eds.), *Handbook of drug abuse* (pp. 337-355). Washington, DC: U.S. Government Printing Office.

Jessor, R., Chase, J. A., & Donovan, J. E. (1980). Psychosocial correlates of marijuana use and problem drinking in a national sample of adolescents. *American Journal of Public Health, 70*, 604-613.

Jessor, R., & Jessor, S. L. (1977). *Problem behavior and psychosocial development: A longitudinal study of youth*. New York: Academic Press.

Johnston, L. D. (1985). The etiology and prevention of substance use: What can we learn from recent historical changes? In C. L. Jones & R. J. Battjes (Eds.), *Etiology of drug abuse: Implications for prevention* (Research Monograph No. 45, pp. 155-177). Rockville, MD: National Institute on Drug Abuse.

Kandel, D. (1975). Stages of adolescent involvement in drug use. *Science, 190*, 912-914.

Kandel, D. B. (1980). Drug and drinking behavior among youth. *Annual Review of Sociology, 6*, 235-285.

Kandel, D. B. (1984). Marijuana users in young adulthood. *Archives of General Psychiatry, 41*, 200-209.

Kandel, D. B. (1985). On processes of peer influences in adolescent drug use: A developmental perspective. *Advances in Alcohol & Substance Abuse, 4*(3/4), 139-163.

Kandel, D. B., Kessler, R. C., & Margulies, R. Z. (1978). Antecedents of adolescent initiation into stages of drug use: A developmental analysis. *Journal of Youth and Adolescence, 7*, 13-40.

Kandel, D. B., & Logan, J. A. (1984). Patterns of drug use from adolescence to young adulthood: I. Periods of risk for initiation, continued use, and discontinuation. *American Journal of Public Health, 74*, 660-666.

Kaplan, H. B., Martin, S. S., & Robbins, C. (1982). Applications of a general theory of deviant behavior: Self-derogation and adolescent drug use. *Journal of Health and Social Behavior, 23*, 274-294.

Kay, E. J., Lyons, A., Newman, W., Mankin, D., & Loeb, R. C. (1978). A longitudinal study of the personality correlates of marijuana use. *Journal of Consulting and Clinical Psychology, 46*, 470-477.

Kellam, S. G., Ensminger, M. E., & Simon, M. B. (1980). Mental health in first grade and teenage drug, alcohol, and cigarette use. *Drug and Alcohol Dependence, 5*, 273-304.

Khavari, K. A., & Harmon, T. M. (1982). The relationship between the degree of professed religious belief and use of drugs. *International Journal of the Addictions, 17*, 847-857.

Kohn, M. L. (1977). *Class and conformity: A study in values* (2nd ed.). Chicago: University of Chicago Press.

Lamb, M. E. (Ed.). (1981). *The role of the father in child development* (2nd ed.). New York: Wiley.

Langner, T. S., Gersten, J. C., Wills, T. A., & Simcha-Fagan, O. (1983). The relative roles of early environment and early behavior as predictors of later child behavior. In D. F. Ricks & B. S. Dohrenwend (Eds.), *Origins of psychopathology* (pp. 43-70). New York: Cambridge University Press.

Laosa, L. M. (1982). Families as facilitators of children's intellectual development at 3 years of age: A causal analysis. In L. M. Laosa & I. E. Sigel (Eds.), *Families as learning environments for children* (pp. 1-45). New York: Plenum Press.

Lerner, J. V., & Vicary, J. R. (1984). Difficult temperament and drug use: Analyses from the New York Longitudinal Study. *Journal of Drug Education, 14*, 1-7.

Lerner, R. M., & Spanier, G. B. (1978). A dynamic interactional view of child and family development. In R. M. Lerner & G. B. Spanier (Eds.), *Child influences on marital and family interaction* (pp. 1-22). New York: Academic Press.

Lettieri, D. J. (1985). Drug abuse: A review of explanations and models of explanation. *Advances in Alcohol & Substance Abuse, 4*(3/4), 41-67.

Liddle, G. (1958). The California Psychological Inventory and certain social and personal factors. *Journal of Educational Psychology, 49*, 144-149.

Lytton, H. (1980). *Parent-child interaction: The socialization process observed in twin and singleton families*. New York: Plenum Press.

Maccoby, E. E., & Martin, J. A. (1983). Socialization in the context of the family: Parent-child interaction. In E. M. Hetherington (Ed.), *Handbook of child psychology: Vol. 4. Socialization, personality, and social development* (pp. 1-101). New York: Wiley.

Masten, A., Garmezy, N., Larkin, K., & Tellegen, A. (1985, August). *Family factors related to stress and competence in children*. Paper presented at the 93rd Annual Convention of the American Psychological Association, Los Angeles, CA.

McCord, J. (1979). Some child-rearing antecedents of criminal behavior in adult men. *Journal of Personality and Social Psychology, 37*, 1477-1486.

Mellinger, G. D., Somers, R. H., & Manheimer, D. I. (1975). Drug use research items pertaining to personality and interpersonal relations: A working paper for research investigators. In D. J. Lettieri, (Ed.), *Predicting adolescent drug abuse: A review of issues, methods and correlates*. (Research Issues No. 11, pp. 301-342). Rockville, MD: National Institute on Drug Abuse.

Mercer, G. W., Hundleby, J. D., & Carpenter, R. A. (1978). Adolescent drug use and attitudes toward the family. *Canadian Journal of Behavioural Science, 10*, 79-90.

Miller, B. (1976). Student drug use: Attitudinal, parental relations and sex differences – A pilot study. *International Journal of the Addictions, 11*, 1079-1084.

Minuchin, P. P., & Shapiro, E. K. (1983). The school as a context for social development. In E. M. Hetherington (Ed.), *Handbook of child psychology: Vol. 4. Socialization, personality, and social development* (pp. 197-274). New York: Wiley.

Morganthau, T., Miller, M., Huckin, J., & DeQuine, J. (1986, March 17). Kids and cocaine. *Newsweek*, pp. 58-65.

Moss, H. A., & Sussman, E. J. (1980). Longitudinal study of personality development. In O. G. Brim, Jr. & J. Kagan (Eds.), *Constancy and change in human development* (pp. 530-595). Cambridge, MA: Harvard University Press.

Needle, R., McCubbin, H., Wilson, M., Reineck, R., Lazar, A., & Mederer, H. (1986). Interpersonal influences in adolescent drug use: The role of older siblings, parents and peers. *International Journal of the Addictions, 21*, 739-766.

O'Donnell, J. A., & Clayton, R. R. (1979). Determinants of early marijuana use. In G. M. Beschner & A. S. Friedman (Eds.), *Youth drug abuse: Problems, issues, and treatment* (pp. 63-110). Lexington, MA: Lexington Books.

Olweus, D. (1980). Familial and temperamental determinants of aggressive behavior in adolescents: A causal analysis. *Developmental Psychology, 16*, 644-660.

Pandina, R. J., & Schuele, J. A. (1983). Psychosocial correlates of alcohol and drug use of adolescent students and adolescents in treatment. *Journal of Studies on Alcohol, 44*, 950-973.

Paton, S., Kessler, R., & Kandel, D. (1977). Depressive mood and adolescent illicit drug use: A longitudinal analysis. *Journal of Genetic Psychology, 131*, 267-289.

Penning, M., & Barnes, G. E. (1982). Adolescent marijuana use: A review. *International Journal of the Addictions, 17*, 749-791.

Pulkkinen, L. (1983). Youthful smoking and drinking in a longitudinal perspective. *Journal of Youth and Adolescence, 12*, 253-283.

Roberts, G. C., Block, J. H., & Block, J. (1984). Continuity and change in parents' child-rearing practices. *Child Development, 55*, 586-597.

Robins, L. N. (1974). *Deviant children grown up.* Huntington, NY: Robert E. Krieger.

Robins, L. N. (1980). The natural history of drug abuse. In D. J. Lettieri, M. Sayers, & Pearson, H. W. (Eds.), *Theories on drug abuse: Selected contemporary perspectives*. (Research Monograph No. 30, pp. 215-224) Rockville, MD: National Institute on Drug Abuse.

Rosenberg, M. (1965). *Society and adolescent self-image*. Princeton, NJ: Princeton University Press.

Rutter, M. (1981). *Maternal deprivation reassessed* (2nd ed.). New York: Penguin Books.

Schaefer, E., & Bayley, N. (1963). Maternal behavior, child behavior and their intercorrelations from infancy through adolescence. *Monographs of the Society for Research in Child Development, 28*, (3, Serial No. 87).

Schwartz, R. H., Hayden, G. F., Getson, P. R., & DiPaola, A. (1986). Drinking patterns and social consequences: A study of middle-class adolescents in two private pediatric practices. *Pediatrics, 77*, 139-143.

Segal, B. (1977). Reasons for marijuana use and personality: A canonical analysis. *Journal of Alcohol and Drug Education, 22*, 64-67.

Smith, G. M., & Fogg, C. P. (1978). Psychological predictors of early use, late use and non-use of marijuana among teenage students. In D. B. Kandel (Ed.), *Longitudinal research on drug use: Empirical findings and methodological issues* (pp. 101-113). Washington, DC: Hemisphere-Wiley.

Vaughn, B., Egeland, B., Waters, E., & Sroufe, L. A. (1979). Individual differences in infant-mother attachment at 12 and 18 months: Stability and change in families under stress. *Child Development, 50*, 971-975.

Wingard, J. A., Huba, G. J., & Bentler, P. M. (1979). The relationship of personality structure to patterns of adolescent substance use. *Multivariate Behavioral Research, 14*, 131-143.

Wingard, J. A., Huba, G. J., & Bentler, P. M. (1980). A longitudinal analysis of personality structure and adolescent substance use. *Personality & Individual Differences, 1*, 259-272.

Wohlwill, J. F. (1983). Physical and social environment as factors in development. In D. Magnusson & V. L. Allen (Eds.), *Human development: An interactional perspective* (pp. 111-129). New York: Academic Press.

Yamaguchi, K., & Kandel, D. B. (1985). On the resolution of role incompatibility: A life event history analysis of family roles and marijuana use. *The American Journal of Sociology, 90*, 1284-1325.

Youniss, J., & Smollar, J. (1985). *Adolescent relations with mothers, fathers, and friends*. Chicago: University of Chicago Press.

Zigler, E., & Child, I. L. (1969). Socialization. In G. Lindzey & E. Aronson (Eds.), *The handbook of social psychology* (2nd ed., pp. 450-589). Redding, MA: Addison-Wesley.

Families with Attention Deficit Disordered Children and Others at Risk

Dennis P. Cantwell, MD

INTRODUCTION

This chapter describes attention deficit disorder (ADD) and related disorders in childhood, adolescence, and adult life. The possible links between attention deficit disorder and later substance abuse are emphasized. The clinical picture, subtypes, and classification of the attention deficit disorder syndrome in childhood are described. Various terms that have been used to describe this condition and their implications are detailed. Possible etiologic factors are discussed. The relationship of the ADD syndrome to other disorders, particularly conduct and affective disorders, and their implications for later substance abuse are emphasized. The attention deficit disorder with hyperactivity (ADDH) syndrome in adolescence and adult life will be reviewed as will alcohol and substance use in adolescents and adults with a previous history of ADD. Family factors in the ADDH syndrome are outlined including a discussion of the possible family genetic factors as etiologic factors and family factors and possible prognostic factors in outcome. Treatment of the ADDH syndrome in childhood are detailed, and its possible effect on later outcome are described. The chapter ends with notions about the treatment of the disorder in adolescence and adult life.

Purely on programmatic grounds there are good reasons to be-

Dennis P. Cantwell is Joseph Campbell Professor of Child Psychiatry, UCLA School of Medicine and Director, Postdoctoral Fellowship Program in Child Psychiatry, UCLA Neuropsychiatric Institute and Hospital, 760 Westwood Plaza, Room C8-867, Los Angeles, CA 90024.

lieve why children with attention deficit disorder and related disorders may be at risk for alcohol and substance abuse.

First of all, exposure to alcohol and other substances is likely to occur in the junior high school and high school years. Children with low self-esteem who are not making it academically in the classroom, who are having difficulty behaviorally in the classroom, who are having difficulty behaviorally at home, who have difficulty with peer relationships, and lack of success in leisure time activities are likely to be at increased risk for substance abuse. Moreover, those adolescents with a driven quality may find some relief from their driven feeling with alcohol or other substances. Thus, for environmental reasons, as well as for psychological reasons, these children are likely to be at increased risk.

Children and adolescents with attention deficit disorder and related syndromes are quite common in the general population. It is important to delineate the clinical picture of these disorders and how they may be related to later substance abuse. It is also important to delineate the proper intervention that may prevent future substance abuse.

THE ATTENTION DEFICIT DISORDER SYNDROME IN CHILDHOOD

The attention deficit disorder syndrome in childhood is a rather common condition. It begins early in life. It is more common in boys than it is in girls, at least in the prepubertal age range. The core clinical symptoms are problems in attentional behavior, impulsivity, and motor activity.

Various terms have been used to describe this syndrome in the past. The term "Attention Deficit Disorder" was used for the first time officially in the *Diagnostic and Statistical Manual of Mental Disorders*, Third Edition (DSM-III) in 1980 (American Psychiatric Association, 1980). Earlier terms tended to be terms that emphasized possible etiologic factors rather than a behavioral picture. The "brain damage behavior syndrome" was an early term used to describe this condition. The implication was that brain damage of one type or another was the etiologic factor that led to this particular cluster of symptoms of attentional, impulsivity, and motor abnormalities.

While it is true that children with definite brain damage have high rates of psychiatric disorder compared to children in the general population, they are not specifically prone to develop this disorder. They are just as likely to develop anxious or neurotic type pictures as they are to develop an overt behavior disorder. Moreover, no particular behavioral picture, including the ADDH syndrome, can be used by itself to indicate that brain damage is indeed present.

As these facts became known with more systematic research, terms were softened. Brain damage behavior syndrome became "minimal brain damage," which implied that brain damage must be the etiology of the disorder, but since it could not be found by standard means, the brain damage must be minimal. This term was later succeeded by minimal brain dysfunction (an even softer term). Here the implication was that there may not be actual central nervous system structural damage, but there was some type of dysfunction or dysfunctions of the central nervous system which were minimal. Obviously, this is a rather grab bag term. Central nervous system function is not a unitary phenomenon, and we have no way of quantifying "brain dysfunction" so that putting a term such as "minimal" in front of a term like "brain dysfunction" really tells us nothing about the disorder.

More behaviorally oriented terms were terms like the "hyperactive child syndrome" or "hyperkinetic reaction of childhood." Rather than indicating some type of brain damage or brain dysfunction as etiologic factors, these terms emphasized the behavioral picture, and in particular they emphasized the motor activity abnormality.

The task force to produce DSM-III reviewed this voluminous literature and selected the term "attention deficit disorder" for a number of reasons. First, it is true that motor activity abnormalities are prominent in young children with the ADD syndrome, but in many cases these dissipate to a great degree later in life although the attentional behavior and impulsivity often remain. However, it should be emphasized that the motor activity abnormalities do not always dissipate over time. They may be persistent as well, and the attention and/or impulsivity abnormalities may dissipate with time.

Secondly, many clinicians who deal with children with this type of picture felt that they were children who were inattentive and impulsive who often presented with learning problems but were not motorically overactive. Many felt that this condition was more common in girls than it was in boys. For this reason, the term attention deficit disorder syndrome was selected for the DSM-III term.

This term is not without its problems either. Attention is not a unitary phenomenon. Children may have problems in coming to attention. They may have problems in sustaining attention. They may have problems in selective attention, and they may have problems in other areas of attentional behavior. Also, the impulsivity abnormalities are probably equally as important and may cause more functional impairment than the attentional abnormalities, yet they are not emphasized in this term.

The DSM-III classification system delineates three specific subtypes with specific diagnostic criteria for each. For attention deficit disorder with hyperactivity (ADDH), the behavioral picture must include significant symptomatology in the attentional area, the impulsivity area, and the motor activity area. They must begin early in life and must be persistent over time. For attention deficit disorder without hyperactivity (ADD), significant symptomatology must be present in the attentional area and the impulsivity area but not in the motor activity area. These likewise must begin early in life and must be persistent over time. DSM-III also lists as a subtype attention deficit disorder, residual state. The diagnostic criteria are that the child must have had attention deficit disorder *with* hyperactivity (ADDH) in childhood and must have continuing functional impairment secondary to continual symptomatology in the attention and impulsivity area, with the motor activity symptoms dissipating with time.

More recent data from follow-up studies indicate that it is not always the motor activity abnormalities which dissipate with time. Any two of the three core symptom areas persisting over time still lead to a syndromal presentation in adolescence and adult life. Thus, the proposed classification scheme for DSM-III-R has reverted back to one disorder, attention deficit-hyperactivity disorder, rather than specifying three separate subtypes. The attention-hyperactivity disorder will be diagnosed by the presence of any 8 out of 15 core symptoms. These core symptoms tap attentional areas, impulsivity areas, and motor activity areas. However, in contrast to DSM-III, the DSM-III-R diagnosis can be made by any permutation and combination of 8 out of the 15 core symptoms. The number 8 was selected on the basis of a field trial of the original 15 symptoms. Thus, there are children who will have 8 symptoms which are primarily attentional and impulsive. There may be children with primarily motor activity and attention symptoms, etc., depending on which 8 out of the 15 are present.

There are many putative etiologic factors described for this syndrome. These have been systematically reviewed by Cantwell (1986) and Whalen (1983). A complete discussion of all possible etiologic theories of this disorder is beyond the scope of this chapter and can be found in the references provided. Certain important issues will be outlined.

The earliest etiologic views of this disorder were that it was a type of brain damage or brain dysfunction (as noted above). It is clear now that only a minority of ADD children have hard signs of brain damage. The minimal brain dysfunction grab bag has given way to more detailed expositions such as involvement of central monoamines by the study of metabolites and studies of central nervous system arousal with neurophysiological studies. Environmental influences such as lead at a subclinical level and various aspects of the diet (sugar, dyes, and food additives) have been implicated by some clinicians and researchers. It seems best to conclude from the available evidence that the ADD syndrome is probably multifactorial in etiology. In a great number of cases, no specific etiologic agent or agents will be able to be determined, and no specific treatment will be given because of a particular etiologic factor. In other cases, more than one factor may be operating.

For the purpose of this chapter, we wish to concentrate on the familial-genetic factors that may be at least partially etiologic in this disorder. Family studies by Cantwell (1972), Morrison and Stewart (1971), and others (Stewart, de Blois, & Cummings, 1980; Stewart & Leone, 1978) have suggested that many parents of ADD children also had the disorder when they were young. Moreover, as adults these parents have been reported in various studies to have higher rates of antisocial personality disorder, alcoholism, somatization disorder, and depression.

In the Cantwell study it is particularly striking that it was the parents who had been ADD in childhood who had higher rates of alcoholism, antisocial behavior, and somatization disorder, suggesting that the ADD syndrome in these parents were predisposed to the development of those disorders. However, familial does not necessarily mean genetic. Thus, Cantwell (1975) and Morrison and Stewart (1973) conducted adoption studies which showed that the adopting parents of adopted ADDH boys did not present with high rates of these problems either in childhood or adult life, suggesting that it was the biologic parents from whom the disorder might have been inherited rather than the biological parents presenting an environmental role model and/or consciously or unconsciously reinforcing certain types of behavior.

Twin studies have been limited in number and in scope, but if anything they tend to support a genetic etiology in some children with this disorder as do half-sibling studies which show that full siblings are more likely than half siblings to show the ADD symptom pattern. Cantwell's family study also shows that the brothers of ADDH boys have higher rates of ADDH themselves than brothers of a normal comparison group, and sisters have higher rates of attention deficit disorder without hyperactivity and learning problems.

Family genetic factors as etiologic factors could obviously overlap with other theories. For example, what might be inherited is some type of deficit or difference in central neurotransmitters and/or some type of neurophysiologic predisposition to ADD. Moreover, a family genetic etiology does not obviate the possibility (in fact, the strong probability) that ADDH children growing up in homes with parents who are psychiatrically disturbed are likely to have problems for environmental reasons as well as for genetic reasons and that there may be a gene-environment interaction producing the ultimate outcome.

Befera and Barkley (1985) have reviewed research suggesting that parents of ADDH children have greater dissatisfaction with their marriage than either parents of normal controls or adopting parents of adopted ADDH children. He also suggests that mothers of ADDH children have more difficulty in managing the ADDH child than fathers do.

Mendelson, Johnson, and Stewart (1971) suggest that ADDH children who are likely to develop conduct symptomatology and antisocial behavior in adolescence are more likely to have parents who have antisocial behavior themselves. The Montreal group (Weiss, Minde, Werry, Douglas, & Nemeth, 1971) examined family factors in relationship to outcome in adolescence and suggest that having psychiatrically ill parents is associated with a poorer outcome, particularly that of antisocial behavior, as is a poor parent-child relationship (particularly with the mother), and child rearing practices that could be considered punitive. The Montreal group also suggests that there is a correlation between outcome of the child and outcome of the family, with the children who do well having family function improve over time and the reverse occurring with children who do poorly.

Thus, there is reason to suspect that family factors may be important in etiology from the genetic standpoint and also possibly from the environmental standpoint. Also, there is reason to suspect from published data that certain family factors may play a role in outcome of the disorder.

The family studies of Cantwell (1972) and Morrison (1971) suggest also a link between the ADDH syndrome in childhood and alcoholism in later life. Many of the parents, particularly fathers, of ADDH boys had ADD themselves when they were younger. This group of parents had higher rates of alcoholism and antisocial personality including substance abuse when they were seen as adults. Mothers also had high rates of alcoholism and high rates of somatization disorder which some investigators think "substitutes" for antisocial personality in females. There is a family relationship between antisocial personality disorder, somatization disorder, and alcoholism in adult life. It has been suggested that whatever family environmental and/or genetic factors lead to antisocial personality disorder in males may lead to somatization disorder in females rather than antisocial personality disorder.

The central question for the purpose of this chapter is: Is there a relationship between the ADDH syndrome in childhood and later substance abuse—either in adolescence or in adult life?

RELATIONSHIP OF ADDH SYNDROME TO OTHER DISORDERS IN CHILDHOOD

Cantwell (1986) has recently reviewed the relationship of the ADDH syndrome of childhood to other disorders. For the purpose of this chapter, three specific disorders are considered: conduct disorders, learning disorders, and affective disorders.

Conduct disorders are disorders in which the individuals have a chronic pattern of violation of society's norms and/or violation of the rights of others. These disorders begin early in life, are more common in males, and have a rather ominous outcome untreated. As Robins' (1966) systematic study shows, a large amount of these children will develop antisocial personality disorder in later life, and many have other types of psychiatric disorders as well. While ADDH does exist as a pure syndrome, many children present with both ADDH and conduct disorder. Many children who present initially with the ADDH syndrome develop significant conduct symptomatology later and antisocial personality disorder in adolescence. Included in this antisocial group are substance abusers, both alcohol and other types of drugs.

Learning disorders are diagnosed when children are not performing academically in one or more academic subjects at the level that would be predicted on the basis of their age and IQ. While learning disorders in children are multifactorially determined, it is clear that there is a relationship between the ADDH syndrome in childhood and learning disorders. Cantwell and Satterfield (1978) show that their ADDH group had a significantly higher rate of learning disorders than a matched comparison group. Not only were more children functioning at a learning disordered level in the ADDH group, but the ADDH group tended to be more academically retarded and in more academic subjects than did the non-ADDH comparison group. Learning disorders and conduct disorders are intimately related as well. We know the most about the relationship with reading disorder, and that relationship suggests that many initially reading disordered children develop antisocial behavior, and many conduct disordered children and antisocial adolescents are found to have high rates of reading disorders.

Rutter's Isle of Wight Study (Rutter, 1970) compared purely

reading disordered children with purely conduct disordered children and with a mixed group. The mixed group, who had both conduct disorders and reading disorders were more like the children with reading disorders than they were like the children with conduct disorders, suggesting that either the reading disorder led to the conduct disorder or there were certain features that characterized both groups. And indeed the reading disordered group and the group with reading and conduct disorders were characterized by inattentiveness, motor activity abnormalities, and impulsivity, all symptoms suggestive of the ADD syndrome, although no attempt was made to make that diagnosis in this group. One possible scenario would be that ADDH children find it difficult to learn in school; thus, they do not get any gratification from the primary source of gratification: rewards from their teachers and rewards from their parents for good grades. Thus, they may drift into delinquent behavior as a way of rebelling against the system or as a reaction to the frustration from their lack of academic success.

Affective disorders are disorders characterized by disturbances of mood – depression and mania. It is common for conduct disordered children, for learning disordered children, and for ADD children independently to demonstrate a demoralization syndrome which looks like a depression. These children are demoralized, have a low self-esteem, due to a series of life defeats. They are children who do not "make it in society" either because they do not do well academically or in extracurricular activities. They also have poor peer relationships. These children tend to develop a demoralization syndrome that is differentiated from a true major depressive disorder by the lack of pervasive anhedonia.

However, there may also be a relationship between the ADD syndrome and true affective disorders. Two recent studies of the children of affectively ill parents report high rates of ADD in their children. Moreover, a more recent family study by Beiderman, Munir, and Knee (1986) suggests high rates of affective disorders in the parents of ADD children as well as the previously reported antisocial spectrum disorders.

There are now data to suggest that some depressed adolescents present with a longstanding history of disruptive behavior suggestive of ADD, conduct disorder, or both, and that these depressed adolescents are highly likely to develop mania in adolescence for the first time.

It is theoretically possible that demoralized and/or depressed adolescents who are grown up ADD children may begin to self-medicate themselves with alcohol and/or other substances to alleviate their depression and demoralization. This has not been systematically studied to any great degree, but it is a theoretical possibility worth exploring.

As Shuckit (1986) has pointed out with adults, anywhere from 5% to 10% of primary alcoholics might have an independent affective disorder, and 3% to 10% of patients with primary affective disorder could independently have alcoholism. It is also true in adult life that alcoholics often present for treatment with symptoms of depression, and patients with major depressive disorder and dysthymic disorder may develop secondary alcohol problems as a result of their depression. Apparently, about a third of individuals with primary alcoholism will have sustained periods of depression qualifying for a diagnosis of secondary affective disorder, but as many as 70% will have periods lasting hours to days at a time in which they are sad, and the sadness is of a great degree of intensity, but it is not persistent enough to qualify for a diagnosis of secondary alcoholism. Somewhere between 5% to 10% of males with alcoholism and 15% to 20% of females with alcoholism give histories of either major depressive disorder or dysthymic disorder that occur during periods of sustained abstinence in which they were not drinking at all, and in many cases the affective disturbance preceded the onset of the alcoholism.

Shuckit also points out that adults with antisocial personality disorder also can develop alcohol and drug-related life problems, as many as 70% during the course of their lifetime. They also can demonstrate mood swings that at times are severe enough and of long enough duration to qualify for a diagnosis of major depressive disorder or dysthymic disorder.

Thus, it can be seen that there is good reason to believe that there may be a relationship between the ADD syndrome in children and later life drug and alcohol problems. This may be through the development of conduct disorder and antisocial personality disorder or maybe through the development of affective disorder—either a demoralization syndrome or a major or minor depressive syndrome which may lead to alcohol and/or substance abuse.

THE ADDH SYNDROME IN ADOLESCENT AND ADULT LIFE

The outcome of childhood ADDH in adolescent and adult life has been the subject of intense research over the last decade. Three rather different types of outcomes have been postulated as the outcome of childhood ADDH in adolescence and adulthood. The earliest view was one best labeled as a developmental delay hypothesis. In essence, this hypothesis stated that ADDH children were developmentally delayed and had a maturational lag or some such term. The implication was that with time, particularly with the advent of puberty, most children would "outgrow their problem." Early writers suggested as a corollary to this hypothesis that ADDH children who were treated with stimulant medication should have their medication stopped at the time of puberty because the effect would be a stimulating one rather than a paradoxical one. There has never been any solid evidence for this view. In fact, current evidence suggests that it is decidedly untrue.

A second hypothesis is the continual display hypothesis. This hypothesis suggests that in adolescence what one sees is a continuation of the core symptoms of the childhood ADDH syndrome, although they may be manifested in somewhat of a modified form.

The developmental decay hypothesis postulates that childhood ADDH is a predisposing factor to psychopathology in adolescence and in adult life. Antisocial personality disorders and alcoholism are particularly singled out as common outcomes. But a variety of other disorders, including affective disorders, anxiety disorders, Tourette's syndrome, other forms of substance abuse besides alcoholism, and some types of schizophrenia are also outcomes of the ADDH syndrome in childhood.

The focus of this chapter is on evidence that there is indeed a relationship between childhood ADDH and various forms of substance abuse in adolescence or in adult life. Before we review the published evidence on this topic, it is important to recognize that there are methodological issues which may play a role in determining some of the results.

The relationship between ADDH in childhood and substance abuse in adolescence (as well as other disorders in adolescence) can be investigated with three different study designs. The first study design is the true prospective study design. In this design, ADDH children are selected in childhood by the investigator, examined by the investigator, and followed over time into adolescence and into adult life looking for prevalence rates of substance use and abuse. This study design is the only one that can answer the question of whether or not any particular types of treatments, singly or in combination, are better than no treatment at all or that one type of treatment is more effective than another type of treatment. This is because this is the only type of study that allows one to randomly assign matched groups to treatment or no treatment conditions.

The true prospective study design does have some problems. Significant attrition may occur over time so that in adolescence and in adult life one does not have a true comprehensive complete sample of the children who were initially seen. There is research evidence to suggest that those who are hardest to find later on may have disproportionate amounts of psychopathology. An investigator must be relatively young if he is going to follow a young child population into adolescence and adult life, and he must be able to obtain funding to do such a long-term prospective study, which is no easy feat. Also, our scientific base of knowledge changes with time. Thus, measurement instruments, classificatory schemes, and other methodologies may look good and may be state-of-the-art when they are initially used on the childhood population, but once one sees the population 10 years later or 20 years later, the initial measures are no longer state-of-the-art. Thus, while the true prospective study design does offer some advantages, there are some limitations as well.

In the true retrospective study design, also called the follow-back design, one selects a particular outcome in adolescence or adult life. In this case, one would select adolescents or adults with alcohol and/or other forms of substance abuse. One can then attempt to make a diagnosis of childhood ADDH either retrospectively from the patient and/or significant others or locate records that would indicate the children were given a diagnosis of childhood ADDH. One could also attempt to make a diagnosis in adult life or in adolescence of attention deficit disorder, residual state, to see if the childhood condition of ADDH was persisting in adolescence or adult life.

This design presents some problems as well. One either has to rely on existing records for data in childhood to support a diagnosis of childhood ADDH or one has to retrospectively make the diagnosis. Retrospective diagnosis may be difficult 10 to 20 years after childhood, and records may not be available that are complete and comprehensive to allow a diagnosis of childhood ADDH to be made comfortably. Also, children who were never seen in childhood who may have had ADDH may be missed because there are no existing records. In addition, appropriate comparison groups must be selected in order to determine whether or not the percentage of adolescent or adult alcoholics or substance abusers may have greater rates of childhood ADDH than those who are not alcohol or substance abusers in adolescence or adult life.

A third type of study design is the catch-up prospective study design. Lee Robins' (1966) *Deviant Children Grown Up* is the classic example of this type of study. Here the sample is identified in childhood, not in adolescence or adult life, and the diagnosis is made in childhood. However, the diagnosis is made from existing records rather than by seeing the patients in childhood and making the diagnosis on a personal examination. This design has the advantage of selecting the patients in childhood as one would do in a prospective study but gets away from the disadvantage of having to wait for the children to reach adolescence or adult life in order to demonstrate links between childhood ADDH and adolescent or adult alcohol or substance abuse.

There are other methodological issues involved in attempting to look at the links between childhood ADDH and later life alcohol and substance abuse. One is the issue of subject selection. A common problem is disorders that the children may have in addition to the ADDH syndrome. As mentioned above, the ADDH syndrome often overlaps with conduct and learning disorders and may be related to affective disorders in some cases as well. Follow-up information then will be complicated by what additional diagnoses the children have. Since it is common for antisocial adolescents and adults to have substance abuse as a complicating system, one might plausibly suggest that ADDH children who also have conduct disorder will be more likely than pure ADDH children to have substance abuse in adolescence or adult life. Thus, the outcome linking ADDH in childhood to later life substance abuse may actually be mediated by the presence of conduct disorder and not ADDH. Prospective study design with careful evaluation generally can eliminate this problem. On the other hand, relying on existing records or retrospective diagnosis may give one a mixed population.

Selection of control and comparison groups is also important. What type of control group should be used—normal children, children with other types of psychiatric and/or learning disorders—is one question. When the control group should be selected is another question. Should they be selected initially, or should they be selected at follow-up? What variables to match the comparison group to the ADDH group is also an issue since if one is going to look for predictors of later life substance abuse in childhood ADDH patients, whatever variables the ADDH and comparison groups are matched on cannot be used as predictor variables.

Interval factors between childhood and adolescence and between childhood and adult life are also important. The longer the follow-up interval, the more difficult it probably is to reliably and validly rate interval factors which may be important in outcome. What types of treatment are given for what length of time and how effective they are is difficult to rate retrospectively. Presence or absence of certain types of life events and life stressors which may complicate the picture in adolescence or adult life may be difficult to rate as well.

With these caveats in mind then, what does the literature show using these three different types of study designs with regard to the issue of childhood ADDH and later life alcohol and/or substance abuse in adolescence and adult life? This issue has recently been reviewed in detail by Weiss and Hechtman (1986), and the interested reader is referred to their book for a detailed description. Some highlights will be reviewed here.

First, there is a series of studies that have looked at adults with alcoholism and other types of psychiatric disorders. Tarter,

McBride, Baonpane, and Schneider (1977), for example, in a study of adult inpatients with alcoholism, suggest that childhood ADDH was more common in individuals whose alcoholism was severe than in those in whom the alcoholism was mild. He also used the distinction primary versus secondary alcoholism, with the primary type being more severe and the secondary being milder; and childhood ADDH was associated with severe primary alcoholism. ADDH in childhood was also greater in these patients with severe primary alcoholism than it was in psychiatric patients who were not alcoholic and in nonpsychiatric patients.

Morrison (1980b), in a study of his private practice suggests that retrospectively one could make a childhood ADDH diagnosis on a subsample of his adult psychiatric patients. Those in his practice who had a childhood ADDH history were much more likely to be alcoholic as adults than in matched patients from his private practice who did not have a childhood ADDH diagnosis.

Wood, Reimherr, Wender, and Johnson (1976) and Wood, Wender, and Reimherr (1983) in Utah report that about a third of adult male alcoholics give a retrospective diagnosis of attention deficit disorder, residual state. However, no comparison groups were used, so the exact difference between the prevalence of attention deficit disorder, residual state, in alcoholic adults versus nonalcoholic adults is not known.

The work of Mattes, Boswell, and Oliver (1984) does not suggest that adult psychiatric patients with childhood ADDH have higher rates of alcohol or substance abuse than adult patients without such a history.

Family studies have been mixed with regard to the link between childhood ADDH and adult alcohol and substance abuse. Earlier studies by Cantwell (1972) and Morrison and Stewart (1971) alluded to above did suggest that biological parents of ADDH children had high rates of ADDH themselves in childhood and were prone to develop alcoholism in adult life. More recently Morrison (1980a) and Offord, Sullivan, Allen, and Abrams (1979) have done similar family studies and have not demonstrated a specific link between childhood ADDH and later alcohol abuse in the parents.

A second set of studies has looked at young adult or slightly older adult ADDH individuals. Some of the studies (Laufer, 1971) are methodologically flawed, and no definitive conclusions can be drawn. Other studies such as those by Feldman, Denhoff, and Denhoff (1979), Borland and Hechtman (1976), and Milman (1979) show no specific link between childhood ADDH and drug or substance abuse in young adult or early adult aged individuals.

Loney's data (Loney, Whaley-Klahn, Kosier, & Conboy, 1981) from the University of Iowa is probably the best controlled study because it used same sexed siblings who were not ADDH in childhood as one comparison group and national survey data on substance use and abuse as another comparison. The Loney study suggests that the ADDH children as young adults and their brothers probably have more drug use than children from a national survey.

Gittelman's data (Gittelman, Mannuzza, Shenker, & Bonagura, in press) is the most interesting in that there was an increase of substance abuse but not alcohol use in grown up ADDH children when compared to a comparison group. What was most interesting were the ADDH children who continued to manifest symptomatology in young adult life who accounted for those with substance abuse, and the link seemed to be through the presence of antisocial symptoms in young adult life. Thus, the Gittelman data would suggest that continuation of the ADDH symptoms in young adult life is associated with the diagnosis of conduct disorder or antisocial personalty, and antisocial personality is associated with a diagnosis of substance abuse.

It should be noted that some of the studies such as those of Feldman and those of Loney do suggest that alcohol use in young adult life in the ADDH population is not low. Indeed it was quite high in both of those studies but not necessarily higher than the brothers or appropriate matches from the general population. But one should not minimize the fact that young adults with ADDH may have alcohol and/or substance abuse as an outcome that may need to enter into the treatment equation.

A somewhat larger group of studies (Blouin, Bornstein, & Trite, 1978; Mendelson, Johnson, & Stewart, 1971; Feldman, Denhoff, & Denhoff, 1979; Beck, Langford, MacKay, & Sum, 1975; Kramer & Loney, 1978; Henker, Whalen, Bugental, & Barker, 1981; Hays, 1976) of adolescents with ADDH does not tend to support the view that alcohol and/or substance abuse is a common outcome of the ADDH syndrome in adolescents. The studies differ in methodological rigor, in patient populations, in the presence or absence of comparison groups, and in other aspects of methodology that make major generalizations difficult.

In summary, a review of the published literature does give rise to some concern that ADDH in childhood may be associated with alcohol and/or substance abuse in adolescence or adult life. Better controlled studies are necessary if we are able to determine which ADDH children are most at risk for developing alcohol and/or other forms of substance abuse in adolescence or adult life. In particular, a positive family history for alcoholism in first-degree relatives is one factor that should be looked at since alcoholism does have some family-genetic etiologic roots.

TREATMENT OF THE ADDH SYNDROME

We will end this chapter with a discussion of treatment of the ADDH syndrome. We will consider separately treatment in childhood, treatment in adolescence, and treatment in adult life. We will begin with a discussion of treatment in childhood. The ADDH syndrome is a multifaceted disorder. In addition to the core symptoms of the disorder (attentional behavior, impulsivity, and motor activity symptoms), different children may present with different associated difficulties such as conduct disorder, aggressive behavior, academic performance problems, family interaction problems, peer relationship difficulties, low self-esteem, depression, demoralization, etc. In addition, these children may come from quite different types of families. For some children, their close family members (particularly their parents) may have high rates of psychopathology themselves which will have to be taken into account in treatment. In other cases, this will not be true.

Thus, the concept that seems most sensible is that the treatment of this disorder will probably employ a multimodal therapeutic intervention design. Certain types of therapeutic interventions may be necessary and useful for some children with the syndrome. They may not be necessary and/or useful for other children with the syndrome. Moreover, for the same child certain types of therapeutic interventions may be necessary at one point in time but may not be useful at other points in time.

Satterfield, Cantwell, and Satterfield (1979) and Satterfield, Satterfield, and Cantwell (1980 and 1981) have demonstrated how a multimodality program can be instituted in childhood and can be effective in ameliorating not only some of the core symptoms but also some of the associated symptoms such as antisocial behavior and academic performance problems.

Treatment in childhood should begin with involvement of the family. The family needs correct information about the nature of the syndrome, what it is, what it is not, what the etiologic factors are likely to be, what the prognosis is likely to be without treatment, and what types of intervention are necessary for this child at this point in time.

Secondly, many families benefit from referrals to local organizations such as the local branch of the National Association for Children with Learning Disabilities. These organizations offer group support. Many parents can offer insights on how to deal with certain kinds of problems having dealt with these themselves with their own children. Most particularly these organizations and the parents who make them up are often the best sources of information about local resources. Some parents have found it useful to read books written for them such as the *Hyperactive and Learning Disabled Child: A Guide for Parents* by Paul and Esther Wender (1980) and/or *Raising a Hyperactive Child* by Mark Stewart and Sally Olds (1971).

Some families will need and benefit from a short course in behavioral observation and behavior modification which can be done routinely with all families to start out treatment. The use of such programmed texts written for parents as *Families* and *Living with Children* by Patterson and his group (Patterson, 1969, 1971) have been found to be helpful in this regard.

If it is discovered that family members do have significant degrees of psychopathology such as alcoholism or antisocial behavior, they should probably be referred for treatment for these problems on their own in addition to whatever types of intervention they may be involved in with their children.

ADDH children who have been enmeshed in difficult family systems may require a more dynamically oriented family therapy approach in addition to the parent training type of approach that seems to be useful for most if not all children with the syndrome.

The next step in treatment of the disorder probably involves skill remediation, and this is multifaceted. Obviously, one of the most important is academic performance skills. If the child is functioning academically at grade level and is able to be maintained in a regular classroom setting, this may solve part of the problem. On the other hand, if the child is already academically behind his peers and is not doing well in a regular classroom setting, some intervention may be necessary. This may be individual tutoring while remaining in the regular classroom. This may be provision of special programs by the public school setting such as a learning disability group, a resource specialist program, or a self-contained learning and/or behavior disorder classroom. In some cases, a special school may be necessary, and the child may not be able to make it in the public school system even with special help. Each case should be taken individually, and there is very little research data to support one type of intervention in the academic skill area over another.

However, skill remediation involves more than simply academic skills through tutoring and/or the public school area. Social skills training has also been found to be useful in helping develop self-control and developing better peer relationships, which is a common problem among children with the ADDH syndrome.

Another type of skill remediation is cognitive training used as an adjunct to help with academic performance problems. This is not simple tutoring or remedial education, but rather an attempt to train the child to overcome disabilities that contribute significantly to academic performance problems.

The next issue is the use of medication. A complete discussion of the issue of medication treatment of children with the ADDH syndrome is beyond the scope of this chapter. It suffices to say that there is a substantial amount of literature suggesting that stimulant medication in childhood is effective for ameliorating the core symptoms of the disorder in a substantial number of the children. There are children who are simply nonresponders, some of whom may benefit from tricyclic medication such as Imipramine or Desipramine. There will always be a subgroup of patients who are nonresponders to any kind of psychopharmacologic intervention. The major question with the use of stimulant medication is whether or not the positive short-term effect seems to have any long-term effect with regard to outcome in adolescence and adult life. This will be discussed below.

The addition of behavior modification, both at home and at school above and beyond that which was described above, may be necessary for certain patients. In particular, aggressive children may need a behavior modification program with self-control procedures in order to be effective. For certain other children other types of therapeutic intervention may be necessary such as therapeutic groups or special physical education programs to help with possible coordination difficulties. For a review of the use of psychopharmacologic intervention in ADDH children that also looks at the addition of multimodality treatment, the reader is referred to recent articles by Hechtman (1985) and by Brown, Borden, and Clingerman (1985). In particular, Hechtman has looked at the issue of stimulant treatment in childhood and whether or not it has any impact on later functioning, particularly in adolescents. The conclusions that she reaches after reviewing this literature include the following: The core ADDH symptoms improve by adolescence, but many of the adolescents still present with significant core symptomatology. Antisocial behavior is a common problem in adolescents, particularly in those who have ADDH symptoms which continue. There is no good evidence that stimulant treatment alone in childhood affects adolescent antisocial behavior. Neither does stimulant treatment in childhood seem to affect the use of alcohol or other forms of substances in adolescence. There is certainly no evidence that the use of stimulants in childhood will sensitize the child to the use of medication and make drug or alcohol abuse more common.

Stimulant treatment in childhood does not seem to have any affect on depression, demoralization, low self-esteem and poor peer relationships later in life. Nor does early stimulant treatment seem to have affect on academic outcome in adolescents which is poor in many children.

There are real problems in reviewing this literature that Hechtman describes including subject selection, the description of drug treatment, what drug was used for how long, how compliance was measured, how effectiveness was measured in childhood, was it the correct dose, etc. Other types of treatment that were given with the medication, which are common in some studies, are often not spelled out. The multimodality studies do seem to have a better outcome in adolescence as might be expected.

Similarly, Weiss and Hechtman (1986) have reviewed the evidence for efficacy of stimulant medication in adolescents and adults with the ADDH syndrome. Clearly there are some adolescents and adults in whom stimulant medication is just as effective in adolescence and adult life as it is in childhood. It is not likely the stimulant medication alone in adolescents or adults will be sufficient to take care of all of the problems that the ADDH adolescent and adult presents with. A multimodality approach is likely to be necessary in adolescents and adults with the ADDH syndrome as it is with children. Nevertheless, there is no reason to stop medication in adolescence or not to consider its use for the first time in adult life based on available evidence. However, in individuals who may be prone to substance abuse, one may want to be more cautious about giving stimulant medication to adolescents and adults. Not only would one be concerned that they may abuse it themselves even though the evidence is not great that they will, but the possibility of selling street drugs to contemporaries must be taken into account. More systematic information is needed about what elements of a multimodality program are necessary for what children, for what adolescents, and for what adults with what components of the ADDH syndrome.

SUMMARY AND CONCLUSIONS

This chapter reviews data suggesting that children with the ADDH syndrome are an at risk group for the development of alcohol and/or substance abuse in adolescence and adult life. It seems that those children who persist with continuation of the core symptoms of the ADDH syndrome in adolescence and adult life are more at risk for antisocial behavior than those in whom the core symptoms of the syndrome resolve. It is those with antisocial behavior who seem to be most at risk for substance abuse, including alcohol. There is no solid evidence that treatment in childhood with stimulant medication alone alters any major facet of adolescent and/or adult outcome. There is suggestive evidence from multimodality studies in childhood that the outcome may be better in later life. A multimodality approach is most likely to be necessary in children, adolescents, and adults with the syndrome and probably more likely to be necessary the older the subject when they present for evaluation and treatment.

REFERENCES

American Psychiatric Association. (1980). *Diagnostic and statistical manual of mental disorders* (3rd ed.). Washington, DC: Author.

Beck, L., Langford, W. S., MacKay, M., & Sum, G. (1975). Childhood chemotherapy and later drug abuse and growth curve: A follow-up study of 30 adolescents. *American Journal of Psychiatry, 132* (4), 436-438.

Befera, M., & Barkley, R. (1985). Hyperactive and normal boys and girls: Mother-child interaction, parent psychiatric status, and child psychophysiology. *Journal of Child Psychology and Psychiatry, 26*, 439-452.

Beiderman, J., Munir, K., & Knee, D. G. (1986). High rates of ADD and major depression in relatives of ADD problands. Presented at the Annual Meeting of the American Academy of Child and Adolescent Psychiatry, Los Angeles, California, October 1986.

Blouin, A. G. A., Bornstein, R., & Trite, R. (1978). Teen-age alcohol use among hyperactive children: A 5-year follow-up study. *Journal of Pediatric Psychology, 3*, 188-194.

Borland, B. L., & Heckman, H. K. (1976). Hyperactive boys and their brothers: A 25-year follow-up study. *Archives of General Psychiatry, 33*, 669-675.

Brown, R. T., Borden, K. A., & Clingerman, S. R. (1985). Pharmacotherapy in ADD adolescents with special attention to multimodality treatments. *Psychopharmacology Bulletin, 21* (2), 192-211.

Cantwell, D. P. (1972). Psychiatric illness in the families of hyperactive children. *Archives of General Psychiatry, 27*, 414-417.

Cantwell, D. P. (1975). Genetics of hyperactivity. *Journal of Child Psychology and Psychiatry, 16*, 216-264.

Cantwell, D. P. (1986). Attention deficit and associated childhood disorders. In T. Millon and G. L. Klerman (Eds.), *Contemporary directions in psychopathology* (pp. 403-428). New York: Guilford Publications.

Cantwell, D. P., & Satterfield, J. H. (1978). The prevalence of academic underachievement in hyperactive children. *Journal of Pediatric Psychology, 3*, 168-171.

Feldman, S., Denhoff, E., & Denhoff, J. (1979). The attention disorders and related syndromes: Outcome in adolescence and young adult life. In E.

Denhoff & L. Stern (Eds.), *Minimal brain dysfunction: A developmental approach*. New York: Masson Publishing (USA).

Gittelman, R., Mannuzza, S., Shenker, R., & Bonagura, N. (in press). Hyperactive boys almost grown up: Psychiatric status. *Archives of General Psychiatry*.

Hays, M. (1976). *Report of the Iowa study of drug attitudes and behavior among youth*. Des Moines: State of Iowa Department of Public Instruction.

Hechtman, L. (1985). Adolescent outcome of hyperactive children treated with stimulants in childhood: A review. *Psychopharmacology Bulletin, 21* (2), 178-191.

Henker, B., Whalen, C., Bugental, D. B., & Barker, C. (1981). Licit and illicit substance use patterns in stimulant-treated children and their peers. In K. Gadow & J. Loney (Eds.), *Psychosocial aspects of drug treatment for hyperactivity*. Boulder, CO: Westview Press.

Kramer, J., & Loney, J. (1978). Predicting adolescent antisocial behavior among hyperactive boys. Paper presented at the Annual Meeting of the American Psychological Association, Toronto, August 1978.

Laufer, M. W. (1971). Long-term management and some follow-up findings on the use of drugs with minimal cerebral syndrome. *Journal of Learning Disabilities, 4*, 55-58.

Loney, J., Whaley-Klahn, M. A., Kosier, T., & Conboy, J. (1981). Hyperactive boys and their brothers at 21: Predictors of aggressive and antisocial outcomes. Paper presented at a meeting of the Society for Life History Research, Monterey, CA, November 1981.

Mattes, J., Boswell, L., & Oliver, H. (1984). Methylphenidate effects on symptoms of attention deficit disorder in adults. *Archives of General Psychiatry, 41*, 1059-1067.

Mendelson, W., Johnson, J., & Stewart, J. (1971). Hyperactive children as teenagers: A follow-up study. *Journal of Nervous Mental Disorders, 153*, 273-279.

Milman, D. H. (1979). Minimal brain dysfunction in childhood: Outcome in late adolescence and early adult years. *Journal of Clinical Psychiatry, 40*, 371-380.

Morrison, J. R. (1980a). Adult psychiatric disorders in parents of hyperactive children. *American Journal of Psychiatry, 137*, 825-827.

Morrison, J. R. (1980b). Childhood hyperactivity in an adult psychiatric population: Social factors. *Journal of Clinical Psychiatry, 41*, 40-43.

Morrison, J. R., & Stewart, M. A. (1971). A family study of the hyperactive child syndrome. *Biological Psychiatry, 3*, 189-195.

Morrison, J. R., & Stewart, M. A. (1973). The psychiatric status of the legal families of adopted hyperactives. *Archives of General Psychiatry, 3*, 888-891.

Offord, D. R., Sullivan, N., Allen, N., & Abrams, N. (1979). Delinquency and hyperactivity. *Journal of Nervous and Mental Disease, 167*, 734-741.

Patterson, G. I. (1969). *Families*. Champaign, IL: Research Press.

Patterson, G. I. (1970). *Living with children*. Champaign, IL: Research Press.

Robins, L. N. (1966). *Deviant children grown up*. Baltimore: Williams & Wilkins.

Rutter, M., Tizard, J., & Whitmore, K. (1970). *Education, health, and behavior*. New York: Wiley & Sons.

Satterfield, J. H., Cantwell, D. P., & Satterfield, B. T. (1979). Multimodality treatment. A one-year follow-up of 84 hyperactive boys. *Archives of General Psychiatry, 36*, 965-974.

Satterfield, J. H., Satterfield, B. T., & Cantwell, D. P. (1980). Multimodality treatment. A two-year evaluation of 61 hyperactive boys. *Archives of General Psychiatry, 37*, 915-919.

Satterfield, J. H., Satterfield, B. T., & Cantwell, D. P. (1981). Three-year multimodality treatment of hyperactive boys. *Pediatrics, 98* (4), 650-655.

Shuckit, M. (1986). Affective disorder and alcoholism. *Psychiatric Times*.

Stewart, M. A., de Blois, C. S., & Cummings, C. (1980). Psychiatric disorder in the parents of hyperactive boys and those with conduct disorder. *Journal of Child Psychology and Psychiatry, 21*, 283-292.

Stewart, M. A., & Leone, L. (1978). A family study of unsocialized-aggressive boys. *Biological Psychiatry, 13*, 10-7-118.

Stewart, M., & Olds, S. (1971). *Raising the hyperactive child*. New York: Basic Books.

Tarter, R. E., McBride, N., Baonpane, N., & Schneider, D. U. (1977). Differentiation of alcoholics: Children history of minimal brain dysfunction, family history, and drinking pattern. *Archives of General Psychiatry, 34*, 761-768.

Weiss, G., & Hechtman, L. T. (1986). *Hyperactive children grown up*. New York: Guilford Press.

Weiss, G., Minde, K., Werry, Douglas, & Nemeth, E. (1971). Studies on the hyperactive child. VIII. Five-year follow-up. *Archives of General Psychiatry*.

Wender, P., & Wender, E. (1980). *The hyperactive and learning disabled child – A guide for parents*. New York: Crown Publishers.

Whalen, C. K. (1983). Hyperactivity, learning problems, and the attention deficit disorders. In T. H. Ollendick & M. Hersen (Eds.), *Handbook of child psychopathology*. New York: Plenum Press.

Wood, D., Reimherr, F. W., Wender, P. H., & Johnson, G. E. (1976). Diagnosis and treatment of minimal brain dysfunction in adults. *Archives of General Psychiatry, 33*, 1453-1460.

Wood, D., Wender, P. H., & Reimherr, F. W. (1983). The prevalence of attention deficit disorder residual type or minimal brain dysfunction in a population of male alcoholic patients. *American Journal of Psychiatry, 140*.

III. FAMILY INTERVENTIONS

Empirical Guidelines for a Family Intervention for Adolescent Drug Use

Thomas J. Dishion, PhD
John B. Reid, PhD
Gerald R. Patterson, PhD

INTRODUCTION

The task of this paper is to discuss the development of empirical guidelines that might be useful in the design and evaluation of interventions for at-risk adolescents and adolescents already involved with drug use. The orientation of the authors, and of this volume, represents the concern that somehow families are important in understanding the process explaining early drug use. The evidence is mixed on the role of families in generating adolescent drug use, with some longitudinal investigators reporting weak statistical effects (e.g., Jessor, 1976; Jessor & Jessor, 1975), while other investigators (e.g., Baumrind, 1985) report stronger statistical effects with more intensive measurement of childrearing factors. However, if one accepts the notion that early drug use and delinquency are somewhat different aspects of a unified behavioral process (Dishion & Loeber, 1985; Elliott, Huizinga, & Ageton, 1985; Jessor & Jessor, 1975), then the evidence linking families to adolescent deviancy is foreboding (e.g., Loeber & Dishion, 1983).

Not to be ignored in thinking about adolescent drug use is the influence of peers. In fact, the most consistent finding across re-

---

Thomas J. Dishion is Research Associate, John B. Reid is Executive Director, and Gerald R. Patterson is Director, The Oregon Social Learning Center, 207 East Fifth, Suite 202, Eugene, OR 97401.

search projects is that knowing the drug use habits of an adolescent's peers is the next best thing to knowing his or her own drug use (Dishion & Loeber, 1985; Donovan, Jessor, & Jessor, 1983; Elliott et al., 1985; Friedman, Lichenstein, & Biglan, 1985; Huba & Bentler, 1983; Huba, Wingard, & Bentler, 1981; Kandel, 1973). Kardel (1978) has identified a process of homophilia and mutual socialization that seems to be involved, in that adolescents who use drugs tend to seek out other adolescents who are also favorable to drugs. When two adolescents are not alike on this dimension, they either desist from friendship, or one of them begins using drugs, or so it seems when summarizing over a large group of young people.

Epidemiological research of this kind is extremely useful for the clinician/researcher in providing an overview of the factors that may be etiologically significant and, therefore, clinically useful. The assumption underlying this last statement is that understanding the process leading to an outcome tells us the factors that need to be addressed to effectively intervene to either prevent or curtail this process.

We have defined for ourselves a number of technical barriers to surmount in the development of empirical guidelines for improving the parent training approach to family intervention. Briefly summarized, these include the following. (1) Conceptualizing families in such a way that maximizes the potential utility of research findings. Thus, Patterson (1982) has defined four family management constructs labeled *discipline*, *monitoring*, *positive reinforcement*, and *problem solving*. Later, Patterson, Reid, and Dishion (in press) included a fifth family management construct called *parent involvement*. (2) Developing multiple indicator measurement strategies for theoretical constructs that, as much as possible, incorporate the unique vantage points of multiple respondents and assessment methods. (3) Developing process models that test the hypothesized interrelations between theoretical constructs in such a way as to constitute both an explanation and a prediction of adolescent problem behavior.

In considering the problem of adolescent drug use, two major factors emerge as important considerations in understanding the social processes underlying this outcome: peers and families. We feel that to adapt the parent training approach to family intervention for adolescent drug use, we would need to account for both these factors and the interrelation between the two in our treatment model. Work summarized by Bry (1985) indicates that family interventions are effective in ameliorating drug use in adolescence. Now the question is, what factors will need to be addressed to effect long-term changes in the adolescent's progression toward early drug use and delinquency? We will now proceed to describe some of our own research aimed at achieving empirical guidelines for designing effective family interventions.

In reporting results from our epidemiological research, two study samples will be referred to: the planning study and the longitudinal study. The planning study refers to a sample of 210 boys and their families in the fourth, seventh, and tenth grades. This cross-sectional study provided the empirical foundation for the ongoing sequential cohort longitudinal study. The longitudinal study sample consists of two cohorts of 100 boys each and their families, initially assessed at age 9 to 10 (1983), with yearly probes since. At the time of this writing, Cohort I is 11 to 12, and Cohort II is 10 to 11. To date, only the first assessment wave has been analyzed for both cohorts.

In our review of the preliminary findings originating from the OSLC group, we will begin with the epidemiological research and then proceed to the clinical outcome studies. Among the epidemiological results, the findings associating family management practices, family interaction, and peer influences to antisocial behavior will be reviewed first, followed by the findings relevant to drug use in preadolescence and adolescence, and approaches to screening at-risk youngsters developed at OSLC. We will then review the clinical outcome studies associated with the effectiveness of parent training approaches to treating families with conduct-problem children, especially as the findings pertain to developing a family-based intervention in preadolescence, focusing on reducing drug abuse.

The assumption underlying all of our research is that a multiagent and multimethod approach to measurement is optimal in terms of providing estimates of covariation that are more generalizable and valid. This approach was used to build all the psychological constructs discussed below, where each construct, whenever possible, is defined on the basis of multiple respondents (e.g., child, parent, teacher) and measurement modalities (e.g., telephone interviews, questionnaires, home observations). The approach for developing constructs is detailed in the Experimental Design Section.

FAMILY MANAGEMENT: A KEY DETERMINANT

Based on 20 years of treating families with antisocial children, we have come to consider family management as a key factor in the development of child problem behavior. Following insights gained from working with troubled families, we began the longitudinal research described below (Patterson, 1982). Our primary hypothesis was that family management skill deficits would be shown to precede the occurrence of more serious and chronic manifestations of problem behavior in adolescence. Secondarily, that treatment programs aimed at improving parenting skill deficits would demonstrate subsequent improvements in the child's problem behavior. A systematic review of previous longitudinal research corroborates the former hypothesis by showing that among the best *predictors* of male adolescent delinquency were early composite measures of family management (Loeber & Dishion, 1983). A treatment process study is in progress at the Oregon Social Learning Center (OSLC), directed by Drs. Gerald Patterson and Patricia Chamberlain, to determine if parent training results in improved family management skills when compared to traditional community intervention that does not have the parent training emphasis.

During the planning study, measures were developed for four family management skills: discipline, monitoring, positive reinforcement, and problem solving. These four skills reflected the emphasis of the parent training treatment agenda. The planning study provided our first opportunity to develop composite measures of parenting practices based on multiple respondents and measurement methods. Subsequently, in the longitudinal study, the measurement of these constructs was improved based on our pilot work. Also, we added a new skill, parent involvement, to our list of four. This dimension of child management reflects the degree to which the parent engages in activities with the child, measured by both the parent and child report.

Evidence supporting the relation between each of these skills to family process and child behavior is reviewed by Patterson, Reid and Dishion (in press). Analysis of the first cohort in the longitudinal study reveals these scores to be moderately intercorrelated (see Table 1). Correlational analyses between family management and composite indices revealed significant correlations between monitoring and discipline to composite measures of child antisocial behavior, drug sampling, academic skills, peer relations, self-esteem, and depression. These scores reflect virtually all the dimensions of child behavior that we have attempted to measure to date. Family problem solving was found to significantly covary with the child's antisocial behavior, academic skills, and depression. Parent involvement was found to covary with the child's peer relations and self-esteem, and positive reinforcement correlated with academic skills and self-esteem.

To understand the multivariate relation between these family management variables and child behavior, a canonical correlation was computed. This involved determining the linear dimensions that best describe the relation between the five family management skills (monitoring, discipline, positive reinforcement, problem solving, and parent involvement) with measures of child behavior (overt antisocial, covert antisocial, drug sampling, academic skills,

Table 1

Intercorrelations of Family-Management Constructs in the Longitudinal Study (Cohort 1, $n = 102$)

(from Patterson et al., in press)

	1	2	3	4	5
1. Monitoring	1.0				
2. Discipline	.29**	1.0			
3. Positive Reinforcement	.23**	.30***	1.0		
4. Problem Solving	.16*	.49***	.39***	1.0	
5. Parent Involvement	.14*	.15*	.33***	.10	1.0

*$p < .10$, **$p < .01$, ***$p < .001$

peer relations, self-esteem, depression). The results of this analysis (see Table 2) revealed that the first canonical dimension described parents who were highly skilled in discipline, monitoring, problem solving, parent involvement, and positive reinforcement. Such families tended to have children who were not antisocial, showed little

Table 2

Structure Coefficients for Canonical Correlations Analysis Relating Family Management to Multiple Measures of Child Adjustment

(from Patterson et al., in press)

	Canonical dimensions		
	1	2	3
Dependent variables			
Overt antisocial	-.67	-.26	-.34
Clandestine antisocial	-.53	-.26	.05
Drug sampling	-.62	.08	.58
Academic skills	.65	.37	.28
Peer relations	.59	-.25	.08
Self-esteem	.55	-.57	.13
Child depression	-.60	-.21	.31
Independent variables			
Monitoring	.76	-.17	-.39
Discipline	.80	.39	.28
Positive reinforcement	.39	-.17	.76
Problem solving	.44	.53	.31
Parent involvement	.40	-.71	.22
Canonical R	.67(44%)	.41(17%)	.24(6%)

drug sampling, and were highly socialized. As can be seen in Table 2, the second and third significant canonical dimensions did not yield patterns of covariation between these two sets of variables that were interpretable, nor were these dimensions especially powerful in terms of the amount of variance accounted for.

The first canonical dimension in the above analysis indicated that disruption in family management is often pervasive and includes all parenting skills, beginning with discipline and monitoring practices. In terms of child behavior, this analysis also revealed that high rates of antisocial behavior, more drug sampling, skill deficits, and lower intrapersonal adjustment accompany a general disruption in parenting practices. This finding is consistent with the hypothesis that early drug use is one of several products of a disrupted family process, as is low self-esteem and depression. The notion that early drug use and antisocial acts are different aspects of the same underlying dimension is consistent with the Jessors' perspective that both reflect adolescent problem behavior (Jessor & Jessor, 1975).

At the heart of the disruption is an underlying array of maladaptive parent-child interactions labelled as *coercive family processes* (Patterson, 1977; 1982). These moment-by-moment interaction sequences often serve as training for youngsters to practice coercive, antisocial, and rule-breaking behavior in other settings (Patterson, 1986; Patterson & Bank, 1986; Patterson, Dishion, & Bank, 1984; Patterson & Reid, 1984).

Early Training for Antisocial Behavior

The central assumption is that the parents' failure to deal effectively with coercive behaviors on an event-by-event basis sets in motion destructive family interactional sequences (Patterson, 1982). The primary process underlying the child's training in coercion is hypothesized to be negative reinforcement. That is, a three-step escape-avoidance sequence (e.g., parent – aversive child counteraversive – positive outcome for child) may occur literally hundreds of times each week in distressed families (Patterson, 1982). For antisocial children, it has been found that about 70% of the time the child's counterattack on a family member was followed by the attacker withdrawing or by a positive or neutral outcome (Patterson, 1982).

It is hypothesized that family management practices, if ineffective or provocative, can set this process in motion and can, in turn, be disrupted by the coercive interchanges with the child. It seems that parents can find themselves in the unhappy position of contributing to their child's behavior problems while trying to reduce them. It is also hypothesized that the more effective the child becomes in undermining the parents' attempts to socialize him or her, the less effective future attempts by the parents will be. Parent discipline practices are hypothesized to form the hub of family management skills; inconsistent, overly harsh, or reluctant discipline practices are hypothesized to initiate the early training process for antisocial behavior. It is also assumed that a wide variety of other variables have the potential to disrupt sound parenting practices. Among these are the child's temperament (Werner & Smith, 1977), economic stress (Dumas & Wahler, 1983; Elder, Caspi, & Van Nguyen, 1985), parental substance abuse (Dishion, Patterson, & Reid, 1985, November), and depression (Forgatch & Patterson, 1986).

The testing of the early training model has progressed through the analysis of the planning and longitudinal study concurrent data. In the planning study, Patterson et al. (1984) tested the above-described hypothesis as it applied to a multiagent and multimethod definition of physical fighting in fourth- and seventh-grade boys. These analyses fit the hypothesis that inconsistent discipline practices contributed to the likelihood of negative social exchanges among siblings (as measured by home observations) which, in turn, disrupted discipline practices (observer impressions). It was found that the child's negative exchanges with siblings were significantly related to a tendency to fight physically with peers at home and school. Poor peer relations were found to correlate with this generalized score of physical fighting. Inconsistent discipline practices were found to be indirectly related to physical fighting through the child's negative interactions with siblings. The model was tested in a structural equation format and was found to fit adequately the observed covariances among the individual measures analyzed.

The model described above was retested with the longitudinal study sample, with the revision of replacing the physical fighting dependent variable with a more generalized construct reflecting the full spectrum of antisocial behavior (e.g., lying, stealing, arguing, fighting) (Patterson & Bank, 1986) (see Figure 1). This generalized model was found to fit the data in Cohort I accurately. When the model was applied to the second cohort of the longitudinal study sample in replication, an adequate fit was obtained. The major divergence between the effect coefficients across the two cohorts was that the relation between inept discipline and the parents' monitoring practices found in Cohort I dropped to zero for Cohort II.

Taken together, the models tested were supported on concurrent data using physical fighting and general antisocial behavior as criterion variables, reflecting the hypothesis that antisocial behavior is trained in the home setting. The data were also consistent with the hypothesis that parent-child coercive interchanges serve to undermine the socialization process, especially in the unfortunate circumstance where the child is trained in a negative reinforcement paradigm to escalate and essentially dissipate the parents' bid to control or supervise his behavior.

Delinquent Behavior in Adolescence

In the general model of adolescent delinquent behavior, we hypothesize changes in the contributions of specific family management practices as the child matures into adolescence. For example, we assume the parents' ability to monitor the whereabouts and behavior of their adolescent is crucial in controlling his range of deviant behavior and peer associates. In regard to the latter influence, a considerable body of findings documents the enormous contribution of peers in the adolescents' patterned involvement in antisocial and illegal acts (Elliott, Huizinga, & Ageton, 1985; Snyder, Dishion, & Patterson, 1986; West & Farrington, 1973, 1977), as well as drug use (Dishion & Loeber, 1985; Huba & Bentler, 1983; Jessor, 1976; Jessor & Jessor, 1975; Kandel, 1973). Rarely, however, has the role of the parents' supervision practices been formulated as a primary determinant of the youngsters' association with delinquent peers and commission of delinquent acts or substance use.

A correlational model was formulated that placed parent monitor-

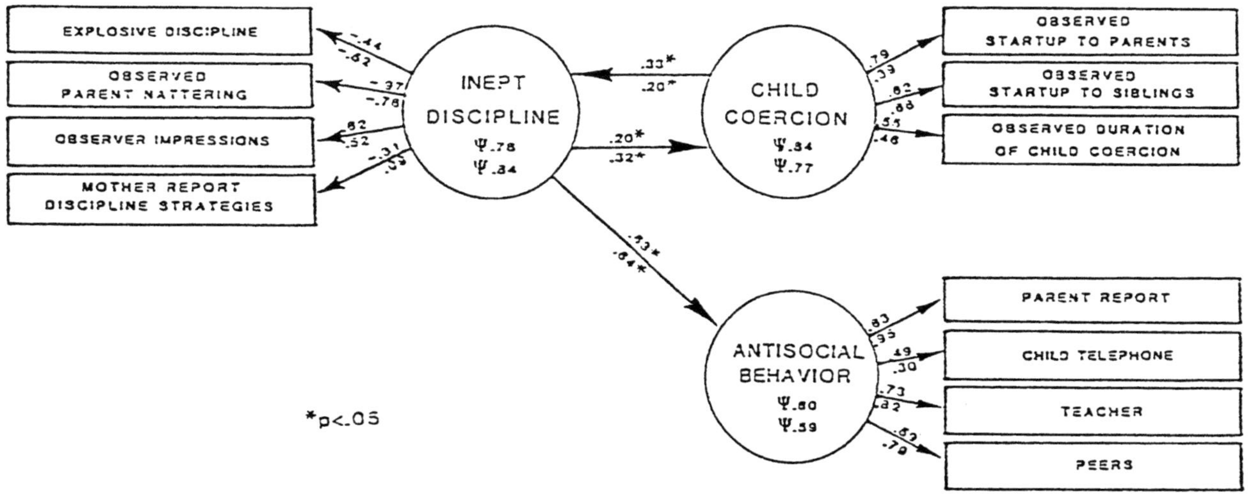

FIGURE 1. Basic Training for Antisocial Behavior (from Patterson et al., in press)

ing as a determinant of both the adolescents' association with deviant peers and delinquent behavior. This model is shown in Figure 2, with data from the adolescents (seventh- and tenth-grade boys) in the planning study. Deviant peers and parent monitoring were hypothesized to codetermine delinquent behavior at this age level. Social skills and academic skill deficits were considered to exacerbate the adolescents' drift towards delinquent behavior and a deviant group of peers. Using structural equation modeling, the model was tested in terms of its fit with the observed correlation matrix. The model was found to be consistent with the data, where effect coefficients emanating from deviant peers and parent monitoring to delinquent behavior were both statistically significant. This model, considered in conjunction with the large body of longitudinal findings on delinquency reviewed by Loeber and Dishion (1983), supports the hypothesis that family management skills are etiologically related to the patterned commitment of delinquent acts. Later, data will be reviewed from studies of the effectiveness of parent training for reducing the antisocial behavior of children that corroborates this conclusion.

It is noteworthy that social skill deficits correlated substantially with the child's association with deviant peers in the model presented in Figure 2. Longitudinal studies on peer affiliation processes indicate that children with poor social behavior and deviant attitudes tend to ally (Cohen, 1976; Kandel, 1978). Snyder, Dishion, and Patterson (1986) extended the delinquency model presented in Figure 2 by performing an in-depth analysis of factors assumed to be determinants of the child's association with deviant peers. In a multiple regression format, a composite measure of deviant peers (based on parent, peer, and child report) was regressed on the composite measures of social skills, poor parent monitoring, and antisocial attitudes (see Table 3). This analysis was computed separately for boys in the fourth, seventh, and tenth grades. It was found that social skill deficits covaried with the child's association with deviant peers in fourth and seventh grades, with poor parent monitoring significantly adding to the variance accounted for in seventh grade. In tenth grade, parent monitoring accounted for most of the explained variance in the deviant peers dependent variable. The

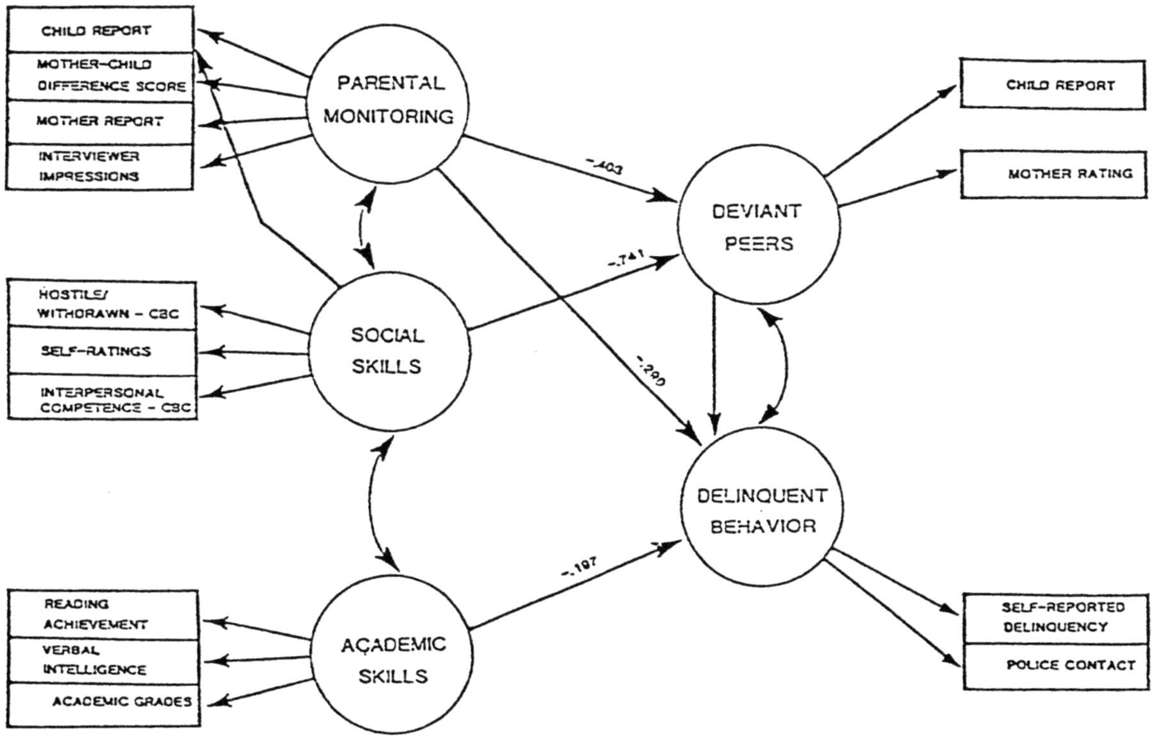

FIGURE 2. Two-Stage Model of Delinquency (from Patterson & Dishion, 1985)

Table 3

Regression of Deviant Peers on Social Skills, Parent Monitoring, and Measures of Attitudes

(from Snyder, Dishion, & Patterson, 1986)

	Grade 4	Grade 7	Grade 10	Across grades
R	.70	.78	.62	.67
F	(3,48)=15.16***	(3,45)=22.77***	(3,38)=7.32***	38.03***
Social skills	-.31**	-.42***	-.16	-.31
Poor monitoring	-.06	.12	.35*	.12[a]
Antisocial attitudes	.58***	.42***	.29*	.44***

[a]$p < .10$, *$p < .05$ **$p < .01$, ***$p < .001$

child's antisocial attitudes covaried with the deviant peers composite at all three grade levels.

It also appears that the effect of child characteristics such as social skill deficits and academic skill deficits may be additive. That is, in addition to deviant peers and poor monitoring, social skill deficits and antisocial attitudes may increase the likelihood that a youngster will commit future delinquent acts. An analysis completed in the Snyder et al. (1986) study provides moderate support for this hypothesis. Using a risk approach, adolescent boys were classified as being at risk (i.e., above the median) on one or more of the following factors: monitoring, peers, academic skills, social skills, and antisocial attitudes. Twenty-seven percent of those children at risk on two or more of these factors had police contact one year following our planning study assessment, compared to 36% of those children with no risk factor. Further, the risk status seemed to increase moderately with the number of risk factors up to four (see Figure 3). Only one child in the study sample was determined to be at risk on all five factors, and did not have a record of police contact.

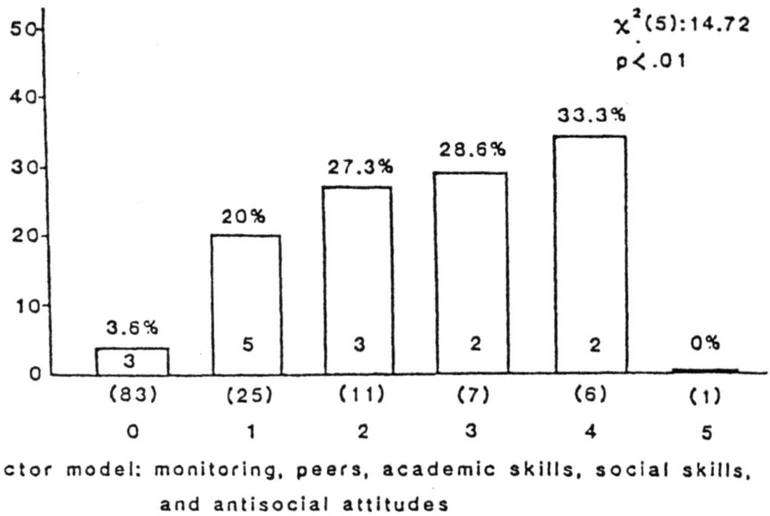

FIGURE 3. Predicting New Arrests for Seventh- and Tenth-Grade Boys (from Snyder, Patterson, & Dishion, in press)

One hypothesis that can be surmised from these findings is that effective interventions for youngsters at risk for delinquency might be enhanced if the interveners targeted both the child's skill deficits and peer associates and the parents' family management practices. We agree that this hypothesis is in need of systematic testing; however, it is assumed that even a minimal amount of change would be difficult to accomplish without the introduction of a treatment program that helped parents improve essential childrearing skills (e.g., supervising their adolescent).

At this point, we will proceed to our findings concerning the role of parents and peers in drug use in preadolescence and adolescence. The findings relating family management to antisocial/delinquent behavior and drug use are so similar that we are proposing that many of the findings on antisocial behavior cited above apply to considerations in designing a treatment intervention for early adolescent drug use. Also to be reviewed in this section are findings concerning our development of a multiple gating method for screening youngsters at risk for antisocial behavior and drug use, and evaluations of the effectiveness of parent training in helping families with conduct problems.

FAMILY MANAGEMENT AND CHILD DRUG USE

We define three phases of drug use referring to the child's *level* (frequency, amount) of use: (1) drug sampling; (2) patterned drug use, and (3) drug abuse. *Drug sampling* refers to experimentation with drugs, where *patterned use* refers to repeated use of any drug, say, at least once a month within a year time period. *Drug abuse* refers to a level of drug use that disrupts the developmental tasks of the adolescent, such as school performance and the establishment and maintenance of peer and familial relations, as well as levels of use that have adverse physiological consequences (Baumrind, Moselle, & Martin, in press).

We will first discuss findings from studies on *drug sampling* in preadolescent boys using data from the longitudinal study. The second set of findings are from the planning study and relate to adolescent *patterned drug use*, the relation between adolescent delinquency and drug use, and the development of screening procedures. The review of treatment outcome data for parent training is based on a series of clinical studies not overlapping with the longitudinal or planning studies.

A Model of Preadolescent Drug Sampling

Very little research has been conducted on the covariates of very early drug sampling prior to adolescence; in fact, we were unable to find in our literature review any research focusing on drug sampling in children approximately 10 years old. This is somewhat surprising in light of the epidemiological fact that individuals most likely to chronically abuse drugs in late adolescence and adulthood are those who began drug use in early adolescence (Robins & Przybeck, 1985). We assume that drug sampling in preadolescence relates to early patterned drug use, and therefore correlates of drug sampling in middle childhood may well become precursors of early drug use and later drug abuse. Longitudinal data are needed, however, before this hypothesis can be tested.

Child drug sampling was derived from a composite of both the parents' and child's reports. The parents' reports correlated reliably with the child's report of drug use ($r = .43$, $df = 99$, $p < .001$). This composite was then correlated with three sets of factors, reflecting the child's behavior (antisocial behavior) and intrapersonal functioning, the parents' childrearing skills, and the parents' own use of substances. These correlational analyses were reported by Dishion et al. (1985, November).

Among the child's characteristics that covaried with drug sampling in middle childhood were, foremost, the child's antisocial behavior ($r = .37$), his observed coercive behavior in the home ($r = .25$), the extent that his peers were characterized as antisocial ($r = .29$), and his low self-esteem ($r = .23$). Marginally correlated with drug sampling in middle childhood were measures of child depression ($r = .22$) and poor peer relations ($r = .14$). These findings accord with data reported by other longitudinal investigators, that drug use in adolescents is most correlated with measures of the child's deviant behavior (Elliott et al., 1985; Huba & Bentler, 1983; Jessor, 1976; Jessor & Jessor, 1975).

The relation between family management and child drug sampling was also examined. In this analysis, composite measures of parent monitoring, discipline, positive reinforcement, parent involvement, and problem solving were correlated with the drug use composite. Significant correlations were found between parent monitoring ($r = -.39$) and discipline ($r = -.28$). A significant correlation was also noted between a composite measure of the parent-child relationship (parent acceptance) and drug sampling in preadolescence ($r = -.31$). The remaining parenting factors described above were not found to correlate with drug sampling.

These data support the hypothesis that generalized measures of family management covary with the child's early drug use. This brings into question previous findings by other investigators showing only marginal and nonsignificant correlations between parenting practices and drug use. Perhaps previous findings were due to incomplete or inadequate measures of child-rearing or over-reliance on one data source, such as self-report questionnaires completed by the child (e.g., Jessor, 1976; Jessor & Jessor, 1975; Zucker, 1976). These findings, albeit correlational, converge with Baumrind's

(1985) research in that drug use among adolescents was associated with lack of monitoring by parents. Her data also identified poor monitoring practices as precursors to later female drug use, but less so for male drug use. As described above, our model assumes that monitoring can have both a direct and an indirect influence on the child's drug use. Low supervision allows the child more opportunity to be involved with peers who use drugs and increased latitude to become increasingly involved with drugs.

An analysis of the covariation between the parent's use of drugs and alcohol and the child's drug sampling proved very interesting. It was found that both the mother's and father's reported frequency of heavy drinking (greater than four drinks) correlated significantly with the youngster's experimentation with drugs, as well as the mother's report of marijuana and hard drug use and the father's score on the Michigan Alcoholism Screening Tests (Selzer, Vinokur, & van Rooijen, 1975). A combination of the scores for mother's and father's report of any drug use, to create a generalized score of parent drug use, also correlated significantly with the child's drug sampling ($r = .32$). It was also found that the parents' drug use covaried with their composite scores on parent monitoring ($r = -.27$, $p < .001$) and parent involvement ($r = -.23$, $p < .001$), reflecting that excessive use of substances may have a disruptive effect on parenting practices, or possibly reflect a generalized parent deviancy factor (Patterson et al., in press).

The strategy for developing a comprehensive structural equation model of the role of parents and peers in the child's early exploration with drugs was to construct a model with data from Cohort I ($n = 100$) of the longitudinal study and replicate it with data from Cohort II ($n = 100$). The model constructed in Cohort I was theory-driven to the extent that the primary hypothesis was that poor parent monitoring was the primary determinant of both deviant peer influences and child drug sampling. Parent drug use was assumed to be a disruptor of the parents' ability to monitor their child, and as we saw earlier, the parents' involvement with the child. The model developed in Cohort I and replicated in Cohort II is shown in Figure 4. Because effect coefficients in structural equation models are sensitive to a small sample size (Dwyer, 1983), the model for the combined sample ($n = 168$) is presented in Figure 1.

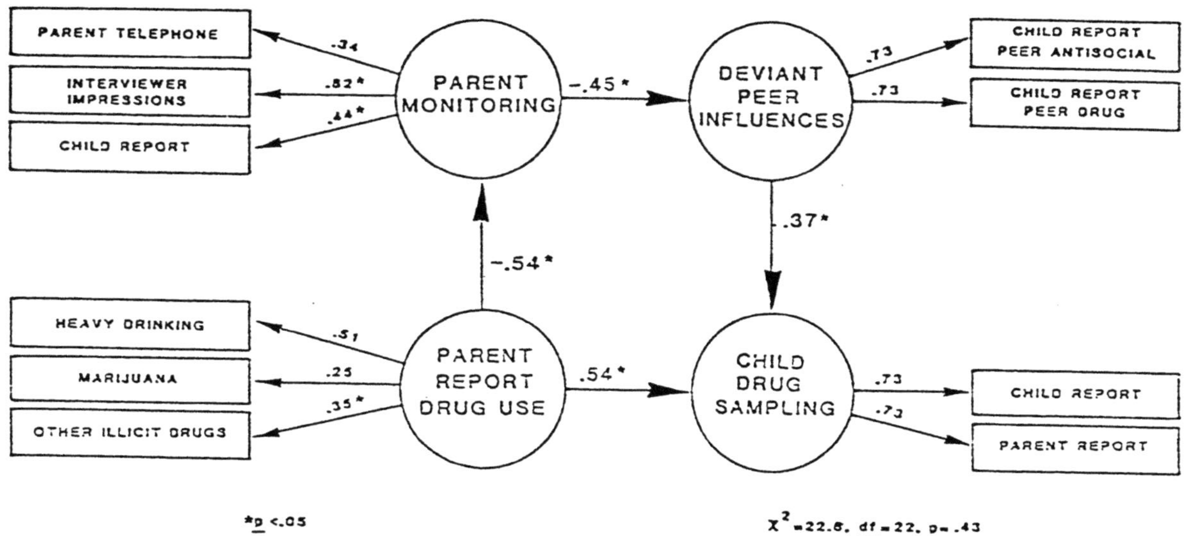

FIGURE 4. Correlation Model of Drug Sampling in Middle Childhood (N = 200) (from Dishion, Patterson, & Reid, 1986)

Two competing versions of this model were examined in Cohort I. The first version was that parent monitoring had a direct effect on the child's early exploration with drugs and an indirect effect through allowing the child increased exposure to deviant peer influences. The direct effect between parent monitoring and child drug sampling was found to approach zero and not contribute to the explanatory power of the model. It was the indirect effect of monitoring on drug exploration, mediated by deviant peer influences, that was found to be significant. Replication in Cohort II confirmed this conclusion. The model shown in Figure 4 accounted for 51% of the variance in the child's drug use in Cohort I and 44% of the variance in Cohort II. Combining the two cohorts yielded results similar to that for Cohort I: 51% of the variance in child drug sampling was accounted for.

The development and testing of the above-described model is a promising first step toward designing an early intervention that has empirical validity. When considering the findings for the relation between family management and preadolescent drug sampling and antisocial behavior together, a reasonable hypothesis is that an intervention targeting both discipline and monitoring practices could have significant bearing on the subsequent drug use of at-risk children. Note in this regard that both inept discipline practices and parent drug use may serve as disruptors of the parents' monitoring practices, as well as other factors impinging on parenting practices such as stress, drug use, marital discord, and single-parent status (Patterson, 1982). For this reason, the parent training intervention at OSLC focuses on helping parents effectively deal with these disruptors of parenting.

ADOLESCENT DRUG USE

The analysis of family and peer factors associated with adolescent drug use reported below were based on the planning study sample of adolescents, representing approximately 70 12- to 13-year-old and 60 15- to 16-year-old boys (Dishion & Loeber, 1985). The purpose of this study was to examine the relative influence of parents and peers on the adolescents' use of marijuana and alcohol, based on data from multiple sources such as child and parent interviews, repeated telephone interviews, and home observer impressions of parenting practices. A number of other researchers have also examined the question of the peers' and parents' influence on drug use in adolescence and generally concur that peers often exert the strongest direct effect (Elliott & Huizinga, 1983; Huba, Wingard, & Bentler, 1981; Jessor, 1976; Jessor & Jessor, 1975; Kandel, 1973; Noll & Zucker, 1983, August; Zucker, 1976; Zucker & Barron, 1973). The assumption has often been that the majority of the influence from parents comes from their own drug use. However, there are some data that address the relation of the role of parenting practices to alcohol use and abuse in adolescence and problem drinking in young adulthood. For example, the Jessors' looked at the relation between the child's report of parental control and marijuana (Jessor & Jessor, 1975) and alcohol use (Jessor, 1976) and found a low but significant effect to marijuana use and a nonsignificant effect to alcohol use. More data exist on the role of early parenting practices and later problem drinking, as reviewed by Zucker (1976). In this review, a very consistent finding was that families characterized by high family conflict and a rejecting mother in early childhood produced both males and females who were problem drinkers. Parental neglect was often a factor that predicted later problem drinking, as well as lax discipline and poor supervision. As might be expected, many of these parents were antisocial themselves, as well as problem drinkers (Zucker, 1976).

The role of exposure to drug use among peers has been consistently shown to be a strong covariate of substance use in adolescence (Elliott et al., 1985; Huba et al., 1981; Huba & Bentler, 1983; Kandel, 1973, Kandel & Faust, 1975; Pederson, Baskerville, & Lefcoe, 1983). An interesting extension of this research is the work reported by Friedman, Lichtenstein, and Biglan (1985), in which intense analyses were executed of the situations where adolescents began smoking. Again, these data implicate unsupervised time with peers as among the situations with the highest risk. In fact, peers were present in 89% of the initial exposure incidents. This percentage breaks down into 57% friends, 20% acquaintances, and 11% siblings. However, in only 30% of the initiating incidents of smoking tobacco did the subject actually feel pressure to smoke from peers. This last datum speaks to the probable limited effectiveness of an exclusive peer influence intervention strategy. It seems likely that the exploration of smoking tobacco was often a mutual adventure on the part of the subject and his/her peers.

In our analysis of adolescent drug use, both alcohol and marijuana use were correlated with measures of deviant peers, parent monitoring, and discipline, and the parents' self-report on alcohol use (Dishion & Loeber, 1985). These correlations revealed a substantial correlation between monitoring, discipline, and deviant peers to both marijuana and alcohol use. However, the parents' use of alcohol was only slightly correlated with the boys' marijuana use, although significantly so for the mother ($r = .17$, $df = 128$, $p < .05$). The strong correlation between monitoring and the adolescent's self-report of alcohol and marijuana use is consistent with our hypothesis that the influence of poor monitoring practices becomes increasingly relevant to drug use in adolescence, especially to drug abuse. As different from during the preadolescent period, parent monitoring should have both a direct and an indirect influence on drug use during adolescence, especially on drug abuse.

The hypothesis that parent monitoring would have a direct and an indirect influence on drug use during adolescence was examined for marijuana and alcohol use separately in a multiple regression format, and is presented in Table 4. The hypothesis was partially confirmed when marijuana use served as the dependent variable but was only partially confirmed for alcohol use. That is, both deviant peers and parent monitoring contributed uniquely to the variance accounted for, producing standard partial beta coefficients of $-.26$ and .31, respectively. The mother's report of her alcohol use did not contribute to the regression on alcohol or marijuana use. In interpreting these findings, it should be kept in mind that the planning study sample was biased, in that deviance was underrepresented and middle and higher socioeconomic status were overrepresented. Also, the age range consisted of seventh and tenth graders, and therefore there may have been restricted ranges on all variables, but especially on the parents' alcohol use and the adolescents' report of drug use. In addition, as noted in the preadolescent model, the frequency of parent drinking was less related to the child's drug sampling than the problems resulting from drinking. Furthermore, the composite score of parent drug use correlated with drug sam-

Table 4

Multiple Regressions of Self-Reported Drug Use on Parent Monitoring, Deviant Peers, and Mother Alcohol Use (N = 91)

(from Loeber & Dishion, 1983)

Dependent variable	Independent variables	Standardized beta coefficient	(R) R^2 Adjusted[a] R^2	F
Self-reported alcohol use	Parent monitoring	−.19	(.41)	
	Mother alcohol use	−.01	.17	5.98**
	Deviant peers	.28*	Adj. R^2=.14	
Self-reported marijuana use	Parent monitoring	−.26*	(.52)	11.01**
	Mother alcohol use	.10	.27	
	Deviant peers	.31*	Adj. R^2=.25	

[a]Adjusted for estimated shrinkage under cross validation

*$p < .05$, **$p < .001$

pling more than any single index. Such a composite measure of drug use was not available on the adolescent sample in the planning study.

ADOLESCENT ANTISOCIAL BEHAVIOR AND DRUG USE

Although considerable evidence has accumulated indicating overlap between the development of antisocial behavior and drug use, the overlap is not perfect. We agree with the position that there are probably multiple pathways leading to drug use in adolescence (Bry, Pedroza, & Pandina, 1985; Elliott et al., 1985), but we hypothesize that family and peer factors define the process the majority of adolescents experience along the way. One useful approach to unraveling possible alternative pathways to drug use in adolescence is dividing a sample into subgroups and looking at profiles on relevant factors related to the child's behavior. For example, Pulkkinen (1983) followed this strategy in a longitudinal study conducted in Finland. Adolescents were divided into subgroups on the basis of their antisocial behavior and substance use. It was found that those youngsters who were not antisocial but used drugs (labeled *revelers*) were very similar to nondeviant youngsters in all respects.

We have found this also in our own research (Dishion & Loeber, 1985). Figure 5 shows the profiles of youngsters classified as delinquent drug users, nondelinquent drug users, and nondelinquent abstainers. In this analysis, drug use was divided into alcohol and marijuana use. As can be seen, those youngsters who use drugs regularly (at least once a month over a year) showed an almost identical profile to that of the nondelinquent abstainer group on the measures of peer deviancy and parent monitoring. It was the adolescents who used drugs and had an official record of police contact for nondrug offenses who were the most pathogenic on these variables.

Noting the consistent covariation between antisocial behavior and drug use across developmental (preadolescence vs. adolescence) periods and the predictive relation between early problem behavior and later drug use and abuse, it follows that at least some of what has been learned about family interventions with conduct-problem children may have a strong application to the treatment and prevention of drug abuse. In the following section, we will review briefly the history of the development of a parent training model for the treatment of conduct problems. We will then discuss possible extensions to designing family-based interventions for early drug users, given the apparent overlap in etiologies.

IDENTIFYING HIGH RISK FAMILIES: MULTIPLE GATING

Approximately 5% of the adolescents in the United States are likely to use drugs at abusive levels, and most of these will be involved in multiple drug use (Brennan, 1979). The problem is, how do you accurately identify a risk sample when the target behavior has such a low base rate? A technical barrier in executing an

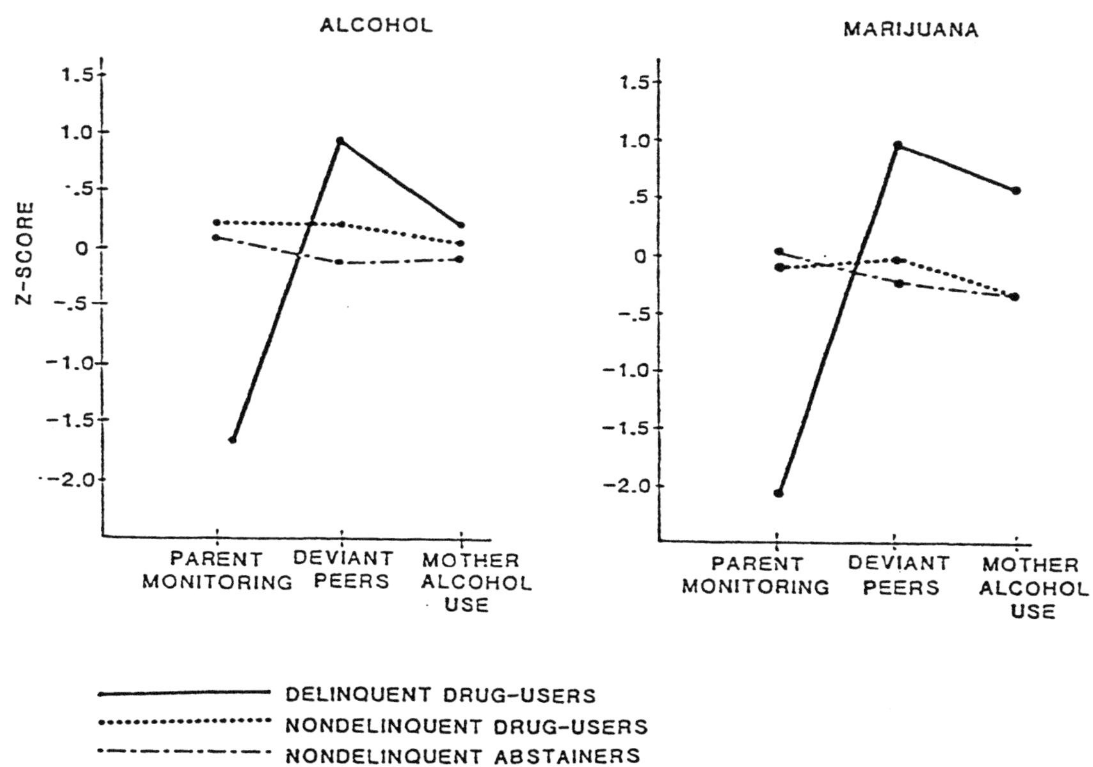

FIGURE 5. Profiles of Deliquent Drug Users Compared to Nondelinquent Drug Users and Abstainers on Family Management, Deviant Peers, and Mother Alcohol Use (from Dishion & Loeber, 1985)

intervention with a risk sample is to identify youngsters most in need of treatment in a cost-effective way. However, progress has been made on the problem of identifying youngsters at risk for chronic delinquency, which can be readily applied to the problem of adolescent drug abuse.

Loeber, Dishion, and Patterson (1984) presented an approach to the problem based on Cronbach's stage-sequential assessment strategy (Cronbach & Gleser, 1965). The idea is straightforward. Conceptualize the assessment as a series of stages or gates, each employing a more powerful, albeit more costly, set of predictors. The strategy is to sequentially apply assessment instruments to a sample of youngsters, successively redefining the risk sample by rejecting youngsters who are clearly not at risk (see Figure 6). In the Loeber et al. (1984) study, the teacher ratings of child school behavior was used as the first gate, the mother report on six brief telephone reports the second gate, and the third gate consisted of a structured interview with the parent and child on family management practices. The three gates combined produced a total hit rate of 88.2%, with a false-positive rate of 43.8%. Furthermore, six of the seven multiple offenders (three or more police contacts, official records) were accurately identified in the risk group (85.7%). In a follow-up study conducted a year later, the same three gates achieved a hit rate of 81.4% and a false-positive rate of 43%. In the follow-up study, 8 of the 10 multiple offenders were correctly identified.

This is an appealing strategy. Its main advantage lies in the possi-

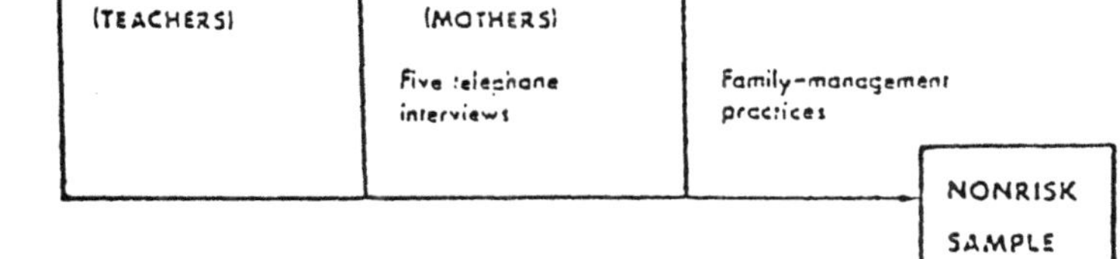

FIGURE 6. Diagram of the Multiple-Gating Design for a Three-Gate Procedure (from Loeber, Dishion, & Patterson, 1984)

bility of using the most powerful assessment battery one can find at minimum cost. Because of the correlation between the child's antisocial behavior and drug sampling behavior in middle childhood (Dishion et al., 1985, November) and because 60% of the adolescent delinquents in our planning study sample were also regular drug users, we assume that the multiple gating screening will apply to screening samples for families with children at risk for early patterned drug use.

To determine the feasibility of screening referrals at intake in the proposed study, the Parent Child Behavior Checklist (Achenbach & Edelbrock, 1983) was examined as a screening measure. In the planning study, the parents' report of their young adolescent (seventh to tenth grade) associating with a deviant peer group and using drugs identified a group, 55% (20/36) of which were *patterned* alcohol or marijuana users. This screening measure, however, missed 51% (21/40) of those youngsters reporting regular drug use ($\chi^2 = 14.7, p < .001$). This false negative error rate would be less of a problem in the proposed study because youngsters reporting regular drug use would be admitted into the study. It is unlikely in this clinical setting that parents would be unaware of their youngster's involvement in a delinquent peer group or drug use, since families are essentially self-referred. This type of screening, however, would reduce the density of low-risk but concerned parents in the treatment samples.

The measures being collected this year on the third year of the longitudinal study reflect an intensive assessment of the child's peer group, based on parent report in the Child Behavior Checklist and the telephone interviews. Prior to the beginning of this study, we would develop a screening measure based on these new measures with the 12-year-old boys in the longitudinal study.

CONCLUSIONS/SUMMARY

The problem of adolescent drug abuse has been addressed by two approaches. The first approach is the use of intensive residential and outpatient treatment groups for youngsters involved in self-destructive levels of drug use (Hubbard, Cavanaugh, Craddock, & Rachal, 1985). Although the outcome data from these treatment facilities is respectable given the multitude of problems these youngsters present, the dropout rate has been estimated at approximately one-third of those admitted, an alarmingly high rate for a population of youngsters with serious adjustment problems. The second approach included the spread of primary prevention programs to ameliorate the conditions hypothesized to cause adolescent drug abuse. This approach is appealing, but considering that only about 5% of adolescents will eventually become involved in drug abuse (Brennan, 1979), over 90% of all adolescents are not at serious risk for abusing drugs. This low base rate problem makes it difficult to concentrate the prevention resources on those youngsters most in need of help. Furthermore, it becomes extremely difficult to evaluate the impact when many of the intervention recipients are either abstainers (approximately 50%) or involved in very low levels of drug use and not at risk for drug abuse.

The research summarized in this chapter reflects the orientation that negative adolescent outcomes, such as delinquency and drug use, arise within the family and are later exacerbated by the influence of peers. The process models described in this chapter are correlational and thus should be interpreted with some caution. However, these models are consistent with longitudinal data showing childrearing factors to precede adolescent problems such as delinquency and drug use. Further, peer variables have been shown to temporally precede adolescent drug use and delinquency (e.g., Elliott et al., 1985).

The empirical guidelines that arise out of this research are that an effective family intervention might target the parent's monitoring practices, the adolescent's peer associates, the parent's use of drugs, and the adolescent's level of social skills and antisocial behavior. However, the cautious reader may have some justifiable reservations at this point. Are we concluding causality on the basis of correlational data? No, we are suggesting that we, as a clinical and research group, are approaching a stage in our development when we are in a position to act on our limited empirical base. As pointed out by Cook and Campbell (1979) and by Dwyer (1983), in the event that longitudinal research showed the temporal ordering of events we hypothesize, the causality inference would be elusive. What is needed at this stage is a more active stance in determining the utility of these ideas in helping prevent maladaptive behavior in youngsters at risk and curtailing those processes for youngsters already experiencing problems. The active stance we refer to is the application of these findings to the design of a randomized longitudinal experiment, a step that would yield clinical as well as theoretical information. We propose two approaches to intervening on these variables that represent the major outpatient intervention modalities in the field of adolescent drug use today.

Progress in Parent Training

Parent training at OSLC is based on social learning principles of child management. The primary assumption underlying the parent training model is that effective child management practices can be taught to parents that will result in a reduction of child problem behavior. The beginning test of this treatment approach took the form of a series of single-subject intervention designs (Patterson & Brodsky, 1966; Patterson, McNeal, Hawkins, & Phelps, 1967; Wahler, Winkle, Peterson, & Morrison, 1965). The parent training procedures used with these pilot cases were buttressed with weekly staff meetings to discuss problems and successes arising in each case and implications for developing a more generalized treatment strategy (Patterson, 1980).

The results of these single-subject interventions warranted testing the more generalized treatment strategy (Patterson, Reid, Jones, & Conger, 1975), as well as the refinement of treatment evaluation criteria, such as home observations (Reid, 1978) and parent daily telephone reports (PDR). Follow-up data for families treated with the more generalized parent training model showed reductions in observed child problem behaviors in the home from treatment to 12-month follow-up (Patterson, 1974; Patterson, Cobb, & Ray, 1973). Investigators joining the OSLC group and receiving training in the OSLC parent training model demonstrated that treatment effects were replicable with a new group of therapists using similar outcome criteria (Fleischman, 1981; Fleischman & Szykula, 1981; Weinrott, Bauske, & Patterson, 1979).

Subsequent studies focused on comparing this parent training program to other approaches in the community geared towards treating families with conduct-disordered children. The most systematic evaluation of this question is reported by Patterson, Chamberlain, and Reid (1982). Pre-post evaluations were conducted on cases randomly assigned to a treatment or waiting-list control group. A two-way analysis of variance for repeated measures was conducted on pre-post observation (i.e., total aversive behavior) scores for the two groups. The interaction of groups by phase was significant. These findings are summarized in Figure 7. At termination, 75% of OSLC-treated cases were within the normal range. Both groups showed significant reductions in symptoms reported to have occurred in the last 24 hours (PDR). Ninety percent of the parents in the experimental group and 25% of the parents in the comparison group provided global ratings of treatment as having been very effective.

The findings supported the hypothesis that the decrease in deviant child behavior was specific to the parent training procedures and not simply to the passage of time or as an outcome of receiving another type of treatment typically employed in the same commu-

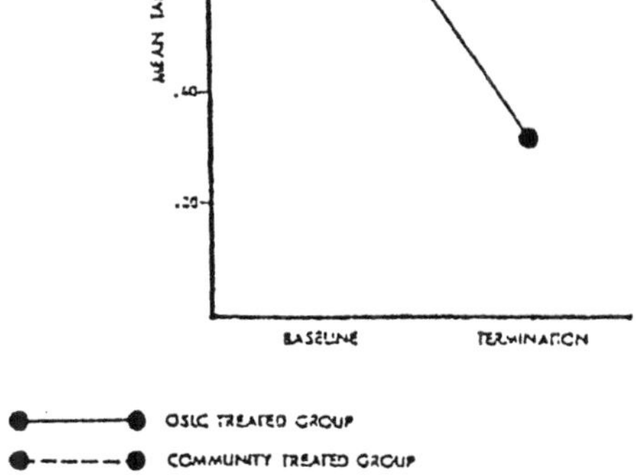

FIGURE 7. Average Rate per Minute of Child Deviant Behavior for Two Groups (from Patterson, Chamberlain, & Reid, 1982)

nity. Other controlled evaluations of the parent training model yielded less optimistic results (e.g., Bernal, Klinnert, & Schultz, 1980). Two characteristics of such studies, however, impede interpretation: (1) the inclusion of time-limited and highly structured treatment agenda, often administered in a group design, and (2) the use of graduate students as therapists as opposed to more highly trained and experienced therapists.

More recently, the parent training family intervention has been extended to the treatment of families with youngsters with documented multiple police contacts and to families referred for child abuse (Reid, 1984). Preliminary evaluations reveal that, for the multiple offending delinquent group, parent training tended to have a long-term effect lowering the recidivism rate to the state institution and the amount of time spent in institutions following treatment (Marlowe, Reid, Patterson, & Weinrott, 1986). In the extension to the treatment of child abuse, preliminary evaluations reveal reductions in the parents' use of high-amplitude physical discipline strategies following treatment (Reid, 1984).

Peer Training Intervention

In the area of substance abuse prevention a number of alternative peer intervention strategies have been developed and found to be effective in reducing the percentages of youngsters initiating tobacco use and becoming regular smokers. Some studies show effects on marijuana use as well (Botvin & Wills, 1985). Most of these interventions have been offered in a school setting, with teachers, counselors, older peers, and interns providing treatment (Botvin & Wills, 1985). Botvin and Wills (1985) reviewed four alternative peer intervention strategies in terms of the intervention target, measures of mediating factors, and outcome data. The approach most consistent with our theoretical/empirical model is the peer-based cognitive-behavioral intervention described by Botvin, Baker, Renick, Filazzola, and Botvin (1984). The intervention developed by Botvin and colleagues has been described as a broad-spectrum intervention design where refusal/assertion skills are developed in youngsters as well as a wide range of other skills deemed crucial for social adjustment and drug-abuse prevention. The target of the Botvin Life Skills Training is to train assertiveness, general social skills, anxiety/stress reduction, decision making/problem solving, and accurate information related to substance use.

This intervention strategy has been extensively evaluated. Evaluation studies reveal that the Life Skills Training program was effective in reducing initiation into tobacco, alcohol, and marijuana use. One evaluation revealed that groups led by older peers were more effective than groups led by teachers (Botvin et al., 1984). The author speculated, however, that the teacher-led condition was characterized by "implementation failure." Peer-led groups were given much more supervision by project staff and were monitored more closely than teacher-led groups. A previous study by Botvin (cited in Botvin & Wills, 1985) did indicate that teachers were successful in effecting reductions in the percentage of children initiating drug use.

Treatment Context and Process Change

Obviously, both the parent training and peer training interventions are viable approaches to intervening to prevent premature drug involvement. Our data indicate that factors such as peer associates, social skills, parent monitoring, and parent drug use need to be addressed for an intervention to be effective. The data also indicate that the process leading to adolescent drug use can potentially be identified earlier than adolescence and that it is theoretically and practically conceivable to identify groups of youngsters at risk for delinquency and possibly drug use.

An example of an experiment that might be conducted is to identify a group of young adolescents (approximately ages 11 to 13) and randomly assign them to one of four treatment conditions: (1) parent training with special emphasis on monitoring skills, (2) peer intervention along the guidelines established by Botvin and others, (3) a combined intervention incorporating both a family and peer intervention, and (4) a no-treatment control group.

An essential ingredient of this study would be to evaluate the effects of each of the interventions on the list of variables implicated as determinants in the process leading to adolescent deviancy. This level of evaluation of a treatment program proposes to look at changes in factors that mediate treatment outcome (Dwyer, 1983; Judd & Kenny, 1981). Of course, treatment outcome is evaluated as well, that is, the specific effect of the intervention on subsequent drug use and problem behavior. We would hypothesize that peer interventions and parent training would effect statistically reliable change in comparison to the no-treatment group, but that the most significant change would most likely be effected by the combined intervention implemented in the context of peers and parents. The rationale underlying this approach is that the combined intervention would more comprehensively address the process factors implicated in the epidemiological research. Thus, the empirical guidelines dictate the next step in the clinical research agenda.

REFERENCES

Achenbach, T. M., & Edelbrock, C. (1983). *Manual for the Child Behavior Checklist and the revised Child Behavior Profile*. Burlington, VT: Thomas M. Achenbach.

Baumrind, D. (1985). Familial antecedents of adolescent drug use: A developmental perspective. In C. L. Jones & R. J. Battjes (Eds.), *Etiology of drug abuse: Implications for prevention* (NIDA Research Monograph 56). Washington, DC: NIDA.

Baumrind, D., Moselle, K., & Martin, J. A. (in press). Adolescent drug abuse research: A critical examination from a developmental perspective. In *Advances in Alcohol & Substance Abuse*.

Bernal, M. E., Klinnert, M. D., & Schultz, L. A. (1980). Outcome evaluation of behavioral parent training and client-centered parent counseling for children with conduct problems. *Journal of Applied Behavioral Analysis, 13*, 677-691.

Botvin, G. J., Baker, E., Renick, N., Filazzola, P. D., & Botvin, E. M. (1984). A cognitive-behavioral approach to substance abuse prevention. *Addictive Behaviors, 9*, 137-147.

Botvin, G. J., & Wills, T. A. (1985). Personal and social skills training: Cognitive-Behavioral approaches to substance abuse prevention. In C. S. Bell & R. Battjes (Eds.), *Prevention research: Deterring drug abuse among children and adolescents*, Research Monograph No. 63. Washington, DC: NIDA.

Brennan, T. (1979). Patterns of multiple drug use in a national adolescent sample: A multivariate approach. *The National Youth Survey Project Report No. 6*. Boulder, CO: Behavioral Research Institute.

Bry, B. H. (1985, November). *Family approaches to the treatment of adolescent drug abuse*. Paper presented at the NIDA Technical Review Meeting on Adolescent Drug Abuse: Analysis of Treatment Research. Bethesda, MD.

Bry, B. H., Pedroza, M., & Pandina, R. J. (1985). Number of risk factors predicts three year probabilities of heavy drug and alcohol use in adolescents. Manuscript. (Available from the Graduate School of Applied Professional Psychology and Center on Alcohol Studies, Rutgers State University, Box 814, Piscataway, NJ 08854.)

Cohen, J. M. (1976). Sources of peer group homogeneity. *Sociology of Education, 50*, 227-241.

Cook, T. D., & Campbell, D. T. (1979). *Quasi-experimentation: Design and analysis issues for field settings*. Boston: Houghton Mifflin Co.

Cronbach, L. J., & Glesar, G. C. (1965). *Psychological tests and personnel decisions*. Urbana: University of Illinois Press.

Dishion, T. J., & Loeber, R. (1985). Male adolescent marijuana and alcohol use: The role of parents and peers revisited. *American Journal of Drug and Alcohol Abuse, 11*, 11-25.

Dishion, T. J., Patterson, G. R., & Reid, J. B. (1985, Nov.). *An applied model of parent and peer factors associated with drug sampling in middle childhood: Implications for the prevention of adolescent drug use*. Paper presented at the Technical Review meeting on Adolescent Drug Abuse: Analyses of Treatment Research, sponsored by the National Institute of Drug Abuse, Bethesda, MD.

Donovan, J. E., Jessor, R., & Jessor, L. (1983). Problem drinking in adolescence and young adulthood: A follow-up study. *Journal of Studies on Alcohol, 44*(1), 109-137.

Dumas, J. E., & Wahler, R. G. (1983). Predictors of treatment outcome in parent training: Mother insularity and socioeconomic disadvantage. *Behavioral Assessment, 5*, 301-313.

Dwyer, J. H. (1983). *Statistical models for the social and behavioral sciences*. New York: Oxford University Press.

Elder, G. H., Caspi, A., & Van Nguyen, T. (1985). Resourceful and vulnerable children: Family influences in hard times. In R. K. Silbereisen & K. Eyforth (Eds.), *Development in context: Integrative perspectives on youth development*.

Elliott, D. S., & Huizinga, D. E. (1983). Social class and delinquent behavior in a national youth panel: 1976-1980. *Criminology, 21*, 149-177.

Elliott, D. S., Huizinga, D., & Ageton, S. S. (1985). *Explaining delinquency and drug use*. Beverly Hills, CA: Sage Publications.

Fleischman, M. J. (1981). A replication of Patterson's "Intervention for boys with conduct problems." *Journal of Consulting and Clinical Psychology, 49*, 342-351.

Fleischman, M. J., & Szykula, S. (1981). A community setting replication of a social learning treatment for aggressive children. *Behavior Therapy, 12*(1), 15.

Forgatch, M. S., & Patterson, G. R. (1986). A process model of maternal depression. Manuscript.

Friedman, L. S., Lichenstein, E., & Biglan, A. (1985). Smoking onset among teens: An empirical analysis of initial situations. *Addictive Behaviors, 10*, 1-13.

Huba, G. J., & Bentler, P. M. (1983). Causal models of the development of law abidance and its relationship to psychosocial factors in drug use. In W. F. Laufer & J. M. Day (Eds.), *Personality theory, moral development and criminal behavior*. Lexington, MA: Lexington Books.

Huba, G. J., Wingard, J. A., & Bentler, P. M. (1981). A comparison of two latent variable causal models for adolescent drug use. *Journal of Personality and Social Psychology, 40*(1), 180-193.

Hubbard, R. L., Cavanaugh, E. R., Craddock, S. G., & Rachal, J. V. (1985). In A. S. Friedmas & G. M. Beschner (Eds.), *NIDA Treatment Monograph Series, DHHS Pub. No. 85-1342*, Treatment services for adolescent substance abusers.

Jessor, R. (1976). Predicting time of onset of marijuana use: A developmental study of high school youth. *Journal of Consulting and Clinical Psychology, 44*(1), 125-134.

Jessor, R., & Jessor, S. L. (1975). Adolescent development and the onset of drinking. *Journal of Studies on Alcohol, 36*(1), 27-51.

Judd, C. M., & Kenny, D. A. (1981). Process analysis: Estimating mediation in treatment evaluations. *Evaluation Review, 5*(5), 602-619.

Kandel, D. (1973). Adolescent marijuana use: Role of parents and peers. *Science, 181*, 1067-1081.

Kandel, D. (Ed.) (1978). *Longitudinal research on drug use*. New York: John Wiley & Sons.

Kandel, D., & Faust, R. (1975). Sequence and stages in patterns of adolescent drug use. *Archives of General Psychiatry, 32*, 923-932.

Loeber, R., & Dishion, T. J. (1983). Boys who fight at home and in school: Family conditions influencing cross-setting consistency. *Journal of Consulting and Clinical Psychology, 52*(5), 759-768.

Loeber, R., Dishion, T. J., & Patterson, G. R. (1984). Multiple gating: A multistage assessment procedure for identifying youths at risk for delinquency. *Journal of Research in Crime and Delinquency, 21*, 7-32.

Marlowe, H., Reid, J. B., Patterson, G. R., & Weinrott, M. (1986). Treating adolescent multiple offenders: A comparison and follow-up of parent training for families of chronic delinquents. Manuscript. Oregon Social Learning Center.

Noll, R. B., & Zucker, R. A. (1983, August). *Developmental findings from an alcoholic vulnerability study: The preschool years*. Paper presented at the Annual Meeting of the American Psychological Association, Anaheim, CA.

Patterson, G. R. (1974). Interventions for boys with conduct problems: Multiple settings, treatments, and criteria. *Journal of Consulting and Clinical Psychology, 42*(4), 471-481.

Patterson, G. R. (1977). A three-stage functional analysis for children's coercive behaviors: A tactic for developing a performance theory. In D. Baer, B. C. Etzel, & J. M. LeBlanc (Eds.), *New developments in behavioral research: Theory, methods, and applications*. Hillsdale, NJ: Lawrence Erlbaum Associates.

Patterson, G. R. (1980). Treatment for children with conduct problems: A review of outcome studies. In J. Fesbach & A. Fraczek (Eds.), *Aggression and behavior change: Biological and social processes* (pp. 83-132). New York: Praeger Publishers.

Patterson, G. R. (1982). *A social learning approach to family intervention. III. Coercive family process*. Eugene, OR: Castalia Publishing Co.

Patterson, G. R. (1986). Performance models for antisocial boys. *American Psychologist, 41*, 432-444.

Patterson, G. R., & Bank, L. (1986). Bootstrapping your way in the nomological thicket. *Behavioral Assessment, 8*, 49-73.

Patterson, G. R., & Brodsky, G. (1966). A behavior modification program for a child with multiple problem behaviors. *Journal of Child Psychology and Psychiatry, 7*, 277-295.

Patterson, G. R., Chamberlain, P., & Reid, J. B. (1982). A comparative evaluation of parent training procedures. *Behavior Therapy, 13*, 638-650.

Patterson, G. R., Cobb, J. A., & Ray, R. S. (1973). A social engineering technology for retraining the families of aggressive boys. In H. E. Adams & I. P. Unikel (Eds.), *Issues and trends in behavior therapy* (pp. 139-224). Springfield, IL: Charles C Thomas.

Patterson, G. R., Dishion, T. J., & Bank, L. (1984). Family interaction: A process model of deviancy training. In L. Eron (Ed.), special edition of *Aggressive Behavior, 10*, 253-267.

Patterson, G. R., McNeal, S., Hawkins, N., & Phelps, R. (1967). Reprogramming the social environment. *Journal of Child Psychology and Psychiatry, 8*, 181-195.

Patterson, G. R., & Reid, J. B. (1984). Social interactional processes within the family: The study of moment-by-moment family transactions in which human social development is imbedded. *Journal of Applied Developmental Psychology, 5*, 237-262.

Patterson, G. R., Reid, J. B., & Dishion, T. J. (in press). *Antisocial boys*. Eugene, OR: Castalia Publishing Co.

Patterson, G. R., Reid, J. B., Jones, R. R., & Conger, R. E. (1975). *A social learning approach to family intervention. I. Families with aggressive children*. Eugene, OR: Castalia Publishing Co.

Pederson, L. L., Baskerville, J. C., & Lefcoe, N. M. (1983). Prevalence of and factors related to cigarette smoking among students in grade 6. *Journal of Drug Education, 13*(4), 305-312.

Pulkkinen, L. (1983). Youthful smoking and drinking in a longitudinal perspective. *Journal of Youth and Adolescence, 12*(4), 253-283.

Reid, J. B. (Ed.) (1978). *A social learning approach to family intervention. II. Observation in home settings*. Eugene, OR: Castalia Publishing Co.

Reid, J. B. (1984). *Final Report: Child abuse: Developmental factors and treatment* (NIMH Grant 7 RO1 MH 37938).

Robins, L. N., & Przybeck, T. R. (1985). Age of onset of drug use as a factor in drug and other disorders. In C. L. Jones & R. J. Battjes (Eds.), *Etiology of drug abuse: Implications for prevention* (NIDA Research Monograph 56). Washington, DC: NIDA.

Selzer, M. L., Vinokur, A., & van Rooijen, L. (1975). A self-administered short Michigan Alcoholism Screening Test (SMAST). *Journal of Studies on Alcohol, 36*(1), 117-126.

Snyder, J., Dishion, T. J., & Patterson, G. R. (1986). Determinants and consequences of associating with deviant peers during preadolescence and adolescence. *Journal of Early Adolescence, 6*, 29-43.

Wahler, R. G., Winkle, G. R., Peterson, R. F., & Morrison, D. C. (1965). Mothers as behavior therapists for their own children. *Behavior Research and Therapy, 3*, 113-124.

Weinrott, M. R., Bauske, B. W., & Patterson, G. R. (1979). Systematic replication of a social learning approach to parent training. In S. L. Bates, P. O. Sjödén, & W. S. Dockens, III (Eds.), *Trends in behavior therapy*. New York: Academic Press.

Werner, E. E., & Smith, R. S. (1977). *Kauai's children come of age*. Honolulu: University Press of Hawaii.

West, D. J., & Farrington, D. P. (1973). *Who becomes delinquent*? London: Heinemann.

West, D. J., & Farrington, D. P. (1977). *The delinquent way of life*. London: Heinemann.

Zucker, R. A. (1976). Parental influences on the drinking patterns of their children. In M. Greenblatt & M. A. Schuckt (Eds.), *Alcoholism problems in women and children*. New York: Grune & Stratton.

Zucker, R. A., & Barron, F. H. (1973). Parental behaviors associated with problem drinking and antisocial behavior among adolescent males. In M. E. Chafetz (Eds.), *Research on alcoholism, I: Clinical problems and special populations* (DHEW publication 74-675). Washington, DC: U.S. Government Printing Office.

Managing Adolescent Behaviors at School: Implications for Families

Thomas J. Glynn, PhD
Marianne Haenlein, PhD

Both the schools and the media have begun to focus increased attention on drug use by adolescents. As both the prevalence and variety of substance use rises, public concern is growing over the significant long- and short-term consequences that threaten the physical and mental health of an entire generation. With substance abuse on the rise and cessation efforts complicated by established behavioral patterns and physiological changes, considerable effort currently is being focused on preventing the initiation of substance use. By preventing the initiation of substance use, the many problems that are associated with continued substance use may be stopped before they start. Following this same logic, and based on research that demonstrates a predictable progression of use from tobacco to alcohol, to marijuana, and potentially to drugs such as depressants or opiates (e.g., Kandel, 1978), the primary focus of a majority of prevention programs has been the prevention of smoking and tobacco use. Additionally, smoking prevention programs may provide an understanding of the fundamental principles of effective drug use prevention, and these principles may then provide the foundation for subsequent drug use prevention and cessation programs aimed at substances other than tobacco. Supporting this approach, some programs that are designed to prevent tobacco use

---

Thomas J. Glynn is Program Director for Smoking Research, Office of the Director, Division of Cancer Prevention and Control, National Cancer Institute, Blair Building, Room 432, 9000 Rockville Pike, Bethesda, MD 20892-4200. Marianne Haenlein is Deputy Project Manager, Prospect Associates, Ltd., 1801 Rockville Pike, Suite 500, Rockville, MD 20852.

have demonstrated significant effects on alcohol and marijuana use as well (e.g., Botvin, 1983).

In the past decade, we have witnessed remarkable accomplishments in the development of effective drug use prevention programs. Although many programs can point to only moderately reduced rates of substance use, the real progress of these early prevention efforts is more dramatically reflected in the volume of knowledge that they have provided. Significant methodological advances have enabled clearer evaluations of program effectiveness and the potential to identify more precisely which features contribute to successful prevention efforts and to what degree they do so (McCaul & Glasgow, 1985; Schinke & Gilchrist, 1985; Snow, Gilchrist, & Schinke, 1985). These accomplishments are particularly impressive in light of the magnitude of these programs in terms of both the program personnel necessary to implement and evaluate programs using such large subject populations and the duration of these programs, many reporting significant follow-up periods.

This chapter will address the implications of school-based prevention programs for families by reviewing the development of these programs and discussing specific contributions that the family can make to the success of these prevention programs. The brief review of these programs will highlight the advances discussed above concerning methodological improvements and identification of program factors that directly affect prevention and provide the theoretical and practical rationale for considering the role of the family in the prevention of drug use.

RESISTANCE TO PROSMOKING PRESSURE PROGRAMS

The earliest drug prevention programs were founded on the premise that knowledge alone would deter adolescent drug use (Goodstadt, 1978). Certainly, it was thought, a clear understanding of the deleterious physical and mental long-term effects of drug use would be sufficient for prevention. However, these fact-based educational programs were largely unsuccessful (as discussed by, e.g., Botvin, 1983; Goodstadt, 1978; Thompson, 1978).

Since the goal of these programs was to prevent the initiation of drug use behavior, subsequent programs attempted to increase their success by focusing more directly on behavior. Reflecting a significant shift in the underlying rationale of previous prevention programs, Evans and his colleagues (e.g., 1976, 1978, 1981) initiated a program based on social inoculation theory (McGuire, 1964, 1968). By viewing films depicting peer pressures to use drugs, adolescents could develop counterarguments to drug use that would better enable them to resist such pressures when encountered. While Evans et al. (1981) found minor long-term effects of their program, their initial investigations did not provide clear direction because positive results were not consistently observed throughout the 3-year follow-up and methodological difficulties allowed alternative interpretations (Flay, 1985; Flay et al., 1985). Programs devoted exclusively to aiding students in resisting prosmoking pressure are not now considered to be a preferred approach to this problem (Johnson, 1982).

While Evans' work provided an important foundation for current prevention programs, the focus of these early programs was limited to a narrow range of behaviors within a limited number of circumstances. Subsequent programs have expanded their focus to include a broader range of behaviors and base of intervention environments. As depicted in Table 1, this review will use these features to organize programs along dimensions of both their focus on an increasing range of behaviors (e.g., resisting prosmoking pressure to personal health and general skills) and their utilization of an increasing number of environmental settings for implementing interventions (e.g., school to school and community settings).

SOCIAL INFLUENCE PROGRAMS

As shown in Table 1, the prevention programs immediately following Evans' work maintained their base within the school setting but expanded their behavioral perspective. These programs included components from social learning (Bandura, 1977), attribution (Jones, Kanouse, Kelley, Nisbett, Valins, & Weiner, 1972), and commitment (Kiesler, 1971) theories. The largest of these programs, often termed social influence programs, were implemented

Table 1

Drug Use Prevention Programs Organized Generally According to Base of Intervention Environment and Specificity of Behaviors Targeted During Intervention

Drug Use Prevention Programs				
Resistance to Prosmoking Pressures	Social Influences	Modified Social Influences	Cognitive-Behavioral	Personal Health and General Skills
-Inoculation Theory Evans et al., 1976, 1978, 1981.	-Stanford (CLASP) McAlister et al., 1979, 1980; Perry, Killen, & Slinkard, 1980; Perry et al., 1980; Telch et al., 1982.	-Waterloo Best et al., 1984; Flay et al., 1983, 1985.	-Social Competence Pentz, 1983.	-North Karelia Youth Project Vartiainen et al., 1983; McAlister et al., 1982.
	-Minnesota (RASP) Arkin et al., 1981; Hurd et al., 1980; Luepker et al., 1983; Murray et al., 1983.		-Problem-Solving Schinke & Gilchrist, 1984; Schinke et al., 1985; Gilchrist & Schinke, 1985.	-Oslo Youth Study Tell et al., 1984.
			-Decision Skills Curriculum Botvin & Wills, 1985.	-Minnesota Heart Health Program Perry & Jessor, 1983, 1985.
	-Western Australia Colquhoun & Cullen, 1981; Fisher et al., 1983.	-USC (TVSP) Flay et al., 1983; Flay & Sobel, 1983.	-Life Skills Training (LST) Botvin & Eng, 1980, 1982; Botvin et al., 1980; Botvin, 1983; Botvin & Wills, 1985.	-NHLBI Stone, 1985.
	-Coe et al., 1982; Gritz, 1977; Killen, 1985; Ledwith, 1985; Murray et al., 1984; Reid, 1985.			

Behavior-Specific Programs ←→ Behavior-General Programs

☐ Generally School-Based Intervention Environment

☐ Generally Community-Based Intervention Environment

at Stanford (CLASP) (McAlister, Perry, & Maccoby, 1979; McAlister, Perry, Killen, Slinkard, & Maccoby, 1980; Perry, Killen, & Slinkard, 1980; Perry, Killen, Telch, Slinkard, & Danaher, 1980; Telch, Killen, McAlister, Perry, & Maccoby, 1982); at Minnesota (RASP) (Arkin, Roemhild, Johnson, Luepker, & Murray, 1981; Hurd et al., 1980; Luepker, Johnson, Murray, & Pechacek, 1983; Murray, Johnson, Luepker, Pechacek, & Jacobs, 1980); and in Western Australia (Colquhoun & Cullen, 1981; Fisher, Armstrong, & deKlerk, 1983). These programs included not only films demonstrating peer pressure resistance techniques but a forum for students to role-play and receive performance feedback as well as to express publicly their commitment to the program. Other investigators implemented variations of the social influences program (Coe, Crouse, Cohen, & Fisher, 1982; Gritz, 1977; Killen, 1985; Ledwith, 1985; Murray, Johnson, Luepker, & Mittelmark, 1984; Reid, 1985). While all programs demonstrate prevention effects, unambiguous interpretation is not possible. Not only did the magnitudes of these effects differ markedly among programs, but more importantly, methodological difficulties, as in the earlier studies, allow for multiple alternative explanations.

Despite these limitations, these programs enumerate several important variables that appear to alter program effectiveness as well as several methodological considerations that could prevent clear interpretation of program effectiveness. For example, a number of these studies evaluate the utility of expanded dependent variable measures (Biglan, cf. Flay, 1985) and the potentially differential influence of teacher versus peer leaders (Fisher et al., 1983; Hurd et al., 1980; Luepker et al., 1983; Murray et al., 1984; Perry et al., 1983), total versus partial class involvement (Dielman, cf. Flay, 1985), and post-intervention booster sessions versus no post-intervention sessions (Botvin, Renick, & Baker, 1983; Williamson & Campbell, 1981). Additionally, methodological issues involving reduced statistical power, inappropriate unit of analysis, high attrition, and within-subject comparison over time have been identified, and solutions have been proposed within the unique limitations of prevention program evaluation.

MODIFIED SOCIAL INFLUENCES PROGRAMS

Expanding upon the behaviors targeted by the social influences programs (Table 1), the Waterloo Smoking Prevention Program added a values clarification/decision-making component (Best et al., 1984; Flay, d'Avernas, Best, Kersell, & Ryan, 1983; Flay et al., 1985). Evaluations of the efficacy of prevention efforts with this added component reveal varied effects over time, contingent upon the smoking history of the student. Students experienced with smoking demonstrate the greatest immediate effects while students having little or no smoking experience demonstrate greater long-term effects.

Using the modified social influences program, Flay and his colleagues (1983) expanded their base of intervention environments by including a series of television segments (TVSP). Additionally, and of particular significance to our interest in the family, they also stimulated parental involvement via homework assignments. Although firm conclusions are illusive from this work as well, results are promising and suggest that with future research, mass media involvement and particularly family involvement may provide an important mechanism in preventing drug use.

COGNITIVE-BEHAVIORAL PROGRAMS

The next series of programs (shown in Table 1) reflect expansion along the behavioral dimension; they targeted more general personal and social skills. Underlying these cognitive-behavioral approaches are assumptions about the etiology of adolescent drug use. Adolescence is viewed within a developmental framework as a period characterized by increasing autonomy and individuality, changing cognitive perspectives, and a progressive decline in parental influence with a corresponding increase in peer influence (Botvin & Wills, 1985). Within this framework, drug use is viewed as a functional behavior resulting from both social and personal factors (Jessor & Jessor, 1977). The family is viewed not only as playing an integral role in the development of these personal factors but as an important social influence. The intervention strategies discussed below attempted to prevent substance use by enhancing social and life skills and by providing alternatives to substance use. The skills targeted within each program reflect certain fundamental assumptions about specific social deficits.

Based on a social competence model, Pentz (1983; Botvin & Wills, 1985) utilized social assertiveness training in her prevention program. Students were taught through modeling, rehearsal, and feedback the skills for dealing with everyday situations. The results indicate increased social competence and reduced alcohol use; no effects, however, are noted for cigarette smoking. Interestingly, the efficacy of this program interacts with grade level and personality style, a finding whose practical application will require more specifically focused research.

At a slightly more general level, Schinke and Gilchrist (1984; Schinke, Gilchrist, & Snow, 1985; Gilchrist & Schinke, 1985) emphasized flexible, situation-independent cognitive and behavioral skills. Their approach has been to teach decision-making and problem-solving skills as well as interpersonal skills to equip adolescents to make better decisions and to communicate those decisions more effectively. This program has consistently proven to be effective as a smoking prevention tool.

In addition to providing decision-making and interpersonal skills training, the Decision Skills Curriculum (Botvin & Wills, 1985) provides a stress management component. The addition of stress management instruction reflected an attempt to deal with findings that poor coping strategies are a predictive factor in substance use (Kandel, 1978). Although this program was found to be very effective in one of the schools that was evaluated, this was not the case for a second school. Further research to determine what school characteristics contribute to marked differences in program effectiveness could prove valuable not only for future use of the Decision Skills Curriculum but to gain a better understanding of the factors that influence cognitive-behavioral training in general.

Perhaps the most extensive cognitive-behavioral approach is the Life Skills Training (LST) program (Botvin & Eng, 1980, 1982; Botvin, Eng, & Williams, 1980; Botvin, 1983; Botvin & Wills, 1985). This program incorporates training to enhance self-esteem, resist persuasive appeals, cope with anxiety, and communicate effectively as well as to gain knowledge and skills specifically related to substance use. The LST program has proven quite successful over a number of investigations. Not only is tobacco use reduced, but alcohol and marijuana use also are shown to decrease.

Consistent with the assumption that drug use is a functional behavior serving to fulfill social and personal needs, alternative activities programs have approached drug use prevention by attempting to substitute activities that are both more rewarding and incompatible with drug use (Olton, 1985; Swisher & Hu, 1983). Alternative activities are selected based upon both the developmental level of the individual and the specific social and personal deficits present. Other variations of cognitive-developmental approaches to prevention also have emphasized the developmental level of the individual (Glynn, Leventhal, & Hirschman, 1985; McCarthy, 1985; Wells, 1985). The efficacy of the alternative activities approach, however, remains uncertain because few evaluation investigations have been conducted.

PERSONAL HEALTH AND GENERAL SKILLS

The most general are those drug use prevention programs that have existed as a component of more general school- and community-based programs designed to influence general health behaviors (Table 1). For example, the North Karelia Youth Project (Vartiainen, Pallonen, McAlister, Koskela, & Puska, 1983; McAlister, Puska, Salonen, Tuomilehto, & Koskela, 1982), the Oslo Youth Study (Tell, Klepp, Vellar, & McAlister, 1984), and the Minnesota Heart Health Program (Perry & Jessor, 1983, 1985) all contained a social influences, school-based smoking prevention program. Additionally, Stone (1985) reviews eight general health programs currently funded by the National Heart, Lung, and Blood Institute, all of which contain a school-based smoking prevention component. Arguments in favor of these more comprehensive prevention programs have been made (Johnson & Solis, 1983); however, a complete review of these programs is beyond the scope of this chapter (see Johnson & Solis, 1983, for review).

In summary, the early school-based prevention programs focused primarily on education as a route to drug use prevention. Following this less than successful approach, programs focused on demonstrating resistance to prosmoking pressure. As a result of this exposure, adolescents were expected to develop and use counterarguments to drug use pressures. Addressing increasingly less specific behaviors, subsequent social influences programs utilized role-playing techniques to instruct students in the use of resistance techniques. The modified social influences programs expanded upon this training to add a values-clarification/decision-making component. Cognitive-behavioral programs incorporated even broader behavioral interventions by adding instruction in interpersonal and coping skills. Finally, personal health and general skills programs focus on very general health behaviors within an expanded school- and community-based intervention environment. The progression from behavior-specific to behavior-general programs and from school-based to school- and community-based intervention environments is reflected in Table 1.

IMPLICATIONS FOR FAMILIES

The fundamental goal of all of these prevention programs is to provide children with the necessary tools to avoid drug use. Similarly, parents are often in the role of trying to provide children with the necessary tools to address everyday life decisions, and drug use has become one of those decisions. Research on the role of the family, particularly parents, in the etiology of drug use and abuse has identified many family-related factors that appear to contribute to the initiation and continuation of drug use behavior, as well as its prevention (e.g., Glynn, 1982, 1984). Based on the evidence presented in the second article of this volume, we will address two of these factors in relation to drug use prevention programs: the parent-child relationship, specifically as it relates to communication, and the parent as teacher, including parental discipline and parental modeling as both relate to the effective instruction of values and problem-solving skills. Although discussed independently, these factors are viewed from a family-systems perspective; the behavior of each member of the family is assumed to affect all other members, and no behavior is without its consequences (Glynn, 1982; Needle, Glynn, & Needle, 1983). A brief discussion of the role of these factors in drug use behavior will provide supportive theoretical rationale for many components of the prevention programs described and will suggest a very specific role for the family in contributing to the efficacy of these programs.

The parent-child relationship has been the focus of considerable research, particularly as it relates to drug use behavior. Although several aspects of this relationship have been identified as potentially predisposing an individual to initiate drug use, one aspect, communication, relates specifically to the target behaviors addressed by many of the drug use prevention programs discussed. The classic "communication-gap" is often characteristic of the interaction between drug users and their parents (Jurich, Polson, Jurich, & Bates, 1985; Kandel, 1978). Additionally, the communication between parents within these families is typically poor (Cannon, 1976; Jurich et al., 1985), and the adolescent often feels in conflict and emotionally distant from his or her parents (Barnes, 1977; Jurich et al., 1985; Vaglum, 1985). This lack of communication and the environment that it creates is considered the rocky foundation upon which decision-making and coping skills fail to develop (Cannon, 1976).

Communication has been one of the behavioral targets of almost all of the prevention programs outlined. Initially, programs focused more narrowly on developing specific skills to resist prosmoking pressures and ultimately expanded in the cognitive-behavioral programs to include general assertiveness and interpersonal communication skills as well as values clarification and decision-making skills. Given the role of the family in the development and support of effective communication and decision-making skills, many researchers and program planners realized that the efficacy of prevention programs in contributing to the development of these skills would certainly be enhanced by support of these efforts from the family. Additionally, programs can provide a natural foundation for establishing topics of communication. Prevention programs and families should act in a reciprocally reinforcing fashion with adolescents contributing to enhanced family communication as a result of their involvement in prevention programs and the family enhancing the efforts of prevention programs to develop communication skills in adolescents by supporting and reinforcing program involvement.

Related to poor communication as a predisposing family-related factor in the initiation and continued use of drugs is the prevalence of discipline problems in families of drug users (Jurich et al., 1985). Specifically, problems arise in relation to both the type of discipline (Jurich et al., 1985) and its consistency (Wittenborn, Smith, & Wittenborn, 1970). Most problematic are situations in which either laissez-faire (Wittenborn et al., 1970) or authoritarian (Cannon, 1976) discipline is implemented. Democratic discipline is thought to be least problematic. This form of discipline affords opportunities for adolescents to engage in joint decision-making with their parents. Thus, not only are effective communication patterns likely to develop but better decision-making skills as well. Adolescents learn rules that enable them to solve problems in a consistent way. Inconsistent rules of discipline produce problems in part because adolescents fail to learn the rules that might aid them in future, independent problem-solving and fail to develop their own value system.

As described earlier, the majority of prevention programs reviewed have attempted to provide a foundation for making a "no" decision regarding drugs, with the cognitive-behavioral programs providing the broadest decision-making and values-clarification training. Similarly, the advantages of reciprocal support between the family and prevention programs hold in relation to problems emanating from discipline problems.

Finally, parental modeling has been identified as yet another family-related factor associated with drug use (Jurich et al., 1985). Here too, one of the results of inconsistent parental modeling is that the adolescent is unable to perceive consistent rules as the foundation for making decisions and clarifying his or her own values. In addition, however, poor modeling, such as parental cigarette smoking (Dobbs & Marsh, 1983; Wilcox & Gillies, 1984) or use of alcohol as a "psychological crutch" (Jurich et al., 1985), teaches adolescents about acceptable behavior and coping mechanisms. The role of a reciprocal family and school-based prevention program approach would perhaps have its most profound effect on this influence of modeling. As evidenced in Flay et al.'s (1983) and Flay and Sobel's (1983) smoking prevention programs in which parents were involved via homework assignments, not only were significant reductions in smoking initiation observed in students, but parental smoking was impressively reduced as well. Other programs have witnessed similarly positive effects as a result of parental involvement (e.g., Aaro, Bruland, Hauknes, & Luchsen, 1982; Rabinowitz, 1978; Sunseri, Alberti, Kent et al., 1983; Wilcox, Engel, & Reid, 1978).

In conclusion, although emanating from different sources within the family such as the parent-child relationship, parental discipline, and parental modeling, family-related factors impact not only on the initiation and continued use of drugs but on its prevention as well via similar skills, including communication, decision-making, values clarification, and coping. Current drug use prevention programs tend to focus on developing these types of skills, although some programs in less general ways. The advantages of a reciprocal relationship between these programs and the family are clear. These programs can help to reduce the magnitude of predisposing family factors, and the family can enhance program involvement and commitment.

FUTURE RESEARCH AND ACTIVITIES AIMED AT THE INVOLVEMENT OF FAMILIES IN SCHOOL-BASED SUBSTANCE USE PREVENTION PROGRAMS

There has been sufficient indication that the family has a potentially significant role, through our schools, in the prevention of youthful substance use. Because this role has been considered almost exclusively in the research setting, however, a number of very practical questions remain. For example, what are the substance use-related issues that parents are most interested in? What type of program will engender the greatest degree of active involvement on the part of families? Is a focus on tobacco use, as a gateway drug and the nation's most important public health problem, a sufficient ingredient to ensure family participation or is a focus on illicit substances necessary as well? What do the schools need to do to interest families in the development of such family-based programs? What do families need to do to interest schools in the development of such programs? What types of activities (e.g., joint parent-child "homework," watching assigned television shows together, community activism, etc.) will have the greatest effect, not only on the subsequent substance use of youth but on other family members as well? What types of programs can address some of the important issues discussed above—family communication, varieties of discipline styles, and parental modeling—without being perceived as undue interference in the family process?

In addition to these program-level questions, another, perhaps more general, series of issues arise when the role that the family plays in the prevention of adolescent substance use is considered in the context of the other major influences on youth today, primarily revolving around the school, media, and one's peers. These major behavioral influences—family, school, media, and peers—are of course highly interactive and have greater or less influence depending upon a variety of factors, including the age of the adolescent and the seriousness of the behavior in question (Kandel, 1978; Glynn, 1981). Nevertheless, the relative power of each of these influences must be considered in the development of any initiative concerning the family. More importantly, specific ways in which the family can best exercise its influence in relation to the influences of the school, media, and peers must be developed.

Finally, research activity in the area of a family and school partnership in the prevention of substance use needs to move beyond the smaller, tightly controlled studies that have, necessarily, dominated the research agenda thus far. A number of well-documented prevention-oriented curricula, reviewed in this chapter, now exist. These ought to be reviewed and, where they do not now provide the means to involve families in their activities, provisions should be made to do so. The role of the family in these curricula should then be evaluated as part of the large trials either now under way (e.g., Stone, 1985; National Cancer Institute, 1986) or soon to be undertaken. Additionally, any new programs should consider family involvement in school-based prevention programs as nothing less than essential to their optimum success. In this way, we can utilize two of the most basic institutions in our society—the family and the educational system—in the prevention of one of the basic threats to the integrity of that society—drug use by our children.

REFERENCES

Aaro, L.E., Bruland, E., Hauknes, S., & Luchsen, P.M. (1983). Smoking among Norwegian schoolchildren, 1975-1980: III. The effect of antismoking campaigns. *Scandinavian Journal of Psychology, 24*, 277-283.

Arkin, R.M., Roemhild, H.F., Johnson, C.A., Luepker, R.V., & Murray, D.M. (1981). The Minnesota Smoking Prevention Program. *Journal of School Health, 51*, 611-616.

Bandura, A. (1977). *Social learning theory*. Englewood Cliffs, NJ: Prentice-Hall.

Barnes, G.M. (1977). The development of adolescent drinking behavior: An evaluation review of the impact of the socialization process within the family. *Adolescence, 12*, 571-591.

Best, J.A., Flay, B.R., Towson, S.M., Ryan, K.B., Perry, C.L., Brown, K.S., Kersell, M.W., & d'Avernas, J.R. (1984). Smoking prevention and the concept of risk. *Journal of Applied Social Psychology, 14*(3), 257-273.

Botvin, G.J. (1983). Prevention of adolescent substance abuse through the development of personal and social competence. *National Institute on Drug Abuse Research Monograph Series Number 47* (DHHS Pub. No. ADM 83-1280). Washington, DC: U.S. Government Printing Office.

Botvin, G. & Eng, A. (1980). A comprehensive school-based smoking prevention program. *Journal of School Health, 11*, 209-213.

Botvin, G. & Eng, A. (1982). The efficacy of a multicomponent approach to the prevention of cigarette smoking. *Preventive Medicine, 11*, 199-211.

Botvin, G.J., Eng, A., & Williams, C. (1980). Preventing the onset of smoking through life skills training. *Preventive Medicine, 9*, 135-143.

Botvin, G.J., Renick, N.L., & Baker, E. (1983). The effects of scheduling format and booster sessions on a broad-spectrum psychosocial approach to smoking prevention. *Journal of Behavioral Medicine, 6*(4), 359-379.

Botvin, G.J., & Wills, T.A. (1985). Personal and social skills training: Cognitive-behavioral approaches to substance abuse prevention. *National Institute on Drug Abuse Monograph Series Number 63* (DHHS Pub. No. ADM 85-1334). Washington, DC: U.S. Government Printing Office.

Cannon, S.R. (1976). *Social functioning patterns in families of offspring receiving treatment for drug abuse*. Roslyn Heights, NY: Libra Publishers.

Coe, R.M., Crouse, E., Cohen, J.D., & Fisher, E.B., Jr. (1982). Patterns of change in adolescent smoking behavior and results of a one year follow-up of a smoking prevention program. *Journal of School Health, 52*, 348-353.

Colquhoun, J. & Cullen, K. (1981). Improved smoking habits in 12- to 14-year-old Busselton children after antismoking programmes. *Medical Journal of Australia, 1*(11), 586-587.

Dobbs, J. & Marsh, A. (1983). *Smoking among secondary school children*. (OPCS Survey). London: HMSO.

Evans, R.I. (1976). Smoking in children: Developing a social psychological strategy of deterrence. *Preventive Medicine, 5*, 122-127.

Evans, R.I., Rozelle, R.M., Mittelmark, M., Hansen, W.B., Bane, A., & Havis,

J. (1978). Deterring the onset of smoking in children: Knowledge of immediate physiological effects and coping with peer pressure, media pressure, and parent modeling. *Journal of Applied Social Psychology, 8*(2), 126-135.

Evans, R.I., Rozelle, R.M., Maxwell, S.E., Raines, B.E., Dill, C.A., Guthrie, T.J., Henderson, A.H., & Hill, P.C. (1981). Social modeling films to deter smoking in adolescents: Results of a three year field investigation. *Journal of Applied Psychology, 66*(4), 399-414.

Fisher, D.A., Armstrong, D.K., & deKlerk, N.H. (1983, July). *A randomized control of education for prevention of smoking in 12-year-old children*. Paper presented at the 5th World Conference of Smoking and Health, Winnipeg, Canada.

Flay, B.R. (1985). What we know about the social influences approach to smoking prevention: Review and recommendations. *National Institute on Drug Abuse Research Monograph Series Number 63* (DHHS Pub. No. ADM 85-1334). Washington, DC: U.S. Government Printing Office.

Flay, B.R., d'Avernas, J.R., Best, J.A., Kersell, M.W., & Ryan, R.B. (1983). Cigarette smoking: Why young people do it and ways of preventing it. In P. McGrath & P. Firestone (Eds.), *Pediatric and adolescent behavioral medicine*. New York: Springer-Verlag.

Flay, B.R., Hansen, W.B., Johnson, C.A., & Sobel, J.L. (1983, July). *Involvement of children in motivating parents to quit smoking with a television programme* (Health Behavior Research Institute, University of Southern California). Paper presented at the 5th World Conference of Smoking and Health, Winnipeg, Canada.

Flay, B.R., Ryan, K.B., Best, A., Brown, K.S., Kersell, M.W., d'Avernas, J.R., & Zanna, M.D. (1985). Are social-psychological smoking prevention programs effective? The Waterloo Study. *Journal of Behavioral Medicine, 8*(1), 37-59.

Flay, B.R. & Sobel, J.L. (1983). The role of mass media in preventing adolescent substance abuse. *National Institute on Drug Abuse Research Monograph Series Number 47* (DHHS Pub. No. ADM 83-1280). Washington, DC: U.S. Government Printing Office.

Gilchrist, L.D. & Schinke, S.P. (1985). Improving smoking prevention programs. *Journal of Psychosocial Oncology, 3*(1), 67-78.

Glynn, T.J. (1981). From Family to Peer: A review of transitions of influence among drug-using youth. *Journal of Youth and Adolescence, 10*, 363-384.

Glynn, T.J. (1982). Families and drugs: A life-span research approach. *American Journal of Drug and Alcohol Abuse, 9*(4), 396-411.

Glynn, T.J. (1984). Adolescent drug use and the family environment: A review. *Journal of Drug Issues, 2*, 271-295.

Glynn, K., Leventhal, H., & Hirschman, R. (1985). A cognitive developmental approach to smoking prevention. *National Institute on Drug Abuse Research Monograph Number 63* (DHHS Pub. No. ADM 85-1334). Washington, DC: U.S. Government Printing Office.

Goodstadt, M.S. (1978). Alcohol and drug education. *Health Education Monographs, 6*(3), 263-279.

Gritz, E.R. (1977). Smoking: The prevention of onset. *National Institute on Drug Abuse Research Monograph Number 17* (DHEW Pub. No. ADM 78-581). Washington, DC: U.S. Government Printing Office.

Hurd, P.D., Johnson, C.A., Pechacek, T., Bast, L.P., Jacobs, D.R., & Luepker, R.V. (1980). Prevention of cigarette smoking in seventh grade students. *Journal of Behavioral Medicine, 3*, 15-92.

Jessor, R. & Jessor, S.L. (1977). *Problem behavior and psychosocial development—A longitudinal study of youth*. New York: Academic Press.

Johnson, C.A. (1982). Untested and erroneous assumptions underlying antismoking programs. In T.C. Coates, A.R. Peterson, & C. Perry, (Eds.), *Promoting adolescent health: A dialog on research and practice* (pp. 149-165). New York: Academic Press.

Johnson, C.A. & Solis, J. (1983). Comprehensive community programs for drug abuse prevention: Implications of the community heart disease prevention programs for future research. *National Institute on Drug Abuse Research Monograph Series Number 47* (DHHS Pub. No. ADM 83-1280). Washington, DC: U.S. Government Printing Office.

Jones, E.E., Kanouse, D.E., Kelley, H.H., Nisbett, R.E., Valins, S., & Weiner, B. (1972). *Attribution: Perceiving the causes of behavior*. Morristown, PA: General Learning Press.

Jurich, A.P., Polson, C.J., Jurich, J.A., & Bates, R.A. (1985). Family factors in the lives of drug users and abusers. *Adolescence, 20*(77), 143-159.

Kandel, D. (1978). Convergences in prospective longitudinal surveys of drug use in normal populations. In D. Kandel (Ed.), *Longitudinal research on drug use: Empirical findings and methodological issues*. Washington, DC: Hemisphere-Wiley.

Kiesler, C.A. (1971). *The psychology of commitment: Experiments linking behavior to beliefs*. New York: Academic Press.

Killen, J.D. (1985). Prevention of adolescent tobacco smoking: The social pressure resistance training approach. *Journal of Child Psychology and Psychiatry and Allied Disciplines, 26*(1), 7-15.

Ledwith, F. (1985). *The evaluation of a secondary school smoking education intervention*. (Report to the Scottish Health Education Group.) Department of Education, University of Manchester.

Luepker, R.V., Johnson, C.A., Murray, D.M., & Pechacek, T.F. (1983). Prevention of cigarette smoking: Three year follow-up of an education program for youth. *Journal of Behavioral Medicine, 6*(1), 53-62.

McAlister, A., Perry, C., Killen, J., Slinkard, L., & Maccoby, N. (1980). Pilot study of smoking, alcohol, and drug abuse prevention. *American Journal of Public Health, 70*, 719-721.

McAlister, A., Perry, C., & Maccoby, N. (1979). Adolescent smoking: Onset and prevention. *Pediatrics, 63*, 650-658.

McAlister, A., Puska, P., Salonen, J.T., Tuomilehto, J., & Koskela, K. (1982).

Theory and action for health promotion: Illustrations from the North Karelia project. *American Journal of Public Health, 72*(1), 43-50.

McCarthy, W.J. (1985). The cognitive developmental model and other alternatives to the social skills deficit model of smoking onset. *National Institute on Drug Abuse Research Monograph Number 63* (DHHS Pub. No. ADM 85-1334). Washington, DC: U.S. Government Printing Office.

McCaul, K.D. & Glasgow, R.E. (1985). Preventing adolescent smoking: What we have learned about treatment construct validity. *Healthy Psychology, 4*(4), 361-87.

McGuire, W.J. (1964). Inducing resistance to persuasion: Some contemporary approaches. In L. Barkowitz (Ed.), *Advances in experimental social psychology* (Vol. 1, pp. 192-227). New York: Academic Press.

McGuire, W.J. (1968). The nature of attitudes and attitude change. In G. Lindsey & E. Aronson (Eds.), *Handbook of social psychology* (pp. 136-314). Reading, MA: Addison-Wesley.

Murray, D.M., Johnson, C.A., Luepker, R.V., & Mittelmark, M.B. (1984). The prevention of cigarette smoking in children: A comparison of four strategies. *Journal of Applied Social Psychology, 14*, 274-288.

Murray, D.M., Johnson, C.A., Luepker, R.V., Pechacek, T.F., & Jacobs, P.R. (1980, September). *Issues in smoking prevention research*. Paper presented at the annual meeting of the American Psychological Association, Montreal, Canada.

National Cancer Institute. (1986). *Smoking, Tobacco, and Cancer Program*. (NIH Publication No. 86-2687). Washington, DC: U.S. Government Printing Office.

Needle, R.H., Glynn, T.J., & Needle, M.P. (1983). Drug abuse: Adolescent activities and the family. In C. Figley & M. McCubbin (Eds.), *Stress and the family*. New York: Bruner/Mazel.

Olton, A.L. (1985). The effect of locus of control and perceptions of school environment on outcome in three school drug abuse prevention programs. *Journal of Drug Education, 15*(2), 157-169.

Pentz, M.A. (1983). Prevention of adolescent substance abuse through social skill development. *National Institute on Drug Abuse Research Monograph Series Number 47* (DHHS Pub. No. ADM 83-1280). Washington, DC: U.S. Government Printing Office.

Perry, C.L. & Jessor, R. (1983). Doing the cube: Preventing drug abuse through adolescent health promotion. *National Institute on Drug Abuse Research Monograph Series Number 47* (DHHS Pub. No. ADM 83-1280). Washington, DC: U.S. Government Printing Office.

Perry, C.L. & Jessor, R. (1985). The concept of health promotion and the prevention of adolescent drug abuse. *Health Education Quarterly, 12*(2), 169-184.

Perry, C.L., Killen, J., & Slinkard, L.A. (1980). Peer teaching and smoking prevention among junior high students. *Adolescence, 15*, 277-281.

Perry, C.L., Killen, J., Telch, M.J., Slinkard, L.A., & Danaher, B.S. (1980).

Modifying smoking behavior of teenagers: A school-based intervention. *American Journal of Public Health, 70*, 722-725.

Perry, C.L., Telch, M.J., Killen, J., Burke, A., & Maccoby, N. (1983). High school smoking prevention: The relative efficacy of varied treatments and instructors. *Adolescence, 18*(71), 561-566.

Rabinowitz, H.S. (1978). Who health educates whom? *International Journal of Health Education, 21*, 183-188.

Reid, D. (1985). Prevention of smoking among school children: Recommendations for policy development. *Health Education Journal, 44*(1), 3-12.

Schinke, S.P. & Gilchrist, L.D. (1984). Preventing cigarette smoking with youth. *Journal of Primary Prevention, 5*, 48-56.

Schinke, S.P. & Gilchrist, L.D. (1985). Preventing substance abuse with children and adolescents. *Journal of Consulting and Clinical Psychology, 53*, 596-602.

Schinke, S.P., Gilchrist, L.D., & Snow, W.H. (1985). Skills intervention to prevent cigarette smoking among adolescents. *American Journal of Public Health, 75*, 665-667.

Snow, W.H., Gilchrist, L.D., & Schinke, S.P. (1985). A critique of progress in adolescent smoking prevention. *Children and Youth Services Review, 7*, 1-19.

Stone, E.J. (1985). School-based health research funded by the National Heart, Lung, and Blood Institute. *Journal of School Health, 55*(5), 168-174.

Sunseri, A.J., Alberti, J.M., Kent, N.O. et al. (1983). Reading, demographic, social, and psychological factors related to pre-adolescent smoking and non-smoking behaviors and attitudes. *Journal of School Health, 53*, 257-263.

Swisher, J.D. & Hu, T.W. (1983). Alternatives to drug abuse: Some are and some are not. *National Institute on Drug Abuse Research Monograph Series Number 47* (DHHS Pub. No. ADM 83-1280). Washington, DC: U.S. Government Printing Office.

Telch, M.J., Killen, J.D., McAlister, A.L., Perry, C.L., & Maccoby, N. (1982). Long-term follow-up of a pilot project on smoking prevention with adolescents. *Journal of Behavioral Medicine, 5*, 1-8.

Tell, G.S., Klepp, K.I., Vellar, O.D., & McAlister, A. (1984). Preventing the onset of cigarette smoking in Norwegian adolescents: The Oslo Youth Study. *Preventive Medicine, 13*(3), 256-275.

Thompson, E.L. (1978). Smoking education programs. *American Journal of Public Health, 68*, 150-157.

Vaglum, P. (1985). Young drug abusers' problems of attachment to the family. *Journal of Oslo City Hospital, 35*, 69-76.

Vartiainen, E., Pallonen, U., McAlister, A., Koskela, K., & Puska, P. (1983). Effect of two years of educational intervention on adolescent smoking (the North Karelia Youth Project). *Bull-WHO, 61*(3), 529-532.

Wells, L.A. (1985). Chemical dependence among adolescents. *Mayo Clinic Proceedings, 60*(8), 557-561.

Wilcox, B., Engel, E., & Reid, D. (1978). Smoking education in children: United Kingdom trials of an international project. *International Journal of Health Education, 21*, 236-244.

Wilcox, B. & Gillies, P. (1984). Prevalence of smoking amongst school children in Sheffield – Planning for prevention. *Health Education Journal, 43*, 57-69.
Williamson, J.A. & Campbell, L.P. (1981). Evaluating the effectiveness of an anti-smoking program. *Journal of School Health, 51*(3), 146-147.
Wittenborn, J.R., Smith, J.R., & Wittenborn, S. (Eds.) (1970). *Communication and Drug Abuse*. Springfield, IL: Charles C Thomas.

Peer Relationships, Social Competence, and Substance Abuse Prevention: Implications for the Family

Gilbert J. Botvin, PhD
Stephanie Tortu, PhD

INTRODUCTION

The implicit assumption underlying most traditional approaches to substance abuse prevention is that if individuals were sufficiently aware of the negative consequences, they would make a rational decision not to smoke, drink excessively, or use drugs. Consequently, the most widespread approach to substance abuse prevention has involved efforts to increase students' awareness of the adverse health, legal, and social consequences of substance use. This may take the form of simply providing factual information about various psychoactive substances or using fear-arousal strategies to "scare" adolescents into not using these substances. Unfortunately, published reviews of evaluation studies testing this general approach have consistently concluded that this type of prevention strategy is not effective (Berberian et al., 1976; Braucht et al., 1973; Dorn and Thompson, 1976; Goodstadt, 1974; Richards, 1969; Schaps et al., 1981; Swisher and Hoffman, 1975).

A close examination of the available data concerning the etiology of substance abuse leads to the conclusion that a variety of factors promote initial experimentation and the subsequent development of compulsive patterns of use (Millman and Botvin, 1983). Psychoso-

Gilbert J. Botvin is Associate Professor of Psychology and Director, Laboratory of Health Behavior Research and Stephanie Tortu is Assistant Professor, Cornell University Medical College, 1300 York Avenue, New York, NY 10021.

cial factors appear to be largely responsible for the initiation of substance use. These include social, cognitive, attitudinal, personality, and developmental factors. Pharmacologic factors help to maintain regular patterns of use, once they are established, in combination with psychosocial factors. These factors all relate to the demand side of the substance abuse equation. However, issues relating to supply are also obviously important and must be considered when developing a conceptual model of substance abuse and its causes.

Although there is still a good deal of controversy over the relative importance played by these various factors and their specific roles in the development of substance abuse, there has been a growing recognition over the past few years of the central role played by social factors—particularly negative influences from friends or peers—in promoting substance abuse. In fact, the most promising substance abuse prevention programs are those which include components designed to increase individuals' resistance to these kinds of pro-substance use influences (Botvin, 1984; Botvin, in press).

This chapter will focus on the onset and early stages of substance abuse from the perspective of peer relations and psychosocial development. Particular attention will be paid to the importance of personal and social competence and the development of healthy peer relationships. Research utilizing intervention strategies designed to enhance the acquisition of general personal and social skills as well as to increase resistance to the negative social influences supporting substance use will be discussed. Finally, implications for the family will be suggested.

ETIOLOGY OF SUBSTANCE ABUSE

Onset and Developmental Course

The use of psychoactive substances generally begins during the adolescent period. Since some degree of experimentation with one or more substances is fairly commonplace, it has come to be viewed as normal adolescent behavior, and perhaps even as part of the coming of age in America. Although many individuals may succeed in limiting their use of these substances to specific occasions (such as concerts or parties) and exercise control over both the frequency and amount of usage, compulsive patterns of use typically develop after an extended period of time. Since most of these substances are dependency-producing, "recreational" use often leads to the development of tolerance and a concomitant escalation of usage characterized by both psychological and physical dependence.

Despite the well-publicized dangers of using psychoactive substances, adolescents typically exhibit a remarkable absence of concern about these dangers. They often downplay the significance of the risks associated with substance use and generally overestimate their ability to avoid personally destructive patterns of use. This "illusion of control" persists often in the face of substantial evidence to the contrary. Even after dependence has developed, substance abusers continue to believe that they can quit whenever they want. Only after they have made a serious effort to quit or reduce their level of usage do adolescent substance abusers begin to appreciate the extent to which they have become psychologically and physiologically dependent.

Experimentation with one substance frequently leads to experimentation with others. The sequence of experimentation and subsequent regular use of psychoactive substances observed in most individuals suggests a natural progression, referred to as a "substance use hierarchy" (Hamburg et al., 1975; Kandel, 1978). The use of tobacco and alcoholic beverages occurs at the beginning of this progression, followed by marijuana use. The use of these "gateway" substances typically precedes the use of depressants, stimulants, psychedelics, and cocaine. The use of opiates generally occurs toward the end of this progression. Although use of any specific substance does not mean that individuals will necessarily progress to the use of other substances, the probabilities for using other substances further along this sequence increase with each step taken.

Etiologic Determinants

A considerable literature exists concerning the etiologic determinants of substance abuse. These include demographic factors, factors relating to the social environment, individual characteristics, factors relating to psychosocial development, and numerous behavioral correlates suggesting the importance of specific lifestyle patterns which may help promote or facilitate substance use (Blum et al., 1979; Braucht et al., 1973; Jessor, 1976; Wechsler, 1976). A detailed discussion of these factors is outside of the scope of this chapter. However, it is appropriate to consider briefly the role played by at least those factors which appear to be the most germane to the central focus of this chapter and which have the potential for being modified through an intervention program.

Perhaps the earliest influence to smoke, drink or use drugs comes from the family. These influences appear to come both from parents and from older siblings. Adolescents who begin using one or more substances may do so because they have seen these behaviors modeled by family members. A related factor is the kind of attitude that is conveyed to adolescents by their parents concerning substance use. In some instances, individuals may actually have their first substance use experience at home. For example, one study (Botvin et al., 1978) indicated that 11% of the adolescents surveyed had their first cigarette given to them by a parent.

An extremely powerful social influence to engage in substance use comes from the media. Because this is an area which has been understudied, little empirical evidence is available concerning the relative importance of the media in promoting substance use. However, the most widespread forms of substance use are those which are portrayed on TV and in movies as being socially acceptable behaviors that carry with them a highly positive images. Another social influence coming from the media takes the form of advertisements for tobacco products and alcoholic beverages. These products are promoted as being the necessary ingredients of social success, sex appeal, relaxation, and good times.

Notwithstanding the obvious importance of both family and media factors, peer pressure is acknowledged to be one of the most important factors promoting substance use. Study after study has found that individuals who smoke, drink, or use drugs nearly always have friends who engage in the same behaviors. In addition, an individual's perception of the surrounding social environment with respect to substance use can also be a powerful influence. The greater an individual's perception that substance use is widespread, the greater the likelihood that he or she will also engage in substance use.

Although existing research evidence does not support theories suggesting that particular substance use patterns are associated with specific personality types, a number of psychological factors have been found to be associated with tobacco, alcohol, or drug use (Botvin, 1984; Millman and Botvin, 1983). These include lower self-esteem, lower belief in personal control (i.e., external locus of control), a higher degree of dissatisfaction and pessimism, a greater need for social approval, less social confidence, more anxiety, lower assertiveness, greater impulsivity, greater rebelliousness, and a greater impatience to assume adult roles than nonusers.

The association of psychological factors with substance abuse initially suggested the possibility of an "addictive personality." However, it is now evident that this is not the case. Available data do not support the existence of a specific personality profile of all substance users/abusers. Indeed, the characteristics found to be associated with substance use/abuse do not occur exclusively in substance users, nor are they totally absent among nonusers. Adolescent substance abusers tend to vary markedly with respect to personality patterns as well as psychological adjustment. Many adolescent substance users are healthy, while some clearly have significant psychopathology.

The role of psychological factors in the etiology of substance abuse may, therefore, also vary. In healthy adolescents, psychological factors may serve as co-factors which, for example, determine vulnerability to social influence. Indeed, differential susceptibility to social influence appears to be mediated by precisely the kind of personality characteristics associated with substance use (Bandura, 1969; Rotter, 1972). In poorly adjusted individuals, psychological factors may function as the primary impetus to use drugs initially or for progressing from casual use to more serious addictive patterns of use. Psychological variables such as low self-esteem, depression, and poor coping skills are notably significant for predicting subsequent progression to problematic drug use (Kandel et al., 1978).

Conceptual Framework

Numerous theories have been developed to explain why and how people become substance abusers (see Lettieri et al., 1980). However, few theories have any direct relevance to the development of effective prevention strategies. In light of the data currently available, social learning theory (Bandura, 1977) provides the most useful theoretical framework. From this perspective, substance use can be conceptualized as a socially learned, purposeful, and functional behavior which results from the interplay of diverse social and personal factors. Substance use behavior appears to be learned through a process of modeling and reinforcement which is mediated by personal factors such as cognitions, attitudes, and beliefs.

For some individuals, social influence factors may play the predominant role in determining substance use status. These individuals may begin smoking, drinking, or using drugs after repeated exposure to high status role models who engage in these behaviors and/or persuasive appeals made by advertisers or peers. For other individuals, substance use may be an effort to cope with real or perceived difficulties. For example, substance use might be viewed as a means of coping with anxiety, social isolation, low self-esteem, a low sense of personal control, or poor academic performance.

This general conceptual framework has several implications for prevention. First, prevention programs should attempt to reduce social influences promoting, facilitating, or supporting substance use. This might be done by decreasing the visibility and perceived attractiveness of negative models or by increasing the visibility and perceived attractiveness of positive models. Second, prevention programs might attempt to increase resistance to social influences through the teaching of refusal skills and media resistance skills. Third, they might attempt to decrease susceptibility to social influence by increasing personal characteristics associated with low susceptibility such as a high self-esteem, high sense of personal control, high self-efficacy, and low anxiety. Fourth, prevention programs might attempt to foster the acquisition of adaptive coping skills in an effort to obviate the need for substance use as a coping response.

ADOLESCENT DEVELOPMENT AND SUBSTANCE USE

The initiation and early stages of substance use among adolescents occur within the context of great physical and psychological change. During the adolescent period, individuals characteristically experiment with a variety of behaviors and lifestyle patterns as part of the natural process of separating from parents, developing a sense of autonomy and independence, establishing an identity, and acquiring the skills needed to function effectively and independently in an increasingly adult world. Much of this experimentation takes place within the peer group, which serves as both a refuge from the adult world and a safe environment in which adolescents may explore a variety of roles and practice important personal and social skills.

Peer Influence

As individuals approach the adolescent period, there is usually a progressive decline in parental influence and a corresponding increase in the influence of peers and other socializing agents (Utech and Hoving, 1969). During early childhood parents exert the most powerful influence on children; however, upon entry into the school environment, this influence decreases somewhat and peers and other socializing agents (e.g., teachers) become increasingly important (Mussen et al., 1974). Generally speaking, in the event of a conflict between the advice provided by parents or peers, there is a gradual but manifest decline with age concerning compliance with parental advice (Russell, 1974). However this is not to say that parents are unable to influence their children; quite simply, it depends on the area of concern. While peers may be more influential with regard to matters of clothing, music and similar lifestyle issues, parents are generally more influential than peers or even best friends concerning areas relating to career and educational choices. Moreover there tends to be considerable overlap between the values of parents and peers because of commonalities in their background (Mussen et al., 1974).

Conformity Behavior

Increased dependence on the peer group is typically accompanied by a corresponding rise in conformity behavior. Preschool children are almost totally impervious to conformity pressure (Hartup, 1970), but the tendency to conform to group norms increases during middle childhood (Costanzo and Shaw, 1966; Piaget, 1932). Conformity needs and corresponding behavior increase rapidly during preadolescence and early adolescence, and decline steadily from middle to late adolescence (Mussen et al., 1974). However, despite this general developmental trend towards increased conformity, individual susceptibility may vary greatly. Thus, if the values of the peer group should be in conflict with those held by the child, the child's susceptibility to change will, to a large extent, depend on the relative importance of peer acceptance. Furthermore, differential susceptibility to conformity pressure has been shown to be a function of personality characteristics and gender. Individuals who are more dependent and anxious (Alters, Marshall, and Shooter, 1960) and who have low self-esteem and high social sensitivity (Hartup, 1983) tend to be more conforming. Girls tend to be more conforming to peer group pressure than boys (Maccoby and Masters, 1970).

Cognitive Development

The way the adolescent sees the world is changed significantly as a consequence of major cognitive developmental shifts taking place during this period. As Piaget (1932) has observed, the thinking of the preadolescent is rigid, literal, and grounded in the "here and now." Adolescent thought, on the other hand, is more relative, abstract, and hypothetical. The new cognitive abilities acquired during this period enable the adolescent to conceive of a wide range of possibilities and logical alternatives, to accept deviations from established rules, and to recognize illogical and inconsistent aspects of adult behavior.

Related to these cognitive changes is a shift in children's notion of right and wrong. Children's moral orientation shifts from a rigid and inflexible notion of right and wrong to one that takes into account a myriad of situational factors. Simply put, children's moral standards gradually become less absolute and more flexible and relative. With this new orientation, children can accept deviations from the established rules and norms, and come to recognize that a behavior might be considered wrong in one situation and right in another (e.g., killing during wartime). As children mature, they become more autonomous and their moral judgements and general conduct become less influenced by parental authority and more the result of their own experience (Kohlberg, 1969). In fact, there is a general decline in the acceptance of authority and in the subordination to adult norms and dictates (Mussen, Conger, and Kagan, 1974).

Identity Formation

One of the major developmental tasks of this period is the formation of an identity separate and distinct from parents and other family members—to discover oneself and define one's own identity. This leads adolescents to be overly concerned with their public image and how they are perceived by others. Elkind (1978) has referred to this phenomenon as "adolescent egocentrism." During this period, individuals tend to have a heightened sense of self-consciousness, the focus of which centers on appearance, personal qualities, and abilities. As a result of this heightened sense of self-consciousness, adolescents may feel so anxious and uncomfortable in social situations that they may begin avoiding them. This can lead not only to social isolation, but may undermine the development of important interpersonal skills.

As adolescents attempt to define who they are, they may actively pursue a specific public image. This often involves using consumer products or engaging in behaviors associated with that image. Thus, for example, adolescents may be motivated to smoke, drink, or use drugs because of the social image factors associated with those behaviors in the media (e.g., that smokers are tough, people who drink are grown-up, people who use cocaine are successful). For this reason, adolescents may be particularly vulnerable to sophisticated advertising appeals designed to associate use of a product with a particular image.

Role of Developmental Factors

Several developmental changes occur, therefore, immediately prior to or during the beginning of the adolescent period which in combination increase the likelihood that an individual will experiment with one or more psychoactive substances. These developmental changes increase adolescents' risk of yielding to direct and indirect social influences to smoke, drink, or use drugs. The decline in parental influence with respect to lifestyle matters, the increased reliance on the peer group, and the increased tendency to conform to peer group norms increase the probability that adolescents will use one or more substances if use is consistent with the norms of their friends or the reference group with which they identify. Concurrent cognitive developmental changes can undermine previously acquired knowledge of the potential risks of using these substances. Adolescents may become cognizant of inconsistencies between adult warnings and behavior or discover logical flaws in the arguments being advanced by adults against substance use. Finally, issues relating to identity and public image may substantially increase general susceptibility to advertising appeals and other social influences promoting substance use.

PEER RELATIONSHIPS AND SOCIAL DEVELOPMENT

Peer relationships contribute significantly to the social development of the child (Piaget, 1932; Sullivan, 1953). The importance of the peer system as a potent and major force in development is rivalled only by the family. This fact is sometimes obscured by conventional theories of social development which tend to emphasize the importance of the role of adults, especially parents, in the socialization of children. Recent work in peer relationships, however, indicates that adult and peer relationships are equally important, although they serve distinct functions in children's social development (Youniss, 1980).

The distinct functions of the child's relationship with adults and peers can best be understood by reflecting upon the nature of each of these relationships. The child-adult relationship is grounded in the unilateral authority of the adult who provides the child with a set of rules which are intended to ensure the adequate socialization of the child. In this relationship between persons of unequal status, the child typically strives to gain adult approval, along with achieving a basic understanding of the world as provided by adults. In contrast, the child-child relationship is grounded in the equality of the participants and the egalitarian nature of their interaction. An understanding of the world is achieved through peer cooperation and the negotiation of different viewpoints. Reciprocity, rather than authority, is the hallmark of this relationship (Youniss, 1980).

Interaction of Family and Peer Systems

During childhood, the family system and the peer system contribute differentially to the social development of the child, but the two systems are seen to be interdependent. Satisfactory relations with the parents provide the emotional and instrumental basis for success within the peer system (Hartup, 1983). Thus, the family system and the peer system are seen as operating synergistically throughout childhood.

It is commonly believed that this synergistic relationship breaks down in adolescence when the family system and the peer system begin to oppose each other and escalate into an intensely conflictual relationship. However, empirical research fails to support the notion of intense opposition between these systems. Most parents and their children agree on important issues like fundamental moral principles, aspirations for the future, and standards of self-control. Sometimes parents take precedence over peers, especially in regard to educational aspirations and job expectations (Kandel and Lesser, 1972). In other instances, peers exceed parents, as in the use of marijuana (Kandel, 1973). Probably the most serious opposition between family and peer values occurs in early adolescence. This opposition focuses on the endorsement of antisocial behavior by young adolescents. While children who have a secure relationship with their parents are able to weather this rebellious phase and remain in tune with parental norms, the distress may be considerable for adolescents who are alienated from their parents and have friends who endorse antisocial behavior (Hartup, 1983).

Friendship

It is impossible to assess the significant contribution of the peer relationship to the social development of the child without considering the special nature of a particular type of peer relationship—friendship. While the child may be accepted within a larger grouping of peers, friendship is a specific attachment to another individual, often emotionally intense. It is acknowledged to be a major and positive force in development because it is specifically through friendship that children learn how to handle intimacy and achieve mutual understanding. In fact, Sullivan (1953) claimed that friendship actually marks the child's first real sensitivity to the needs of another human being. This sensitivity is markedly absent in the child's reaction to its parents, for example.

Friendship is also viewed as one important way in which children learn the rules and norms by which society functions. Research has demonstrated that having friends promotes social skills development (Corsaro, 1981) and facilitates complex forms of play (Gottman and Parkhurst, 1980). Friends also help children learn to manage their aggressive inclinations and sexual feelings (Fine, 1981; Hartup, 1978). Several theorists of children's peer relations suggest that equity and justice motives, the norm of reciprocity, and the need for affiliation originate in the interactions of children within the bonds of friendship (Piaget, 1932; Sullivan, 1953). During adolescence, friendship provides a supportive structure within which individuals can work through the feelings often associated with the physiological changes of puberty (Fine, 1981). Friendship can also potentiate personal growth and identity formation (Donelson and Gullahorn, 1977).

Although the notion of reciprocity appears to be a critical aspect of friendship across all ages, important developmental changes also take place in terms of how friendship is viewed (Hartup, 1983). Younger children view friendship in concrete terms and use specific overt behaviors to define the relationship. With increasing age, friendship comes to be seen in more abstract terms and there is a greater appreciation of the deeper qualities of the relationship, such as loyalty and trust. Finally, at the stage of cognitive maturity, which generally occurs in preadolescence, the first adult-like representation of friendship emerges. At this point, children recognize the uniqueness of special friends and value the intimacy of such relationships.

Selecting Potential Friends

Substantial data indicate that children tend to become friends with those of the same age (Hartup, 1983; Tuma and Hallinan, 1977), same sex (Asher, 1973; Duck, 1975; Tuma and Hallinan, 1977), and the same race (Schofield and Whitley, 1983; Singleton and Asher, 1979). Aside from research on demographic variables such as age, sex, and race, evidence for the similarity of friends on other dimensions is not very strong. Some studies indicate that friends have similar I.Q. scores, but other research does not support this relationship (Hartup, 1970). Data on similarity of sociometric status in children's friendships are also mixed (Hartup, 1983). Finally, physical proximity has been found to have an effect on friendship formation. For example, Byrne (1961) found that students who sat near each other in a classroom were more likely to become friends than were students who did not sit near each other.

Becoming Acquainted

The formation of friendships begins with the process of becoming acquainted. For young children this may first involve simply observing each other (Furman, 1982). The next step is the sharing of superficial information about themselves as a means of getting to know each other. To successfully negotiate their way through the acquaintanceship process, children must possess the necessary social skills. The acquaintanceship process is bi-directional: each overture on the part of one child must be met by the appropriate response on the part of the other child if the acquaintanceship process is to continue. A lack of adequate social skills in either child can stop the process at any point and block further development of the relationship.

It is likely that some children lack friends because they cannot handle the social interactions necessary to move through the acquaintanceship stage. Thus, they experience repeated endings during this early stage of friendship. This type of ending is not due to choice, as when a child decides that he/she will not become friends with another because the other person lacks similar interests. Rather, this type of ending is due to the inability of a child to respond appropriately to the overtures of another child who may be attempting to become acquainted. Repeated endings at this stage in the relationship may have negative effects on the child's social development. First, it prevents the child from learning more sophisticated social skills, such as reciprocity and cooperation, which are acquired later. Second, because the child is probably unaware of the specific inadequacy of his/her behavior, the child may have great difficulty changing this behavior, even after repeated rejection by others. Finally, repeated breakups at this stage may lead to feelings of rejection and loneliness.

Forming Friendships

Though the mechanisms by which an acquaintanceship becomes a friendship have not been directly studied, it is possible to speculate about this process. It is probable that repeated contact over time, increased self-disclosure, the discovery of similarities, and the coordination of activity push the relationship into the friendship stage (Altman and Taylor, 1973). Moreover, children of all ages report that friendships form through continuing adherence to the norm of reciprocity (Hartup, 1983; Mannarino, 1980; Youniss, 1980).

Some acquaintanceships do not develop into friendships. In some instances, children may simply cease all interaction with each other. In others, they may continue interacting as acquaintances rather than friends. Sex differences also appear to occur with respect to friendship formation. Girls tend to make friends less rapidly than boys, and have fewer friends (Eder and Hallinan, 1978).

Maintaining Friendships

Very little data are available concerning what causes friendship to endure or even develop further. However, it seems likely that friendships are easier to maintain if the children involved are socially skilled (Asher and Renshaw, 1981). It is also likely that continued friendship involves attention to reciprocity, equity, and cooperation (Furman, 1982; Mannarino, 1980; Piaget, 1932;

Sullivan, 1953). As friendships endure, the quantity of prosocial intentions and prosocial behavior between close friends increases (Berndt, 1981). Additionally, children's friendships can progress to increasing levels of intimacy characterized by joint behavioral involvement (Levinger and Snoek, 1972) and mutual self-disclosure (Altman and Taylor, 1973). In retrospective reports, for example, adults tend to characterize their childhood friendships as more intimate than their adult friendships (Steuve and Gerson, 1977). This intimacy is probably more characteristic of older children's friendships, because these friendships tend to be more stable than those of younger children (Hallinan, 1978/1979). Permanence is not regarded as a facet of friendship until the child is about twelve years old (Bigelow and La Gaipa, 1980).

Once children enter into a friendship, there are a number of behavioral differences between those who are friends and those who are not. However, because the relevant research is correlational, it is not clear whether these differences between friends and nonfriends are a result or a cause of the friendship relationship. At this point, it is best to consider this work as providing a behavioral description of how children "practice" friendship. As such, some of the relevant observations parallel the reports given by children when they describe the friendship relationship. Children of all ages spend more time interacting with individuals labelled as "friends" than with those not so labelled (McCandless and Marshall, 1957; Medrich, Rosen, Rubin, and Buckley, 1982). More positive exchanges, mutuality, and sharing are observed among school-age friends than among nonfriends (Furman and Masters, 1980). Also, in strange situations, friends are more likely to reduce anxiety, promote verbalization, and share positive affect than are nonfriends (Ipsa, 1977; Schwartz, 1972). Finally, children tend to laugh, smile, talk, and look at each other more if they are friends than if they are only acquaintances (Foot, Chapman, and Smith, 1977).

Enhancing Personal Growth and Social Competence

The acquisition of adequate social skills appears to play an important role in both psychological adjustment and psychosocial development. Basic interpersonal skills are indeed necessary for confident, responsive, and mutually beneficial relationships, and are perhaps among the most important skills an individual must learn. A lack of social competence may lead to rejection and social isolation, which may in turn result in poor psychological adjustment.

Individuals generally begin the acquisition of basic social skills during childhood, and as they mature their social skills generally increase. By the time individuals become adolescents, many have acquired a repertoire of social skills such as initiating and maintaining conversations, communicating effectively, giving and receiving compliments, refusing unreasonable requests, expressing feelings and so forth. Although like other behaviors, social skills are learned through a combination of modeling and reinforcement, the development of these skills is dependent upon having the opportunity to observe and practice them. In addition to acquiring general social skills, it is important that adolescents learn the kind of refusal skills that will enable them to resist peer pressure to engage in behaviors that they might otherwise choose to avoid.

Social Skills Training

Most individuals acquire some degree of social competence with little difficulty. However, some individuals do not sufficiently master the basic social skills needed to function effectively in everyday social situations. For this reason, there has been considerable interest on the part of researchers and clinicians concerning the development of effective strategies for helping individuals improve their social competence. Numerous studies have been reported involving attempts to teach a variety of social skills to adult psychiatric patients, college students, adolescents, and children. Social skills training has been applied to a number of different areas involving interpersonal interaction. This has involved such things as attempting to decrease anxiety and enhance social skills involved in dating (Curran, 1976; Curran and Gilbert, 1975), to teach conversational skills (Minkin et al., 1976), and to teach problem solving and communication skills to parents and adolescents (Robin et al., 1977).

The most common application of social skills training involves teaching individuals how to be more assertive—that is, how to express their feelings, needs, preferences or opinions directly and honestly. Although assertive difficulties were initially viewed by researchers from the perspective of social anxiety, they have come to be viewed primarily as behavioral deficits quite independent of anxiety (Hersen et al., 1973; McFall and Twentyman, 1973). Assertiveness training focuses on both verbal and nonverbal assertive behaviors. Verbal assertive skills involve learning what to say (no statements, refusals), whereas nonverbal (paralinguistic) assertive skills include eye contact, loudness of voice, facial expressions, distance, and body expression. Assertive skills are typically taught using a combination of instruction, modeling or demonstration, feedback, social reinforcement, and behavior rehearsal.

Social skills training has been used with psychiatric patients as well as college students and children. Studies conducted with college students have demonstrated the effectiveness of social skills training procedures for increasing assertive behaviors (McFall and Twentyman, 1973; McFall and Marston, 1970; McFall and Lillysand, 1971; Wolfe, Foder, and Iris, 1977). These studies not only demonstrate the short-term effectiveness of social skills training, but have also shown that significant improvements can be achieved with very brief training (McFall and Twentyman, 1973; Schinke et al., 1979). While practice has generally been found to maximize the effects of social skills training, Kazdin (1974) found that even covert practice could facilitate the learning of these skills.

Assertive behaviors have also been taught to children (Bower et al., 1976; Bornstein et al., 1977). Several excellent reviews of adolescent social skills training have been published (Gilchrist, 1981; Goldstein et al., 1979). Much of the early social skills training research was conducted with clinical populations and, therefore, focused on the remediation of specific deficits. More recently, social skills training approaches have also been used with normal adolescent populations as a means of enhancing personal growth and developing social confidence (Pentz and Tolan, 1983). Not surprisingly, better results have generally been obtained when social skills training has been conducted with normal adolescent populations in schools or community settings.

Coping with Anxiety

Social situations, as well as a variety of "performance" situations, produce a considerable anxiety for adolescents. Two different types of techniques have been utilized to help individuals cope with anxiety: relaxation training and cognitive restructuring. The first type of technique involves learning to exercise conscious control over physiological functions associated with tension or anxiety. Progressive relaxation or deep muscle relaxation (DMR) was initially developed by Jacobsen (1938), and is probably the most widely used technique. This technique involves the systematic tensing and relaxing of specific muscle groups. The main objective of progressive relaxation is to allow individuals to identify the presence of even mild tension and to provide them with a means of eliminating it. In addition, practicing this technique on a daily basis may also result in a general lowering of physiological arousal.

The effectiveness of progressive relaxation for reducing physiological arousal as well as subjective assessments of tension has been demonstrated in a number of studies (Lehrer, 1972; Matthews and Gelder, 1969; Israel and Ieiman, 1977). Moreover, brief or taped training procedures have been found to produce significant relaxation effects when used with normal populations. Still, multisession live procedures which can be paced at a rate that is suitable for individual patients are necessary when used with clinical populations (Borkovec and Sides, 1979).

Many studies have demonstrated the ability of relaxation training procedures to decrease anxiety both during treatment and beyond the treatment session (Weil and Goldfried, 1973). Analysis of post-treatment questionnaires in several well-controlled outcome studies indicated that the most effective approach to anxiety reduction is to use the relaxation skills acquired as active coping strategies (Bootzin and Kazdin, 1972; Sherman, 1972). Such an approach is not only effective in dealing with specific types of anxiety, but it facilitates generalization to other anxiety-producing situations (Goldfried and Trier, 1974). The evidence, therefore, indicates that presenting relaxation as an active coping skill can increase its effectiveness beyond that of the more traditional relaxation approaches.

The other type of anxiety-reduction technique found to be effective involves modifying irrational or negative cognitions and is called "cognitive restructuring." To a large extent, this is based on the recognition that much anxiety is a result of irrational thinking. Ellis (1962) suggested that such problems can be solved if changes are made in one's internal dialogue (e.g., if negative self statements are replaced by positive ones). Several studies have largely supported this hypothesis and have demonstrated the effectiveness of cognitive restructuring strategies when applied, for example, to test anxiety (Meichenbaum, 1972) or social anxiety (DiLoreto, 1971; Kanter and Goldfried, 1976).

The findings of several studies support the use of relaxation training and cognitive restructuring as a means of reducing several types of anxiety. Teaching relaxation as an active coping skill tends to increase its effectiveness and facilitates transfer to other anxiety-provoking situations. Cognitive approaches to anxiety reduction involving specific strategies for eliminating irrational thoughts or replacing negative self statements with positive ones also have been effective in reducing various types of anxiety. Moreover, cognitive restructuring tends to transfer to situations other than the one targeted during training, and long-term results show that it is at least as effective as self-control relaxation techniques.

Application to Substance Abuse Prevention

The acquisition of basic social skills is an important prerequisite for the formation of friendships and healthy peer relationships, which in turn facilitate personal growth and development. Several studies have tested the extent to which enhancing social competence can be effective either alone or in combination with other components as a substance abuse prevention strategy. A review of these studies was published by Botvin and Wills (1985).

Studies testing this type of prevention strategy have generally produced the most impressive results of any school-based substance abuse prevention programs, yielding reductions in new substance use ranging from 42% to 75% (Botvin, in press). Data from two studies (Botvin and Eng, 1982; Botvin et al., 1983) demonstrated reductions ranging from 56% to 67% in the proportion of nonsmokers becoming regular smokers one year after the conclusion of the program without additional booster sessions. One study (Botvin et al., 1983) reported an 87% reduction in the initiation of regular smoking for students who participated in the prevention program in Grade 7 and received additional booster sessions in Grade 8.

Evidence also exists indicating that this type of skills acquisition/

competency enhancement approach can impact on more than a single behavioral domain. In our own work, we have found significant effects for alcohol use (Botvin et al., 1984a; Botvin et al., 1984b) and marijuana use (Botvin et al., 1984b; Botvin et al., 1985). Pentz (1985) reported that her prevention strategy involving social skills training reduced alcohol use and improved academic performance. Finally, Schinke and his colleagues (cf. Schinke, 1984) have found that an approach similar to the one found effective for cigarette smoking was also effective as a strategy for changing variables related to the prevention of teenage pregnancy.

Our own research at Cornell has involved testing the effectiveness of a substance abuse prevention approach designed to teach adolescents skills for resisting the various social influence to smoke, drink, or use drugs within the context of a program designed to enhance general personal and social competence. The goal of this approach is to both *increase resistance* to direct and indirect social influences to engage in substance use, and to *decrease potential motivations*.

The prevention program is designed to be implemented with seventh graders, with booster sessions in the eighth and ninth grades. The intervention consists of 15 sessions which are conceptualized as three different components. The first component includes information concerning the adverse consequences of substance use and its generally low prevalence among both adults and adolescents (i.e., although some teenagers use drugs, most do not). The major focus of this component is the application of general pressure resistance skills to situations related to substance use. These include skills for resisting negative media influences as well as skills for resisting peer pressure to smoke, drink, or use drugs. Students are taught how to identify the appeals used in cigarette ads and how to formulate counterarguments against those appeals. Students are also taught to identify "high risk" situations and avoid them if necessary and are taught the application of general assertive skills to peer pressure situations.

The second component contains material concerning decision making, techniques for coping with anxiety, and material designed to provide students with the basic principles of personal behavior change and self-improvement. In this component students are taught a systematic decision making strategy designed to foster the development of critical thinking and responsible decision-making. Students are also taught specific cognitive-behavioral skills for coping with anxiety, including systematic relaxation, diaphragmatic breathing, and cognitive restructuring techniques. In addition, students are taught the basic principles of self-guided behavior change and self-improvement. Included is material concerning goal-setting, self-monitoring, and self-reinforcement.

The third component contains material designed to improve general interpersonal skills. Included is material concerning effective communications, general social skills (e.g., initiating social interactions, conversational skills, complimenting) as well as social skills related to boy/girl relationships. In addition, students are taught both verbal and nonverbal assertive skills. Students are taught these skills using a combination of instruction, demonstration, feedback, reinforcement, behavior rehearsal, and behavioral "homework" assignments.

IMPLICATIONS FOR THE FAMILY

The material discussed in this chapter has several important implications for the family. First, the early family experience relative to substance use can have a profound impact on whether adolescents will become substance users. Parents, as well as older siblings, play an important role in substance use initiation in terms of both the behaviors that they model and their attitudes toward substance use. Additionally, if any substance is used by a family member, it means that the particular substance will generally be present (i.e., available) in the home, increasing the likelihood that experimentation will occur at an early age.

Second, the family provides the first opportunity for individuals to learn basic social skills. Since family members serve as models, the skills displayed by them will determine, at least initially, the range and type of skills available to children. The development of basic social skills is crucial to the development of healthy peer relationships. Without basic social competence children will have great difficulty forming and maintaining friendships. Family members, particularly parents, can facilitate the development of these important skills by attending to and reinforcing the acquisition of social skills, as they would with respect to language or academic skills.

Third, the family should generally be a supportive environment in which children can develop a sense of self-esteem, self-confidence, self-mastery, and autonomy. Parents have a responsibility to instill a set of norms and values in their children, both in a general sense and with respect to substance use. As the developmental shift begins to occur during the early part of adolescence which results in a more relative view of right and wrong, children need to be provided with help and guidance by their parents in weighing the complex situations that might affect a determination of something's moral rectitude. As issues arise, parents can facilitate more effective decision-making in a manner consistent with basic family or community values. Children not only need to learn and internalize a rule system for guiding their behavior, but they need to progressively move toward more independent decision-making as they approach adolescence. An overreliance on an external decision-making/disciplinary structure imposed by parents may prevent the development of the autonomy and independence necessary to enable adolescents to make appropriate decisions once that structure is no longer present.

Fourth, a high quality parent-child relationship can offset or attenuate negative influences coming from the peer group. Within the family, a sense of mutual trust and concern should be developed so that adolescents will feel free to discuss difficult issues with their parents, such as those surrounding drug use. Adolescents will feel a greater propensity to raise sensitive issues or discuss problems relating to life-style choices in a caring environment.

Fifth, the development of peer relationships should not be viewed as antithetical to a healthy family. Healthy peer relationships provide individuals with the opportunity to learn additional social skills or refine existing ones. Healthy peer relationships play a critical role in psychosocial development. Individuals are able to learn cooperation, negotiation, tolerance, sensitivity to the needs of others, the management of aggressive inclinations and sexual feelings, and reciprocity within the context of healthy peer relationships. Healthy peer relationships can serve as a natural complement to a healthy family relationship. Together, they can foster personal growth and development.

SUMMARY AND CONCLUSIONS

The initiation, early stages, and maintenance of patterns of substance use characterized by psychological and physiological dependence is generally viewed as are adolescent phenomena. A complex array of psychological factors appears to promote substance use, while both psychosocial and pharmacologic factors help maintain it. Substance use onset occurs within the context of great physical and psychological change. Some developmental factors increase the risk of substance use/abuse by increasing susceptibility to social factors promoting substance use.

Central concerns of the adolescent period include the development of an individual identity and the acquisition of important social skills. The peer group provides a context within which these and other issues can be addressed. Peer relationships can be a mechanism for personal growth and development, but they also can be a source of negative influences to smoke, drink excessively, or use drugs. The family and the peer group are two powerful socializing systems. Although conflict between them, particularly with respect to lifestyle matters such as substance use, may arise, they can interact in a positive and synergistic manner. By modeling and reinforcing nonsubstance use behaviors and adequate personal and social skills, the family can both foster the acquisition of positive behaviors and facilitate the development of healthy peer relationships.

REFERENCES

Altman, I., and Taylor, D. A. (1973). *Social penetration: The development of interpersonal relationships.* New York: Holt, Rinehart, & Winston.

Asher, S. (1973). The influence of race and sex on children's sociometric choices across the school year. Manuscript, University of Illinois.

Asher, S. R., and Renshaw, P. D. (1981). Children without friends: Social knowledge and social skill training. In S. R. Asher and J. M. Gottman (Eds.), *The development of children's friendships* (pp. 273-296). Cambridge: Cambridge University Press.

Bandura, A. (1969). *Principles of behavior modification*. New York: Holt, Rinehart & Winston.

Bandura, A. (1977). *Social learning theory*. Englewood Cliffs, NJ: Prentice-Hall.

Berberian, R. M., Gross, C., LoveJoy, J., and Paparella, S. (1976). The effectiveness of drug education programs: A critical review. *Health Education Monographs, 4*, 377-398, Winter.

Berndt, T. J. (1981). Relations between social cognition, non-social cognition, and social behavior: The case of friendship. In J. H. Flavell and L. Ross (Eds.), *Social cognitive development* (pp. 176-199). Cambridge: Cambridge University Press.

Bigelow, B. J., and La Gaipa, J. J. (1980). The development of friendship, values and choice. In H. C. Foot, A. J. Chapman, and J. R. Smith (Eds.), *Friendship and social relations in children* (pp. 15-44). New York: Wiley.

Blum, R., and Richards, L. (1979). Youthful drug use. In R. I. Dupont, A. Goldstein, and J. O'Donnell (Eds.), *Handbook on Drug Abuse* (pp. 257-267). National Institute on Drug Abuse. Washington, DC: Supt. of Docs., U.S. Govt. Print. Off.

Bootzin, R. R., and Kazdin, A. E. (1972). A comparison of systemic desensitization with systematic habituation for fear of heights. Paper presented at the Midwestern Psychological Association.

Borkovec, T. D., and Sides, J. K. (1979). Critical procedural variables related to the physiological effects of progressive relaxation: A review. *Behavior Research Ther, 17*, 119-125.

Bornstein, M., Bellack, A., and Hersen, M. (1977). Social skills training for unassertive children: A multiple baseline analysis. *Journal of Applied Behavioral Analysis, 10*, 183-195.

Botvin, G. J., Eng, A., and Williams, C. L. (1978). The ethnography of teenage cigarette smoking. Presented at the annual meeting of the American Public Health Association. Los Angeles, October, 1978.

Botvin, G. J., Baker, E., Renick, N. L., Filazzola, A. D., and Botvin, E. M. (1984). A cognitive-behavioral approach to substance abuse prevention. *Addictive Behaviors, 9*, 137-147.

Botvin, G. J., Baker, E., Botvin, E. M., Filazzola, A., and Millman, R. (1984a). Alcohol abuse prevention through the development of personal and social competence: A pilot study. *Journal of Studies on Alcohol, 45*, 550-552.

Botvin, G. J., Baker, E., Filazzola, A., Botvin, E., Danilo, M., and Dusenbury, L. (1985). A cognitive-behavioral approach into substance abuse prevention: A one year follow-up. Paper presented at the 93rd annual meeting of the American Psychological Association, August 23-27, Los Angeles.

Botvin, G. J., Baker, E., Renick, N., Filazzola, A. D., and Botvin, E. M. (1984b). A cognitive-behavioral approach to substance abuse prevention. *Addictive Behaviors, 9*, 137-147.

Botvin, G. J., and Eng, A. (1982). The efficacy of a multicomponent approach to the prevention of cigarette smoking. *Preventive Medicine, 11*, 199-211.

Botvin, G. J., Renick, N., and Baker, E. (1983). The effects of scheduling format and booster sessions on a broad-spectrum psychosocial approach to smoking prevention. *Journal of Behavioral Medicine, 6*, 359-379.

Botvin, G. J. (in press). Substance abuse prevention research: Recent developments and future directions. In *Drug Abuse and Drug Abuse Research: The Second Triennial Report to Congress*. National Institute on Drug Abuse. Public Health Service. Department of Health and Human Services.

Botvin, G. J., and Wills, T. A. (1985). Personal and social skills training: Cognitive-behavioral approaches to substance abuse prevention. In C. Bell, and R. Battjes (Eds), *Prevention research: Deterring drug abuse among children and adolescents*. Washington, DC: NIDA Research Monograph.

Bower, S., Amatea, E., and Anderson, R. (1976). Assertiveness training with children. *Elementary School Guidance and Counseling, 4*, 235-245.

Braucht, G. N., Gollingstad, D., Brakarsh, D., and Berry, K. L. (1973). Drug education: A review of goals, approaches and effectiveness, and a paradigm for evaluation. *Quarterly Journal of Studies on Alcohol, 34*, 1279-1292.

Byrne, D. (1961). Interpersonal attraction and attitude similarity. *Journal of Abnormal and Social Psychology, 62*, 713-715.

Corsaro, W. A. (1981). Friendship in the nursery school: Socialization in a peer environment. In S. W. Asher and J. M. Gottman (Eds.), *The development of children's friendship* (pp. 207-241). Cambridge: Cambridge University Press.

Costanzo, P. and Shaw, M. (1966). Conformity as a function of age level. *Child Development, 37*, 967-975.

Curran, J. P. (1976). Social skills training and systematic desensitization in reducing dating anxiety. *Behav Res Ther*, 7, 453-462.

Curran, J. P. and Gilbert, F. A. (1975). A test of the relative effectiveness of a systematic desensitization program and an interpersonal skills training program with date anxious subjects. *Behav Ther, 6*, 510-521.

DiLoreto, A. O. (1971). *Comparative psychotherapy: An experimental analysis*. Chicago: Aldine-Atherton, Inc.

Donelson, E., and Gullahorn, J. (1977). *Women: A psychological perspective*. New York: Wiley.

Dorn, N., and Thompson, A. (1976). Evaluation of drug education in the longer term is not an optional extra. *Community Health, 7*, 154-161.

Duck, S. W. (1975). Personality similarity and friendship choices by adolescents. *European Journal of Social Psychology, 5*, 351-365.

Eder, D., and Hallinan, M. T. (1978). Sex differences in children's friendship. *American Sociological Review, 43*, 237-250.

Elkind, D. (1978). Understanding the young adolescent. *Adolescence, 8*, 127-134.

Ellis, A. (1962). *Reason and emotion in psychotherapy*. New York: Lyle Stuart.

Fine, G. A. (1981). Friends, impression management, and pre-adolescent behavior. In S. R. Asher, and J. M. Gottman (Eds.), *The development of children's friendship* (pp. 29-52). Cambridge: Cambridge University Press.

Foot, H. C., Chapman, A. J., and Smith, J. R. (1977). Friendship and social responsiveness in boys and girls. *Journal of Personality and Social Psychology, 35*, 401-411.

Furman, W. (1982). Children's friendships. In T. Field, G. Finley, A. Huston, H. Quay, and L. Troll (Eds.), *Review of human development* (pp. 327-342). New York: Wiley.

Furman, W., and Masters, J. C. (1980). Peer interactions, sociometric status, and resistance to deviation in young children. *Developmental Psychology, 16*, 229-236.

Gilchrist, L. D. (1981). Social competence in adolescence. In S. P. Schinke (Ed.), *Behavioral methods in social welfare*. New York: Aldine.

Goldfried, M. R., and Trier, C. S. (1974). Effectiveness of relaxation as an active coping skill. *Journal of Abnormal Psychology, 83*, 348-355.

Goldstein, A. P., Sparfkin, R. P., Gershaw, N. J., and Klein, P. (1979). *Skill-streaming the adolescent: A structured learning approach to teaching prosocial behavior*. Champaign, IL: Research Press.

Goodstadt, M. S. (1974). Myths and methodology in drug education: A critical review of the research evidence. In M. S. Goodstadt (Ed.), *Research on methods and programs of drug education*. Toronto: Addiction Research Foundation.

Gottman, J. M., and Parkhurst, J. T. (1980). A developmental theory of friendship and acquaintanceship processes. In W. A. Collins (Ed.), *Minnesota symposium on child psychology: Vol. 13* (pp. 197-253). New York: Erlbaum.

Hallinan, M. T. (1978/79). The process of friendship formation. *Social Networks, 1*, 193-210.

Hamburg, B. A., Braemer, H. C., and Jahnke, W. A. (1975). Hierarchy of drug use in adolescence: Behavioral and attitudinal correlates of substantial drug use. *American Journai of Psychiatry, 132*, 1155-1167.

Hartup, W. W. (1970). Peer interaction & social organization. In P. H. Mussen (Ed.), *Charmichael's manual of child psychology* (Vol. 2), New York: Wiley.

Hartup, W. W. (1978). Children and their friends. In H. McGurk (Ed.), *Issues in childhood social development* (pp. 11-26). New York: Wiley.

Hartup, W. W. (1983). The peer system. In P. H. Mussen, and E. M. Hetherington (Eds.), *Carmichael's manual of child psychology, 4th Edition, Volume 4* (pp. 103-196). New York: Wiley.

Hersen, M., Eisler, R. M., and Miller, P. M. (1973). Development of assertive responses: Clinical, measurement and research considerations. *Behav Res Ther, 11*, 505-521.

Ipsa, J. (1977). Familiar and unfamiliar peers as "havens of security" for Soviet nursery children. Paper presented at the biennial meeting of the Society for Research in Child Development, New Orleans.

Israel, E., and Ieiman, I. (1977). Live versus recorded relaxation training: A controlled investigation. *Behav Ther, 8*, 251-254.

Jacobsen, E. (1938). *Progressive relaxation*. University of Chicago, Chicago (2nd edition).

Jessor, R. (1976). Predicting time of onset of marijuana use: A developmental study of high school youth. In D. Lettieri (Ed.), *Predicting adolescent drug abuse: A review of issues, methods and correlates* (pp. 285-298). National Institute on Drug Abuse Research Issues 11. DHEW Pub. No. (ADM) 77-299. Washington, DC: Supt. of Docs., U.S. Govt. Print. Off.

Kandel, D. (1973). Adolescent marijuana use: Role of parents & peers. *Science, 181*, 1067-1070.

Kandel, D. B. (1978). Convergences in perspective longitudinal surveys of drug use in normal populations. In D. Kandel (Ed.), *Longitudinal research on drug use: Empirical findings and methodological issues* (pp. 3-38). New York: Wiley.

Kandel, D. B., Kessler, R. C., and Margulies, R. Z. (1978). Antecedents of adolescent initiation into stages of drug abuse: A developmental analysis. In D. Kandel (Ed.), *Longitudinal research on drug use: Empirical findings and methodological issues* (pp. 73-99). New York: Wiley, 1978.

Kandel, S., and Lesser, G. S. (1972). *Youth in two worlds*. San Francisco: Jossey-Bass.

Kanter, N. J., and Goldfried, M. R. (1976). Relative effectiveness of rational restructuring and self-control desensitization for the reduction of interpersonal anxiety. Manuscript, State University of New York at Stony Brook.

Kazdin, A. (1974). Effects of covert modeling and model reinforcement on assertive behavior. *Journal of Abnormal Psychology, 83*, 240-252.

Kohlberg, L. (1969). A cognitive development approach to socialization. In D. Gosline (Ed.), *Handbook of socialization theory and research*. Chicago: Rand McNally.

Lehrer, P. M. (1972). Physiological effects of relaxation in a doublebind analog of desensitization. *Behav Ther, 3*, 193-208.

Lettieri, D. J., Sayers, M., and Pearson, H. W. (1980). *Theories on Drug Abuse: Selected Contemporary Perspectives*. National Institute on Drug Abuse Research Monograph 30. DHEW Pub. No. (ADM) 80-967. Washington, DC: Supt. of Docs., U.S. Govt. Print. Off.

Levinger, G., and Snoek, J. (1972). *Attraction in relationships: A new look at interpersonal attraction*. Morristown, NJ: General Learning Press.

Maccoby, E., and Masters, J. (1970). Attachment and dependency. In P. H. Mussen (Ed.), *Carmichael's manual of child psychology, 3rd ed. Vol. 2*. New York: Wiley.

Mannarino, A. P. (1980). The development of children's friendships. In H. Foot, A. H. Chapman, and J. Smith (Eds.), *Childhood and friendship relations* (pp. 45-63). Chichester: Wiley.

Matthews, A., and Gelder, M. G. (1969). Psycho-physiological investigation of brief relaxation training. *Journal of Psychosometric Research, 13*, 1-12.

McCandless, B. R., and Marshall, H. R. (1957). Sex differences in social acceptance and participation of preschool children. *Child Development, 28*, 421-425.

McFall, R. M., and Lillesand, D. B. (1971). Behavioral rehearsal with modeling and coaching in assertion training. *Journal of Abnormal Psychology, 77*, 313-323.

McFall, R. M., and Marston, A. R. (1970). An experimental analysis of behavior rehearsal in assertive training. *Journal of Abnormal Psychology, 76*, 295-303.

McFall, R. M., and Twentyman, D. T. (1973). Four experiments on the relative contribution of rehearsal modeling, and coaching to assertion training. *Journal of Abnormal Psychology, 81*, 199-218.

Medrich, E. A., Rosen, S., Rubin, V., and Buckley, S. (1982). *The serious business of growing up: A study of children's lives outside of school.* Berkeley, CA: University of California Press.

Meichenbaum, D. H. (1972). Cognitive modification of test anxious college students. *Journal of Consulting and Clinical Psychology, 39*, 370-380.

Millman, R. B., and Botvin, G. J. (1983). Substance use, abuse, and dependence. In M. D. Levine, W. B. Carey, A. C. Crocker, and R. T. Gross (Eds.), *Developmental-Behavioral Pediatrics* (pp. 683-708). Philadelphia: W. B. Saunders Co.

Minkin, N., Braukman, C. J., Minkin, B. L., Timbers, G. D., Timbers, B. J., Fixsen, D. L., Phillips, E. L., and Wolf, M. M. (1976). The social validation and training of conversational skills. *Journal of Applied Behavioral Analysis, 9*, 127-139.

Mussen, P., Conger, J., and Kagan, J. (1974). *Child development and personality, 4th ed.* New York: Harper & Row.

Pentz, M. A. (1985). Social competence skills and self-efficacy as determinants of substance use in adolescence. In S. Shiffman, and T. A. Wills (Eds.), *Coping and substance abuse* (pp. 117-142). New York: Academic Press.

Pentz, M. A., and Tolan, P. (1983). Social skills training with adolescents: A critical review of time trends, dimensions and outcome, 1972-1982. Submitted for publication, January.

Piaget, J. (1932). *The moral judgment of the child.* Glencoe, IL: Free Press.

Richards, L. G. (1969). Government programs and psychological principals in drug abuse education. Paper presented at Annual Convention of American Psychological Association, Washington, DC, September.

Robin, A. L., Kent, R., O'Leary, D., Foster, S., and Prinz, R. (1977). An approach to teaching parents and adolescents problem-solving communication skills. A preliminary report. *Behav Ther, 8*, 639-643.

Rotter, J. B. (1972). Generalized expectancies for internal versus external control of reinforcement. In J. B. Rotter, J. E. Chance, and E. J. Phares (Eds.), *Applications of a social learning theory of personality* (pp. 260-295). New York: Holt, Reinhart & Winston.

Russell, M. A. H. (1974). Realistic goals for smoking and health: A case for safer smoking. *Lancet, 1*, 254-258.

Schaps, E., Bartolo, R. D., Moskowitz, J., Palley, C. S., and Churgin, S. (1981). A review of 127 drug abuse prevention program evaluations. *Journal of Drug Issues*, 17-43, Winter.

Schinke, S. P., and Gilchrist, L. D. (1984). Preventing prevention of tobacco smoking. *Journal of Primary Prevention, 5*, 48-56.

Schinke, S. P., Gilchrist, L. D., and Small, R. W. (1979). Preventing unwanted adolescent pregnancy: A cognitive-behavioral approach. *American Journal of Orthopsychiatry, 49*, 81-88.

Schinke, S. P. (1984). Preventing teenage pregnancy. In M. Hersen, R. M. Eisler, and P. M. Miller (Eds.), *Progress in Behavior Modification* (pp. 31-64). New York: Academic Press.

Schofield, J., and Whitley, B. (1983). Peer nomination vs. rating scale measurement of children's peer preference in desegregated schools. *Social Psychology, 3*, 242-251.

Schwartz, J. (1972). Effects of peer familiarity on the behavior of preschoolers in a novel situation. *Journal of Personality and Social Psychology, 24*, 276-284.

Sherman, A. R. (1972). Real-life exposure as primary therapeutic factor in the desensitization treatment of fear. *Journal of Abnormal Psychology, 79*, 19-28.

Singleton, L. C., and Asher, S. R. (1979). Racial integration and children's peer preferences: An investigation of developmental and cohort differences. *Child Development, 47*, 1159-1165.

Steuve, C., and Gerson, K. (1977). Personal relations across the life cycle. In C. Fischer (Ed.), *Networks and places* (pp. 79-98). New York: Free Press.

Sullivan, H. S. (1953). *The interpersonal theory of psychiatry*. New York: W. W. Norton.

Swisher, J. D., and Hoffman, A. (1975). Information: The irrelevant variable in drug education. In B. W. Corder, R. A. Smith, and J. D. Swisher (Eds.), *Drug abuse prevention: Perspectives and approaches for educators* (pp. 49-62). Dubuque, IA: William C. Brown.

Tuma, N. B., and Hallinan, M. T. (1977). The effects of similarity and status on change in schoolchildren's friendships. Manuscript, Stanford University.

Utech, D., and Hoving, K. L. (1969). Parents and peers as competing influences in the decisions on children of differing ages. *Journal of Social Psychology, 78*, 267-274.

Walters, R., Marshall, W., and Shooter, J. (1960). Anxiety, isolation, and susceptibility to social influence. *Journal of Personality, 28*, 518-529.

Wechsler, H. (1976). Alcohol intoxication and drug use among teenagers. *Journal of Studies on Alcohol, 37*, 1672-1677.

Weil, G., and Goldfried, M. R. (1973). Treatment of insomnia in an eleven-year-old child through self-relaxation. *Behavior Therapy, 4*, 282-284.

Wolfe, J. C., Fodor, D., and Iris, G. (1977). Modifying assertive behavior in women: A comparison of three approaches. *Behav Ther, 8*, 567-574.

Youniss, J. (1980). *Parents and peers in social development: A Sullivan-Piaget perspective*. Chicago: The University of Chicago Press.

For Product Safety Concerns and Information please contact our EU
representative GPSR@taylorandfrancis.com
Taylor & Francis Verlag GmbH, Kaufingerstraße 24, 80331 München, Germany

www.ingramcontent.com/pod-product-compliance
Ingram Content Group UK Ltd.
Pitfield, Milton Keynes, MK11 3LW, UK
UKHW022117190926
475702UK00013B/1490
9780866568289